Spaniel on one of the eight library mahogany chairs provided by Ince & Mayhew to the Earl of Exeter at Burghley in 1767.

William Ince

Cabinet Maker

1737 – 1804

SECOND EDITION

Sarah Ingle

with illustrations by
Derry Mountford & Jennifer Evans

Dedicated to the Ince cousins and our descendants

~ may creativity continue to flourish ~

Copyright © Sarah Ingle 2020

All rights reserved. No part of this book may be reproduced or transmitted in any form or by any means, electronic or mechanical, including photocopying, recording or by any information storage and retrieval system, without written permission of the publisher.

ISBN 978-1-9163387-0-8

Contents

Chapter 1 1547-1604 3
   Elmley Lovett and an Elizabethan wife 3

Chapter 2 1564-1619 14
   Swords and Daggers – Servant to Sir John Acton 14

Chapter 3 1620-1715 19
   Plague and Civil War - the 17th century 19

Chapter 4 1660s to 1730s 27
   The Property in Shell 27

Chapter 5 1699-1745 39
   John Ince Glass-Grinder 39

Chapter 6 1737-1804 45
   William Ince Cabinet Maker – His Life 45
   Childhood 46
   Apprenticeship 48
   Family 49
   Ann Ince 53
   Faith and Burial 54
   House Auction 56

Chapter 7 Ince & Mayhew 61
   William Ince Cabinet Maker – His Work 61
   The Universal System of Household Furniture 62
   Work with Architects 64
   Serpentine Commodes 67
   Other furniture 70
   Family Accounts 72
   Marquetry 78
   Fire! 82
   William in Worcestershire 84

The Firm's Property 86

End of the Partnership 91

Chancery 91

Final settlement 95

Ince and Mayhew or Mayhew and Ince? 96

Legacy 98

Reflections on William's life 100

Chapter 8 Colourful descendants of William Ince 102

Frederick Ince (1769-1836) 102

Martha de Bar (1774-1850) 104

Other children of William Ince 107

Other notable descendants of William Ince 110

Chapter 9 John Mayhew's Life and Family 118

John Mayhew 1736-1811 118

Isabella Mayhew 1762-1822 123

John George Winsley Mayhew 1766-1853 124

James Gray Mayhew 1771-1845 124

Joshua Dorset Joseph Mayhew 1778-1858 125

Jane Margery Mayhew 1780-1863 127

Irenaeus Mayhew 1782-1855 128

Ince and Mayhew children 129

Summing up 130

Postscript: 132

The story of Frederick Ince in Virginia and Martha, his long-suffering wife 132

Sources & Picture Credits 166

Index 174

Foreword

In this fascinating and painstakingly researched study of the Ince family, Sarah Ingle, herself of this family, vividly brings to life a quintessential English story, with roots stretching far back into rural Worcestershire in the sixteenth century. In this early period, the redoubtable Maude Ince stands out, and over succeeding generations, the fabric of English life unfolds in this splendid account, embracing as varied a crop of individuals as could well be imagined, including wheelwrights, glovers, weavers, glass grinders and cabinet-makers. Not the least of these was William Ince, partner of John Mayhew in one of the most important and influential cabinet-making concerns of the eighteenth century.

William Ince's own family and their descendants tell a rich and varied story, reflecting some of the extraordinary changes brought about in England by the Industrial Revolution in the 18th century and the rise of the British Empire in the 19th century, and in this delightfully illustrated book is to be found a unique and invaluable record of a family with connections that eventually stretched as far afield as America, South Africa and India.

Sir Hugh Roberts
Surveyor Emeritus of The Queen's Works of Art

Foreword to the Second Edition

As a passionate admirer of the design and construction of furniture of the 18th century, it was a great privilege to be asked to write a foreword for the second edition of this absolutely fascinating book.

Ince and Mayhew does not roll off the tongue to the average person in the street as Chippendale does, but William Ince was every much as great a cabinet maker and designer as Thomas Chippendale. The quality and design of his work is superb and the firm was patronised by just as many society people as Chippendale was. They even openly followed Chippendale by publishing their own catalogue called *The Universal System of Household Furniture*.

Mayhew was the businessman and Ince was the creative partner and his use of fine inlays and incredible detail were second to none. This sets the firm above many who followed them as they were leaders in this field. Unfortunately, many items from the workshop were never signed, but the fine detailing in their furniture will back the name up.

This book provides the reader with a real sense of how life was lived during that great period of English furniture making, when so many of the great cabinet makers of the day worked almost alongside each other around Golden Square.

Sarah has put an enormous amount of effort into researching pieces made by the firm and who they were made for, as well as her family history and that of John Mayhew. Like her predecessor, she seems to have inherited his humble and fair-minded characteristic, as she has presented both sides of their story in a fair and equal way.

You will now need to read on to find out the full history!

Lennox Cato
Antiques Roadshow Furniture Specialist

Acknowledgements

I am most grateful to my family for all their support and interest. Special thanks to cousin Derry for her enthusiasm, ideas and talent for the drawings and to cousin Jennifer for her lovely watercolours. I am indebted to the people who have written about Ince & Mayhew in the past, especially Sir Hugh Roberts, who has so kindly provided a foreword to this book. He also provided some insightful and constructive comments on the manuscript. I also acknowledge the help of various people at the National Archives and County Record Offices and Family History Centres around the UK.

Second Edition: It's been a pleasure to make the acquaintance of Lennox Cato and I am most grateful to him for providing a foreword for this edition. Many thanks to cousin Nigel Ince who made contact after reading the first edition and has provided the wonderful letters written by Frederick Ince from America as well as information about the Ince house auction. Special thanks to Chris Ingle for his professional help with editing and file preparation. Many people have contributed ideas and advice, both here and in America, for which I am most grateful. All errors are my own.

Introduction

William Ince the cabinet-maker was a partner in the important eighteenth century firm Ince & Mayhew. He lived all his life in London, but his father, a glass-grinder, whose business was in Covent Garden, had come to the city from Worcestershire and his ancestors can be traced to the village of Elmley Lovett, not far from Kidderminster in the north of the county, about fifty miles south of Birmingham.

This book looks at the lives of this family from the time the Parish Registers began in 1539 to the lives of William's surviving children in the mid-nineteenth century.

The name 'Ince' means people from the island and is thought to refer to people who came from Ince, a village on the south of the river Mersey now directly opposite John Lennon airport in Liverpool.

The Ince family had some status in the village of Elmley Lovett. Thomas Ince was a weaver and his widow Maude left money to the poor. Several of the Ince men were Church Wardens and one, Stephen, appears to have been some sort of bodyguard to the Lord of the Manor.

The book begins with Thomas and Maude in sixteenth century Worcestershire, then follows the trail through six generations to the life of William and Ann Ince in eighteenth century London.

The overall theme is one of increasing adventure as members of the Ince family travel more widely and expand their horizons, moving from the little village of Elmley Lovett to London, Birmingham, India, America and briefly, South Africa in the three hundred years covered.

Coming from a well-to-do Elizabethan family may well have influenced the choices and determination of their successors. Did one William deliberately go in search of a wife with property? Did one John embark on the migration to London in the expectation of riches?

There is a remarkable amount of documentation which has been used to create this tale: Parish Records, Marriage Bonds, Wills, Deeds and Indentures going back to 1622, Quarter Sessions Recognizances, the Diary of Henry Townshend including a lot of detail about Elmley Lovett during the Civil War, Hearth Tax Returns and a number of court cases, including two heard at the Star Chamber of James I.

Introduction to the Second edition

Inevitably with family history more research reveals more information and the need to correct previous statements. The main corrections in this edition focus on William Ince's immediate family, his father, his siblings and his wife's family. I also wanted to celebrate his furniture as it deserves to be better known so I have included many more examples.

John Mayhew became sufficiently interesting to deserve a chapter to himself and his family, including information on the State Trials for High Treason held in 1794 and royal dentists. It then seemed appropriate to include more of the Ince descendants of note, especially the artists who continue William's expression of taste and beauty. Two renowned actors in America have also been included; Ben de Bar and Annette Ince. Cousin Derry Mountford has produced two more wonderful drawings to illustrate the adventures in America of William's son Frederick and it was fun to recreate his story and that of his wife left behind in England.

Following the long drawn out Chancery case to settle the dissolution of the Ince & Mayhew partnership, it is not surprising that a number of descendants of both William Ince and John Mayhew entered the law as a profession. However, not many stayed, moving on to enterprises such as bringing electricity to the home, Francis Ince, and being involved in workers' rights and social justice issues, such as Thomas Mayhew and Henry Mayhew.

Finding out about eighteenth century fire engines and fire chutes was simply icing on the cake!

Chapter 1 1547-1604

Elmley Lovett and an Elizabethan wife

The village of Elmley Lovett was far from a quiet backwater in the sixteenth century when Maude and Thomas Ince were resident. The Lord of the Manor was Sir Robert Acton, one of the knights of Henry VIII.

Sir Robert Acton had had a colourful career. He worked his way up in the royal household of Henry VIII and became the King's Saddler. He was returned to Parliament for Southwark in 1529 and went to Calais with Henry VIII in October 1532. He was taken ill and wrote to Thomas Cromwell from Elmley Lovett to be excused the next session. He was sent to Marshalsea prison for debt that summer but was released by the Marshal and went back to parliament. He was returned again for Southwark in 1539 and 1542, but then disappeared; possibly due to his worsening financial situation and the death of the Duke of Suffolk in 1545, who may have been his patron in Southwark.

In 1536 Sir Robert served against the northern rebels, in 1540 he attended the reception of Anne of Cleves and in 1544 he fought in France. He bought the manor of Elmley Lovett in 1543 after living there for some time. The sale included a 62 acre deer park and a mill. He was buried in St Michael's churchyard in 1558.

The parson at that time was Philip Hawford who was also Dean of Worcester Cathedral. He baptised the first four children of Maude and Thomas. He had been the last Abbot of Evesham from 1538, having been appointed from the position of Cellarer of the Abbey probably through bribing Thomas Cromwell. Hawford surrendered the monastery to the king in 1540, receiving a pension of £240 a year as his reward, and then being given the deanery of Worcester in 1553 instead of his pension[i]. The abbey church was destroyed immediately on the surrender. Hawford died in 1557 with probate valued at £260. He had a large and well-furnished house in Elmley Lovett, presumably The Old Rectory, and another estate at Crowle with sheep and oxen[ii].

When staying in Elmley Lovett, Sir Robert Acton and his family would most likely have lived in the fortified manor with a moat next to the church in the deserted medieval village.

Deserted Village

In Elmley Lovett there is an area of clearly defined earthworks and the buried remains of a variety of settlement features including a moated manorial complex[iii]. The site has not yet been excavated but it is expected that the remains would contain buried evidence for houses, barns and other structures, together with their boundaries, refuse pits, wells and drainage channels. Artefacts buried with the buildings would give further information about the life of the villagers at that time.

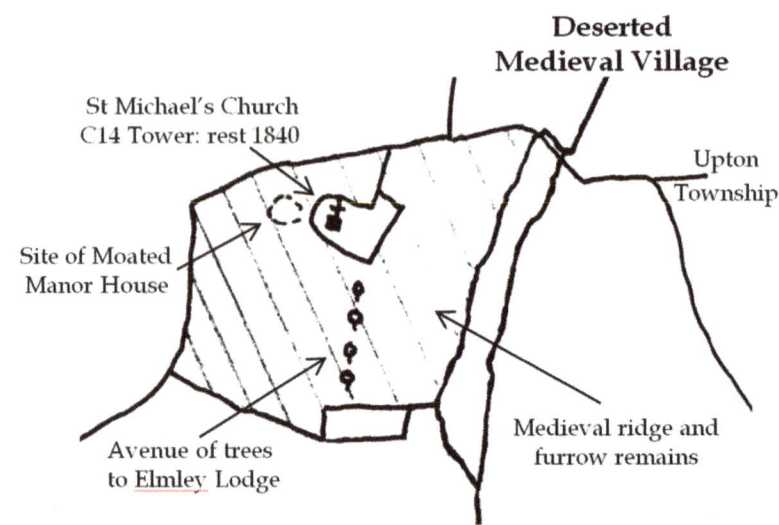

Settlement remains include an area of irregular tofts, (house sites including building platforms and yards), and crofts (the allotments or extended garden plots associated with the dwellings), defined by banks and ditches, lying to the south and west of the church. To the south of the platforms are a number of irregular enclosures, which were used for cultivation, and may have also included stock pens and sheds for animals.

The remains of the Moat

The settlement was surrounded to the south and east by the remains of medieval ridge and furrow cultivation to the edge of Elmley Brook. These remains suggest that this area formed part of the village plough lands.

It is not known exactly when the village was deserted but it is thought the villagers migrated to the Cutnall Green area of the parish, which is on the road between Droitwich and Kidderminster and away from the lower-lying river area. Certainly parts of it had been deserted by the time Henry Townshend planted the avenue of elm trees from the churchyard to his new manor house, Elmley Lodge which was built in 1635.

Maude

Maude was born Maude Dowman and married Thomas Ince of Elmley Lovett around 1545. There was a surprising amount of documentation for this period – the Parish Register[1], three marriage bonds for children of Maude and Thomas, and the wonderful will of Maude Ince, written in 1602.

The marriage of Maude and Thomas did not take place in Elmley Lovett which suggests she was living in another parish, possibly Kidderminster as there were a number of people called Dowman living there in the sixteenth century. Their first child baptised in Elmley Lovett was recorded as *Alis d. of Thomas Ynse* in 1547. There are no records for children of his before that date.

Thomas Ince

Thomas Ince was a weaver, which we know from the marriage bond of their daughter, Mary, dated 1577. We also know from Maude's will that the family had land, pastures and meadows, which they would have farmed.

Weaver, Jost Amman 1568

Worcester was the centre of broadcloth making in England in the sixteenth century producing some of the finest cloth in the world. This cloth would be sent to Blackwell Hall in London via the river Severn to be sold, much of it being bought by the Turks. In 1534 the Worcestershire Cloth Act prohibited people making cloth except in the towns of Worcester, Bromsgrove, Kidderminster, Droitwich and Evesham, unless the cloth was for their own wear or that of their children or servants, in order to preserve the high standards and not allow the rural weavers to compete with the city. In 1561 a man from Hartlebury was fined £80 for making 40 cloths outside a market town, but there was an increase in rural weavers later on, often men with considerable stocks of animals who also farmed on a modest scale.

---

[1] Parish Register entries began in 1539 following a decree of Thomas Cromwell.

The rural weaver had a narrow loom and would have produced narrowcloth, rather than broadcloth, probably of lower quality. He would have produced linen as well as woollen cloth for local consumption.[iv]

Thomas Ince would have fitted this description. He had probably inherited land in Elmley Lovett from his forebears and may have added to it with his earnings from weaving.

The earliest Ince record in the Parish Registers is for the baptism of Francis the son of An Ynse on 13 November 1542. Alys Ynse was buried on 26 December 1573 and Margery Ynse, described as a singlewoman, was buried on 1 August 1588. These women may have been sisters of Thomas.

The Children

Thomas was named as the father of seven daughters and two sons in the Parish Register. Two daughters sadly died, Anne born 1551 died 1557 age 6, and Elizabeth born 1553 died 1569 age 16. The other five girls all survived and married, and appear to have then left the village, except the second Anne, born 1562, who married Phillip Barnard in 1579 and is named in Maude's will as her chosen heir for the lands *and their appurtenances*. Thomas and Maude's son, Charles, their second child, was born in 1548 and Stephen in 1564.

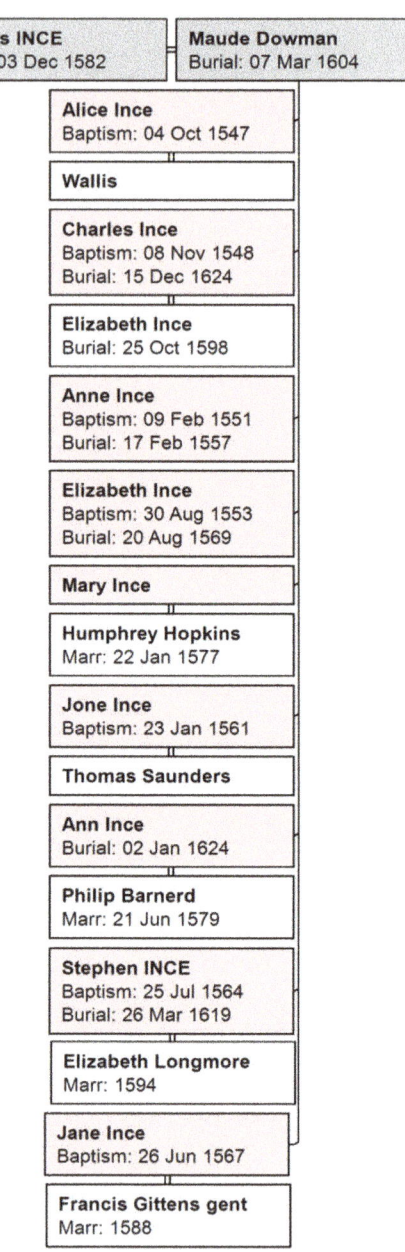

Charles had seven children baptised in Elmley Lovett with his wife Elizabeth. Sadly she died when the youngest surviving child was four in 1598. The following year Charles was Church Warden at Elmley Lovett, and his oldest son Humfrey was

St Michael's Church, Elmley Lovett

married there in 1609, but there are no further records for Charles's family in the village until his burial at St Michael's in 1624. His children may have left or died.

The first marriage bond was for Mary (Marie) Ince, the second-oldest surviving daughter, though her older sister, Alice may have married before then. The only reference to her marriage was in Maude Ince's will when she was referred to as *my daughter Alice Wallis*. The marriage bond for Mary was dated 9th January 1577 and the two bondsmen were John Hopkins of Hartlebury, farmer (*agricola*) and Thomas Ince, weaver, who agreed to a bond of £40 to be paid should Humfrey Hopkins and Marie Ince not marry. She probably moved to Hartlebury on her marriage.

The second bond was for the last child, Jane, and was dated 26th October 1588. It was for one hundred pounds. Thomas Ince had died in 1582 and was buried in Elmley Lovett on 3rd December, so the bondsmen were Francis Gittins, gent of Ribbesford and Thomas Saunders of Ombersley, farmer. We can deduce that Thomas Saunders was the husband of daughter Jone – he was referred to in Maude's will as her son-in-law and Jone is the only daughter whose husband is unaccounted for.

Francis Gittins was the man who married Jane. In a deed dated 27th August 1588[2] v, he was described as a servant of Robert Acton, of Ribisford, Esquire. In the deed Robert Acton conveyed a messuage or tenement, garden, orchard and eight meadows/fields in Ribbesford to Francis Gittyns and Jane Ynse, *in consideration of 32l.(£32) fine and the good and diligent service of Francis Gittyns, his servant ... for the term of their lives*. They were to pay 35s rent *with the best beast* or 40s at deaths. A provisio was given: *proviso for the surrender of the lease if Robert provide them with 'as good a lyvinge as the premisses is in every respecte at the judgement of two or four men yndifferently chosen*. Both Jane Ynse and Francis Gittyns signed the deed.

To be given such a large amount of property implied that Francis Gittins had been of particular help to his master. It was interesting that Jane Ynse was included in the deed, and signed it, two months before the wedding, showing that the Ince family were literate. The Robert Acton that Francis Gittyns worked for was not the same man as the Lord of the Manor of Elmley Lovett, Sir Robert Acton, but was probably related.

---

[2] The Spanish Armada took place in August 1588.

Maude's Life

Maude lived for another twenty years in the village after her husband's death. All her life she would have had to work hard, though we know from her will that she had servants. Fitzherbert's The Book of Husbandry published in 1534 gave a long list of housewifely duties.[vi] After prayers she was to: *sweep the house, dress up thy dishboard, and set all things in good order within thy house; milk the cows, suckle thy calves, sye up they milk, take up thy children and array them, and provide for thy husbands breakfast, dinner, supper and for thy childrens and servants, and take thy part with them.* She would also be taking grain to the mill and making sure the miller did not cheat her, baking, brewing, processing butter and cheese, feeding the pigs, caring for the poultry, planting the herb and vegetable garden; perhaps sowing flax and hemp and helping to make the linen and wool cloth. Sometimes she may have helped her husband *fill the dung cart, drive the plough, load hay, corn.* She may also have gone to the local market to buy and sell. She would have had to plan for the whole year, eg making rennet and salting meat and fish for winter.

Maude had nine children to feed and clothe as well as her weaver husband. The oldest was twenty when the youngest was born so would have helped, and as she had two servants remaining in her house when she wrote her will, she may well have had more help earlier.

There were two deaths to be mourned, Anne who died when she was six in 1557 and Elizabeth who died in 1569 aged 16. Both would have brought sadness and grief.

Maude lived through remarkable religious changes in England. Although it would take time for the changes to reach the countryside, the Protestant reformation would have had an effect on their way of life.

When Henry VIII split with the Pope in 1531, mass would have gone on as before, though no candles were allowed. There was then the dissolution of the monasteries; altars were removed and stained-glass windows smashed. By 1545 every parish had a copy of the Bible in English. Edward came to the throne in 1547 and was a pious and cold Protestant. He abolished the Mass, ordered the smashing of images and the white-washing over of any wall-paintings and the destruction of maypoles. When Mary Tudor became Queen in 1553, she was Catholic, so sung Latin Masses were allowed, and feasting and dancing. With the arrival of Elizabeth on the throne in 1558 there was another swing back to Protestantism.

Queen Elizabeth was determined to remove all traces of Catholicism, perhaps because of the riots and protests, as Protestants were in a minority. In 1559 the Act of Uniformity of Common Prayer and Administration of the Sacrament was passed in which attendance at services in the Church of England became compulsory and non-attendance was punishable by fine or imprisonment. For a long time, the confusion of change was made worse by the lack of any replacements for the rituals that had been lost. By 1600 Maude would have had a new religion based on individual relationship with God, and would have been taught that the Crown and the Church were now one and the same[vii].

Historical Events during Maude's Life

1509	Henry VIII		Bet. 1509–1547	Still Catholic services
1547	Birth	Alis	1547	
1547	Edward VI		Bet. 1547–1553	Strict Protestant
1548	Birth	Charles	1548	
1551	Birth	Anne	1551 d 1557	
1553	Birth	Elizabeth	1553 d 1569	
1553	Mary		Bet. 1553–1558	Catholic
1556	Birth	Mary	Abt. 1556	
1557	Death	Anne	1557	
1558	Elizabeth		Bet. 1558–1603	Protestant
1561	Birth	Jone	1561	
1562	Birth	Ann	Abt. 1562	
1564	Birth	Stephen	1564	
1567	Birth	Jane	1567	
1569	Death	Elizabeth	1569	
1577	Marriage	Mary	1577	
1579	Marriage	Ann	1579	
1580	Francis Drake		Sep 1580	World Navigation
1582	Death Spouse	Thomas	1582	
1588	Marriage	Jane	1588	Spanish Armada
1590s	England			Poor Harvests
1594	Marriage	Stephen	1594	
1602	Will		10 Sep 1602	
1603	James I		Bet. 1603–1625	
1604	Death & Burial		07 Mar 1604	

Maude Ince's Will

Maude wrote her will in September 1602, although she was not buried until 7 March 1604. The impression from her will was that she was fairly wealthy. She came across as well-organised with a keen eye on the business, knowing exactly where her money was, including the £8 that her son-in-law Thomas Saunders owed her[3][viii].

Unfortunately there was no inventory with her will, as that would have given a list of everything she owned and possibly a clue to the layout of the Ince house. It is likely that they still had a great hall as the main room, but by that time they probably also had one or two private chambers such as a parlour and kitchen, with bedrooms above. Access would have been via a ladder from the hall. They would almost certainly have had a dairy and barns, and possibly a brewery.

---

[3] The Average Annual Wage in 1600 was £8 4s 2d (£8.22)

Maude's will began with a statement of faith, commending her soul into the hands of her Creator, and committing her body to the earth. She then listed the disposing of her worldly goods: first to the poor of the parish a total of 6s 8d, then her god-children 4d each, then her servants 12d a piece. She then identified three of her sons-in-law; Humphrey Hopkins husband of Mary, Philip Barnard, husband of Anne, and Francis Gittin, husband of Jane; giving each ten pounds. Then she bequeathed ten pounds to her two sons, Charles and Stephen. Her daughter Alice was named as Alice Wallis, implying that she was a widow and she also received ten pounds. Maude wanted each ten pound gift to be shared with her grandchildren.

Her son-in-law Thomas Saunders was not left any money; instead Philip Barnard, the husband of daughter Anne, was given the eight pounds that Maude had lent to Thomas. It may be that her daughter Jone, who by a process of elimination would have been the child who married Thomas, had already died, and there were no grand-children.

Interestingly she assigns to her daughter Anne *all those my lands medows and pars heyes* (pastures) *and two acres and twoe pieces of land with and singler their appurtenances which my said sonne Stephen now occupies my will intent and meaning is that after my decease the said Anne Barnard my daughter or her assignes shall have hold occupy and enjoy the five lands meadows and pastures and every parte therof with all and singler their appurtenances according to the terme effect and true meaning of the said deede of assignment* in the same way that Maude had occupied and enjoyed it. Poor Stephen. He was appointed executor of the will and was required to give the land he

Summary of the Will of Maude Ince

Dated 10th September 1602
Buried 7th March 1604

1. To the poor of Elmley Lovett [...] Full sum of six shillings and eight pence
2. Godchildren fourpence each
3. Two servants now remaining in my house twelve pence a piece
4. Sonnes in Laws Humfrey Hopkins, Phillip Barnard, Francis Gittin £10
Sons Charles Ince, Stephen Ince £10
Daughter Alys Wallis £10
The ten pounds to be given and distributed amongst their children
Total: three score pounds remaining in hands of Stephen Ince 'by mine appointment'
5. Phillip Barnard the £8 lent to sonne in law Thomas Saunders of Ombersley
6. Daughter Anne Barnard – all rent and money due by son Stephen Ince
Given to Anne Barnard all lands, meadows and pastures and two acres and four pieces of land + appurtenances
7. Linen to remain
8. To such shall ring at the time of my burying 2s to be distributed amongst them
9. Stephen Ince – Executor
10. Charles Ince – one greate brasse panne given by his grandmother Dowman
To Anne Barnard's daughter Bridgett pair hookes and eyes of silver
To Anne Barnard – my best gown

had been occupying to Anne. He must have already had his own land and perhaps only took on Maude's when she was taken ill. Certainly Maude had faith in him to do the job properly *not doubting but that he will carefully and [...] perform the same*. He was also required to pay Anne all rent, annuities and other sums of money owing to Maude during her life.

Maude was concerned that her linen should remain in her house, and that no other person should pretend *any right title or interest thereunto*. It must have been precious to her. She gave to *such ringers as shall ring at the tyme of my buryall two shillings to be distributed amongst them*, which seems a relatively large amount. She bequeathed to her son Charles *one greate brasse panne which is the biggest in my house* writing that this was given to him by his grandmother Dowman, and thereby revealing her maiden name. She also gives her granddaughter Bridget Barnard *one pare hookes and eyes of silver* and her daughter Anne Barnard *her best gowne*. It would seem likely that she had gone to live with her daughter Anne and that Bridget was especially kind to her. Bridget was fifteen when the will was written and the only girl in the family.

Maude's will revealed a great deal of information about the family and the lands, and it highlighted that she was a bright woman and not afraid to show support for her female relatives, especially her daughter Anne. Anne's husband, Philip, may not have been in the best of health, though he was not buried until 1616.

Maude was buried at St Michael's church in Elmley Lovett on 7th March 1604.

In the tax return for January 1642 during the Civil War, the list of payers includes a John Barnard in Upton Township. It seems likely that this was the son or grandson of Anne Barnard who still owned the Ince family farm.

Chapter 2 1564-1619

Swords and Daggers – Servant to Sir John Acton

Stephen Ince lived from 1564 to 1619. There was a surprising amount of written evidence about his life: not only the parish register, recording his baptism and burial, but also his role as executor in his mother's will, his marriage bond, a Quarter Sessions recognizance, and involvement in two cases heard at the Star Chamber of James I.

Stephen was baptised on 25 July 1564 in St Michael's, Elmley Lovett. The parish register described him as the son of Thomas Ince, and we know from her will that his mother was Maude Dowman. It is likely that the family lived in the Upton Township to the east of the parish, very near the deserted village.

A marriage bond was drawn up on 6 November 1594 for his marriage to Elizabeth Longmore of the parish of Wolverley. The document described the bondsmen as Stephen Ince of Elmley Lovett, husbandman and Thomas Saunders of Ombersley, husbandman, who agreed to be bound for £100 *bone et leglis monete Anglie*[4]. The bond meant they did not have to ask for Banns of Marriage. People used Bonds if they wanted to marry in a hurry or in private, or it might have simply been a sign of social status. In 1597 the recommended fee for a license was ten shillings and two of Stephen's older sisters had already been married by bond. Thomas Saunders of Ombersley was his brother-in-law.

As husbandmen, Stephen and Thomas would have had their own land to farm as tenants of the Lord of the Manor, but would have been of lower status than yeomen.

The life of a husbandman involved ploughing, harvesting, and tending the livestock. There would have been three ploughings a year: autumn, spring and summer, with the winter corn being sown as soon as harvest was over. In the Midlands a two-wheeled plough was used with oxen. Oats were sown in January and beans, peas and fitches (vetch) in February. Wheat was important in the Midlands. There may have been a fodder crop for cattle and sheep, and the sheep would have been used to fertilise the arable lands overnight. It is possible that some of the corn was traded, being transported to Worcester and then by the river Severn. In the 1590s there were

---

[4] Good and legal English money

four successive bad harvests in England caused by rain, bringing an economic crisis with the price of flour tripling[ix].

Stephen's next documented listing was on 11th August 1601 in the Quarter Sessions Recognizances, when he and two other villagers were summoned to appear concerning a death in Mitton, a parish about six miles west of Elmley Lovett. There were three recognizances, each with two of the parties saying that the third would appear e.g. *Recognizance before Gervase Bishop of Worcester by Stephen Ince of Elmly and Thomas Best of Pydhill for the appearance of William Best of Elmley to testifie to Fowler's death at Mitton.* Then Stephen Ince and William Best for the appearance of Thomas Best, then William and Thomas Best that Stephen will appear. The outcome is unknown.

From his mother's will, we discover that Stephen and Elizabeth were living in her house and occupying her lands. She appointed Stephen as her Executor, though he was the younger son. At the time of writing she had already given him the sixty pounds to be distributed amongst her family *which he had and took in my house by mine appointment.* She also gave twelve pence apiece to the *two servants nowe remayning in my house with my sonne Stephen.* Maude wished to bequeath her property to her daughter Anne Barnard and Stephen was required to give to Anne *all rentes annuities and other summes of money eyther now due or which shallbe due hereafter unto me duringe my life by my said sonne Stephen.* Maude also assigned to Anne all her lands and pastures.

By 1602 Stephen had three children with another four yet to be born. It would seem that his mother was concerned that her daughter should be provided for. Perhaps her husband was ill or otherwise unable to maintain the household which included five children in 1602. Presumably Stephen would continue to look after the lands and have his share of what he produced, and Anne would receive an income. It seems likely that this arrangement was in place until Stephen's death in 1619. By then his eldest son, John Ince, would have been 27 and he and his widowed mother may then have moved to Walton. One of Anne's sons, probably John Barnard, would have taken over the Upton land. In the 1642 tax assessment the Ince household's yardland in Walton is valued at £9, and that of John Barnard in Upton was valued at £20.

In his later years Stephen Ince also took on the role of helping Sir John Acton[x], the Lord of the Manor at that time. Sir John Acton (c1578-1621) was the grandson of Sir Robert Acton, and was one of the two MPs for Droitwich in 1597, his eligibility being that the family owned a salt pan in the borough. He succeeded his father Charles as Lord of the Manor of Elmley Lovett in 1599 and was knighted in 1603. He became a Catholic in 1607. It would appear that Stephen travelled round with him, and certainly visited Kidderminster and Worcester with him.

In the spring of 1612 there was a dispute between Edward Broade, gent of Dunclent in Stone and Sir John Acton[xi].

In a case that was heard by the Star Chamber[5] of James I, Edward Broade and Philip Smyth, yeoman, accused Sir John Acton, his wife Anne, William Ward, Stephen Ince and others of destroying the corn that had been brought to Edward Broade's mill in Stone in order to favour Sir John's mill at Elmley Lovett.

---

[5]The Star Chamber was established to ensure the fair enforcement of laws against socially and politically prominent people that ordinary courts may hesitate to convict of their crimes. Most cases were really private disputes about property rights [National Archives guide].

Site of the Mill at Elmley Lovett

They were accused of *ploughing up the waste of Elmley Lovett wherein plaintiffs Edward Broade and Philip Smyth claim common, and destruction of the said Philip Smyth's house there.* This was in April. In May the tables were turned as Sir John took out a case against Edward Broad and others with regard to assaults on the servants of Sir John hindering them from ploughing land called Sneades Green. The outcome of the trial is not clear but it is possible that Stephen was required to travel to London to face the charges.

Four years later in May 1616, Stephen Ince was again in court with Sir John Acton, again at the Star Chamber, this time on the more serious charge of assault at Worcester and attempted assault at Kidderminster on William Amphlett who was an attorney against Sir John[xii]. They were also accused of unlawful assembly and conspiracy. The prosecution accused Stephen and another servant, John Talbot, of using unlawful weapons to assault the plaintiff in a chamber in Worcester on 21 October 1615, and then that they *most did as took the life* of the plaintiff *being all of them again arraigned and weaponed with swords and daggers… in the said town of Kidderminster*. They were also accused of *unlawful plotte warfare and conspiracies*.

In both cases Sir John appeared to have stood by Stephen as the defence case is written in both their names. In the second case they completely deny any wrong-doing and say they only used *words of heat and passion* and that in a private chamber. They *pray to be dismissed with their and every of their reasonable costs*. The outcome of this trial is not known as the only papers available are the complaint and the defence. Many of the decree and order books, which gave final judgements by the court, have been lost. Or it may be that the case was settled outside the court.

Stephen Ince died in 1619 aged 55, and was buried at St Michael's church on 26 March. His widow, Elizabeth, was still alive in 1642 when the tax assessment took place, living with their eldest son John in the Walton area of Elmley Lovett. Stephen had seven children, four sons and three daughters, who were baptised at St Michael's. Of these seven children, John's story is told next, Joane (b.1603) married a Richard Yappe in 1627 and Elizabeth was buried aged 10 in 1619, but nothing further is known of the others. No more is known about Elizabeth Longmore, Stephen's wife, either, but it is likely she was buried during the Civil War when no church records were kept.

Chapter 3 1620-1715
Plague and Civil War - the 17th century

In the seventeenth century Elmley Lovett went through many changes. At its centre was the deserted medieval village, probably mostly empty by the beginning of the century with many of the villagers having migrated away from the low-lying river area to Cutnall Green which was on the road from Droitwich to Bromsgrove. Other villagers would have moved away as the increase of pasture led to less arable land, which meant there was less work to be had.

Nationally, England declared war on Spain in 1624, and Charles I came to the throne the following year. It was a time of financial demands on the nation as the war was unsuccessful, and there was increasing political tension between parliament and the king.

John Ince
John, the son of Stephen and Elizabeth, was born in 1591 so he would have known his grandmother Maude, and lived in her house in Upton before moving to Walton. He married Joan Walderne on 30th September 1621 in Elmley Lovett, so she was probably a local woman. They had six children baptised in St Michael's.

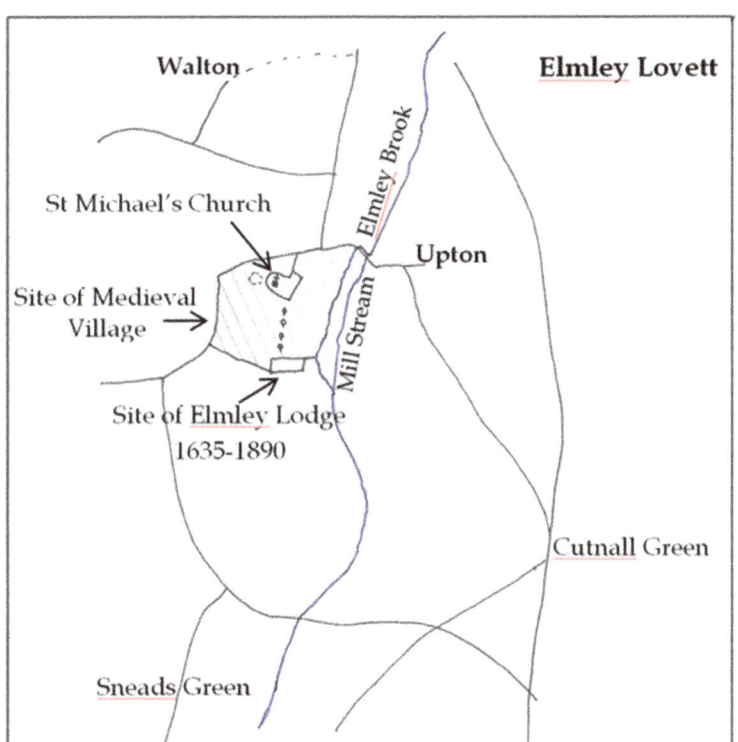

John was Church Warden in 1624 and 1634, so the family had some status in the village. On 29th December 1634 John appeared before William Warmstry at the Quarter Sessions and was sworn to appear at Sessions, presumably the Petty or General Sessions, which were held in between the Quarter Sessions. The Recognizance described him as a yeoman of Elmsley[xiii]. It may be that he was being sworn in to serve on the jury. He was again summoned to appear at the General Sessions in a Recognizance dated 26th September 1640 before Sir William Russell at the Quarter Sessions[xiv]. For these appearances he would have had to travel to Worcester.

Elmley Lodge

In 1634 a new house was built for the Lord of the Manor in Elmley Lovett, Henry Townshend,[6] to replace the fortified manor house in the deserted village. It would seem likely that many of the old houses were already in ruins as an avenue of elm trees was planted on top of some of the earthworks from the new house to the church. This house was a half-timbered mansion, which had sixteen hearths, as shown in the 1664 Hearth Tax return. It also featured a quotation from the psalms: *Nisi Dominus* [7] beneath one of the ornamented gables. In *A handbook for travellers in Gloucestershire, Worcestershire, and Herefordshire* dated 1872 the Manor was described as *one of the best examples of a half-timbered structure in the county*.

Plague Year

Three years later in 1637 the village was struck by the plague. The first burial from plague in the city of Worcester was on 3rd June[xv] and it seems likely it was carried to the village by someone fleeing the pestilence, or visiting from the city. In the Parish Register for Elmley Lovett the first burial with the note *de peste suspecta* was on 30th June. There were forty-seven burials in that year, of which thirty-nine were *of the plague*. There was a peak of fifteen deaths in August, and another sixteen people buried from September to January, the plague continuing because of a mild autumn. The Rector put a note in the Register to say he was grateful his daughter who was buried in November, had not died from the plague. It would have been a horrible death. Sadly three of John and Joan Ince's children died – the two oldest boys, Stephen and Thomas, and their baby girl, Elizabeth. It would have been a time of great fear.

---

[6] Henry Townshend had married one of the four daughters of Sir John Acton, who died in 1621 without a male heir. Henry bought the shares of two of the other daughters, so was Lord of three-quarters of the village. The Snead's Green area remained in the hands of the fourth daughter, Penelope Lench, until she sold it to the tenants.

[7] Psalm 127 Unless the Lord (builds the house, their labour is in vain who build it).

Elmley Lodge: built 1635, destroyed 1890

Civil War

Following on the heels of the plague, the whole of the county was upset by the start of the Civil War. Worcester was the site of the first and last clashes, starting in 1642 at Powick Bridge and ending in 1651. The county was under military occupation for much of that time , either Royalist or Parliamentarian. The Parishes were constantly having demands made on them for quartering and providing the troops with supplies, and they would also have been subject to plundering by the soldiers especially after they were disbanded.

Henry Townshend kept a diary[8][xvi] during the Civil War, which provided a lot of detail about the impact of the war on Elmley Lovett. Taxes were constantly being raised, first to pay for the three men who were mustered in 1640, then to support the soldiers

---

[8] Henry Townshend was one of the garrison of Worcester at the time of its surrender in 1646, and was in the city throughout the siege. He kept a regular diary. He was a commissioner for raising money for the king's forces, but in 1646 he proved before the Parliamentary Commissioners that he had never borne arms in the war and had paid contributions to both sides. He was fined £285 (source: Victoria County History).

on both sides. An assessment of landowners in 1641 gives the names of 19 people in Elmley Lovett, including a John Barnard who was assessed at 20s and had to pay 8d. He was the son of Ann Barnard (neé Ince), who had inherited the Ince lands when her own mother died in 1604.

In 1642 the Royalist Commissioners, who included Henry Townshend, set the sum each parish was to contribute. Elmley Lovett was required to pay £10 a month and in his diary, Henry Townshend gave the details for the 50 villagers who were required to contribute for five separate dates[9]. The first document outlined the yearly values and yard lands which were used to make the assessments. It also gave the detail of where each household lived. John Ince (Ints) and his mother Elizabeth, who was described as a widow, were one of the eight households at Walton, in the north of the parish. They had one yardland valued at £9 and for that month paid 2s 6d. John Barnard was in the Upton Township, and had one yardland and one nook assessed at £20 for which he paid 3s 6d. Francis Gittins, either the husband or son of Mary Ince, was also in the Upton Township, assessed at yardland worth £7, paying 1s 4d. The rates went steadily up, so the Ince family paid 3s 4d the first time, then 4s 4d. For the final assessment in 1644, they were not listed, but John Ince is back in Walton by the time of the Hearth Tax twenty years later. John Barnard was one of the assessors for the Civil War tax.

Taxes were back-dated after Parliament's troops took control in 1645: Elmley Lovett received a demand to pay £10 a month, having already paid the King that amount. The contribution was said to be twelve months in arrears and the parish were told unless they paid on the 9th October they would be *at peril of pillaging, plundering, your houses fired and your persons imprisoned.*

The parishes were also required to provide supplies. In 1643 the constable of Elmley Lovett was ordered to provide *one load of Hay, one quarter of oats, six cheeses, six loaves of bread, and two bushels of meal and deliver that same at the Foregate for the relief of His Majesty's garrison within the city of Worcester.*

When Charles I marched through the county he stayed at Droitwich from the 11th to the 14th March and seven commissioners from the Commission of Array were quartered at Henry Townshend's house in nearby Elmley Lovett with their servants and horses[10]. The rest of the parish was assigned to Colonel Wray for his quarters and

---

[9] The dates were 29th January and 26th June 1642, 20th January and 4th March 1643 and 10th February 1644.
[10] Order from Prince Maurice that no-one else to be quartered there dated 11 May 1645.

sixty of Colonel Wray's horses were turned out on Henry's meadows, a huge cost to the parish.

Henry Townshend wrote about the effects of the war after the Royalist troops had been disbanded: *The country is fallen into such want and extremity through the number and oppression of the Horse lying upon free quarter that the people are necessitated (their hay being spent) to feed their Horses with corn, whilst their children are ready to starve for want of bread; exacting free quarter and extorting sums of money from the time of their absence from their quarters, mingled with threats of firing their houses, their persons with death, their goods with pillaging...... That the insolencies, oppression and cruelties have already so dis-affected and disheartened the people that they are grown desperate and are already upon the point of rising everywhere, and do not stick to say they can find more justice and more money in the enemy's quarters than in the King's.*

Life for the villagers was very hard. John and Joan Ince had already suffered the loss of three of their children from the plague. During the Civil War they had to put up with constant taxation, the demands of the soldiers[11], shortages of food and supplies for themselves and their family and the danger of being caught up in the fighting. A note in the Parish Register Burials for 1642 read: *Robert Lucas wife, shott by a soldier at Tho. Camells was buried Jan 1.* Her burial was one of the last recorded before the Commonwealth Gap, when civil records were kept rather than church ones.

The parson, Edward Best, made a note in the Parish Register that he had kept it faithfully *until the begineing of the late plundering warres and unhappy jarres.* He had then given it to the Church Wardens who had put it into an iron chest in the church *where it remained locked up whilst the wicked Rebellion and Usurpation of the Tyrant Cromwell continued.* He then reported that *In the yeare 1660 when King Charles the Second was happily Restored... this Book was taken out of the Chest.* The only entries from 1643 to 1660 are for the family of Henry Townshend.

During the War there were skirmishes at nearby Kidderminster and Ombersley. William Ince, the son of John and Joan, was only nine years old when the fighting began, and had reached eighteen when the Battle of Worcester took place in 1651 and Charles II fled the country.

---

[11] In parts of Worcestershire groups known as Clubmen were set up, formed of farmers and peasantry. These were neutral gangs trying to protect themselves from both Royalist and Parliamentarian troops.

Commonwealth and Restoration

As the county slowly recovered the inhabitants would have been getting used to the rules of the Commonwealth under the Puritans and Oliver Cromwell. It must have seemed that anything enjoyable was shut down or forbidden; no alehouses, no theatres, no dancing, no ornaments or jewellery. There was no Christmas and no Church of England, though dozens of new sects flourished, including the Quakers. On the positive side there was an improved justice system, new schools and universities, and improved overseas trade. Not surprisingly after Oliver Cromwell's death and the ineptitude of his son as Protector, the country asked for a return to King and Parliament and Charles II was duly enthroned in May 1660.

John Ince lived to see this, and was back living in Walton at the time of the Hearth Tax in 1664 if not before, given that he was listed next to several of his previous neighbours[xvii]. The Hearth Tax[12] was a levy of 2s a year on each fireplace, hearth or stove in properties worth 20s a year or more, to be taken on 25th March and 29th September. The Ince family had one hearth, as did 59% of the households in Elmley Lovett. Henry Townshend had sixteen hearths and there were only two others with more than ten hearths.

In 1666 John Ince was buried at St Michael's church. He was 75. His wife, Joan lived another eleven years, most probably with their son William and his wife, Elizabeth.

William Ince 1633-1715

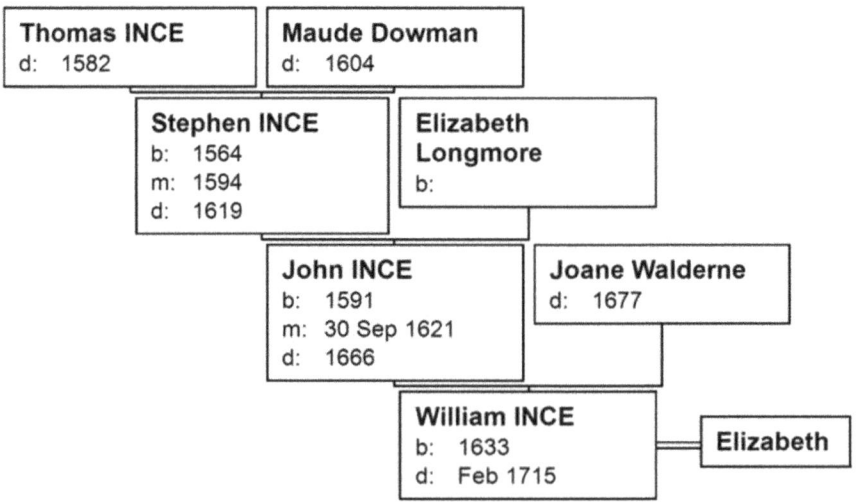

---

[12] The Hearth Tax returns are not completely reliable as it was a very unpopular tax and false returns were made in some instances.

William Ince was baptised in Elmley Lovett on 23rd April 1633. He was the fourth of six children baptised, but three of his siblings died in the plague. Another son, Thomas, was born in 1640.

William probably married during the Commonwealth as there is no record of a marriage and there was no information about his wife, other than the name Elizabeth, which was given as the name of the mother of their son, William (1667-1728). At that time a couple had only to make a statement that they intended to marry at a Market Cross or they could go to a Justice of the Peace to be legally joined. There are no records of baptisms for any other children of that marriage, but there may have been some who were born during the Commonwealth, so were not recorded, and then either moved away to marry or died.

In 1680 according to the Parish Register William Ints married Jane Newman, so Elizabeth must have died. William was Church Warden in that year, as well as in 1666 and 1697.

Church Bell

There is an outstanding memorial to William Ince, son of John and Joan, in the form of an inscription on one of the church bells. The inscription reads: *Peace to the church William Ince Hugh Arden Churchwardens 1696.* The bell is C#, weighs 4cwt 1qr 20lbs and is 28½" in diameter. The six bells installed in 1697 were made by William Bagley.

As Church Warden, William was presumably very involved in the arrangements for the commissioning and hanging of the bells. He must have been very gratified to hear the bells ring out each Sunday.

It is just possible to read URCH WILLI on this side of the bell

This peal of bells replaced the bells that would have rung for Maude Ince. According to the 1552 Inventory for the church, there were three bells and a sanctus, which would have been rung as the Mass was celebrated.

William was buried at St Michael's on 13th February 1715 aged 82. He had witnessed huge changes in his lifetime and had survived the hardships of the Plague, the Civil War and the era of the Commonwealth.

Peace to the church William Ince Hugh Arden Churchwardens 1696

Chapter 4 1660s to 1730s
The Property in Shell

Shell Cottage

William Ince was born in the village of Elmley Lovett in 1667 during the Restoration. He and his wife, Elianor Eaton did not move out of Worcestershire, but they did live in different villages within the county.

The Church of England had been restored following the Commonwealth and under the Act of Uniformity clergy were required to follow the orders of service in the Book of Common Prayer. Those who refused left the church leading to the concept of non-conformists. With the Restoration people were able to relax and enjoy life. They danced round maypoles, theatres reopened and for the first time, women were allowed on stage.

William of Orange and Mary came to the throne in 1688. England and Wales then had a population of around 5 million, and the internal economy was still largely based on agricultural work and production. Domestic industry flourished, with many workers carrying out more than one occupation on a seasonal basis in both industry and agriculture. English society had the largest middling sector of any western country.

William Ince was baptised on 7th July 1667[xviii] the son of William Ince and Elizabeth. It seems likely that his family were living with his grandmother, Joan Ince in Walton, as only his grandfather's name, John Ince, appeared in the 1664 Hearth Tax. John died in 1666. William was the only child of William and Elizabeth recorded in the Parish Register, but it is quite likely that he had older siblings who were born during the Protectorate whose details have been lost[13].

The remarkable fact about William Ince (1667-1728) is that he was a landowner. According to the Poll Books in 1714 he voted in the County of Worcester election. His abode was given as Stone but his place of freehold was Shell, a tiny hamlet near Himbleton, some four hours walk from Stone (13 miles). The electoral roll in the eighteenth century was based on land taxation, so William had to own land in Shell to be able to vote.

The Deed Box

A box of deeds dating from 1622[xix] at the County Record Office in Worcester revealed that William had married an heiress! His wife Elianor Eaton had inherited land in Shell from her father and also some land in Feckenham from her uncle, Humphrey Eaton. An indenture of 1719 revealed the full story, with the details contained in the individual documents.

---

[13] The period 1649-1660 is known as the Commonwealth Gap. Records were poorly kept and many are now missing after being destroyed or hidden by the clergy.

Map of North East Worcestershire
Based on Robert Morden's map of 1695

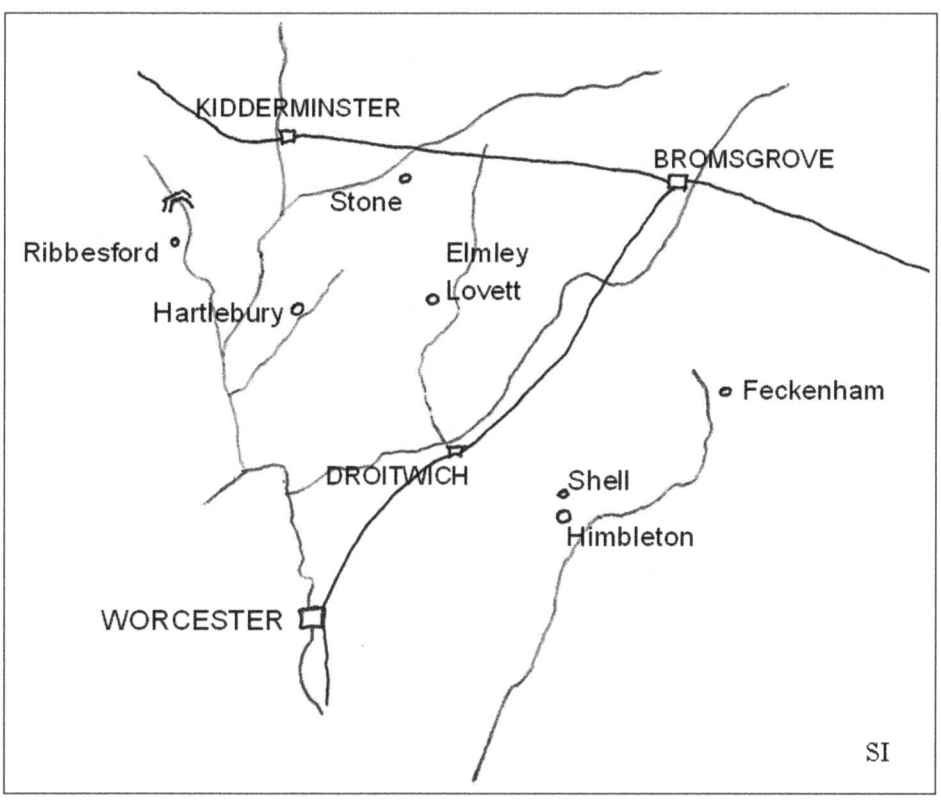

On 6th July 1622 during the reign of James I, William Mowle, a yeoman, paid John Jowe, Mabell his wife and Royeade their eldest son, the sum of thirty pounds for *all that messuage or dwelling house .. wherein they now do dwell and inhabit with the orchards, yardages, .. foldyards[14] outbuildings and appurtenances in Shelve[15].. and all of one acre of arable land.. named Grobson in a field called Millfield'*. This would have been rich agricultural land. The indenture was shown to and agreed by Philip Bearcoft and Edward Davis on 8th August 1638. They may have been local magistrates.

Following the marriage of his daughter Dorothy to John Eaton, the son of Humphrey Eaton of Feckenham, a glover, William Mowle gave one half of this property to his son-in-law and to *the heirs of the body of John Eaton and his wife Dorothy* in an Indenture dated 23rd February 1647 during the Civil War when Charles I was still King.

---

[14] A foldyard is an enclosure for sheep or cattle.
[15] In early records Shell is also recorded as Shelve. The village was in the parish of Inkberrow, although Himbleton was less than a mile away and the church there was used by the Shell inhabitants.

Ancestors revealed by the Deeds

[Family tree diagram:

- Humphrey Eaton — Occupation: Glover; Burial: 22 Jul 1670, Feckenham, Worcestershire
- William Mowle — 1622 Bought land in Shell; 1647 Gave land to Dorothy

Children of Humphrey Eaton:
- Humphrey Eaton — b: 1618; Baptism: 16 May 1618 Alcester, Warwickshire; Occupation: Skinner/Glover; Burial: 18 Jul 1687 Feckenham, Worcestershire. 1687 Bequeathed land to niece Elianor. Married Elianor Boone.
- John Eaton — b: Abt. 1625; Occupation: Glover; Burial: 20 Apr 1688 Himbleton, Worcestershire. Married Dorothy Mowle — m: Abt. 1645 Worcestershire, England; Burial: 1686 Himbleton, Worcestershire.

Children of William Mowle:
- Dorothy Mowle (above)
- Mary Mowle

Children of John Eaton and Dorothy Mowle:
- Elianor Eaton — Burial: 06 Jan 1739 Stone, Worcestershire. Grandmother of William Ince 1737-1804.
- Humphrey Eaton — Burial: 27 Apr 1688 Himbleton, Worcestershire.]

John Eaton was recorded as living in the Parish of Inkberrrow, which included Shell, in the Hearth Tax return of 1664. He was a glover by trade but would have farmed the land as well.

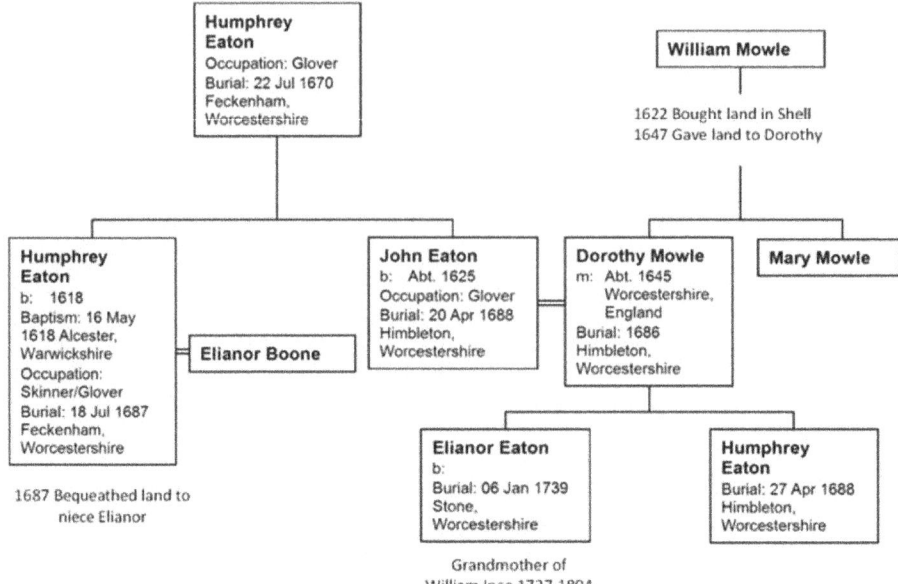

Shell is a tiny hamlet and there are very few houses there even now. It is likely that the Hearth Tax return was written down in the order of the recorder going round.

John Eaton was recorded as having one hearth, above him was Mrs Fincher with six, then Mrs Lench with eight, below him was Wm Chandler with one.

It is likely that Mrs Fincher and Mrs Lench were living in Shell Manor, John Eaton was living in the next building, Shell Cottage, and William Chandler was living in Shell Mill Farm.

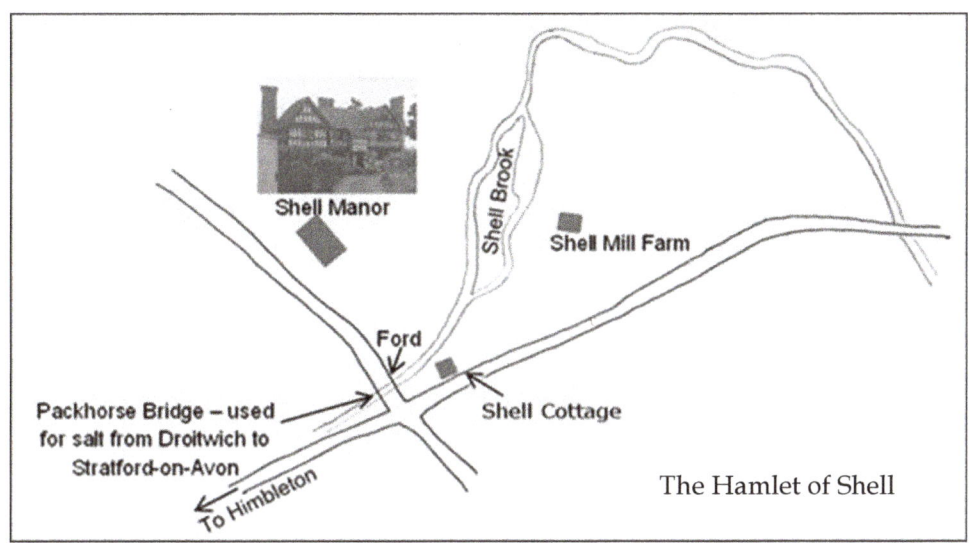

Elianor Eaton

Elianor was the daughter of John and Dorothy, but she was not born until late in their marriage. She probably had older brothers and sisters but there is no record of their baptisms, marriages or burials. This is primarily due to the Commonwealth Gap (1640 to 1662), when no church records were kept, but there are now no parish records for Himbleton before 1713 and the Bishop's Transcripts, which go back to 1611, have many years missing. No baptism has been found for Elianor, but as she bore four children between 1689 and 1699 she was probably born during the 1660s or 1670s.

Entrance to Himbleton church

She would have lived a fairly quiet life, presumably helping with the glove-making and on the land. She probably went to market with her family, possibly taking the gloves to Feckenham where Uncle Humphrey was also a glove-maker. The family would have walked the mile to Himbleton church each Sunday.

Dorothy, Elianor's mother, died and was buried at St Mary Magdalene's Himbleton on 9th April 1686. John Eaton, her father, died and was buried on 20th April 1688[xx]. Her brother, Humphrey, died a week after their father. A total of thirteen burials took place from March to May that year, more than for the whole of 1686, so there may have been some disease, which Elianor managed to survive. In May 1688 she would have been living on her own in Shell, having inherited the land.

The Packhorse Bridge at Shell

Elianor was also the beneficiary of her uncle Humphrey Eaton's will. Humphrey had taken on his father's trade as a glover/skinner in Feckenham, and he and his wife did not have any children.

In his will dated 3rd July 1684 Uncle Humphrey left his house and lands to his wife, then to John Haines, then to Humphrey and Elianor Eaton, son and daughter of John Eaton of Shell, with five pounds, all to be divided equally between them. Uncle Humphrey died and was buried in Feckenham[16] on 18th July 1687.

The name Humphrey Eaton, carried by at least three generations of the Eaton family, was remembered and honoured by John Ince, the glass-grinder, who called the baby brother of William the cabinet-maker Humphrey Eaton Ince. Humphrey Eaton Ince was baptised and buried in St Paul Covent Garden in 1740.[17]

---

[16] Feckenham was a Royal Manor and at one time the rights belonged to Elizabeth I. She may have hunted in Feckenham Forest. Himbleton church has the Tudor Royal Arms painted above the East window, possibly to celebrate a visit by Elizabeth I, or as a statement of loyalty.
[17] This information gives further proof of the connection of the Ince family to the Elmley Lovett line.

Feckenham church interior

An Inventory of Humphrey Eaton's property was taken by John Eaton and two others showing that he had a shop, a hall, and a parlour, with a chamber over the shop and a chamber over the hall. His possessions included two flock beds and two pairs of bed steads, seven pairs of sheets, one table and forms, two chyers two ioyn stools and four cusins, nine pewter dishes, two plates, two saucepans, half a dozen spoons. The Hall was where the cooking took place as that contained three kettles, two pots, one skillet and one scummer, along with two coules, two barrels, one grate, one pound of cobirons, one spit, one gridiron, one chafering dish and one pair of pothooks. He had two loads of hard wood, one load of kids and half a tunn of coals, skips of leather, horse leather, six hogs of goose (fat?), timber and varnish. A deed written in 1719 gives proof that Elianor eventually inherited his house and land in Feckenham.

William and Elianor

So in 1688 we have a young orphaned heiress, and the next known record is a baptism for *Mary y daughter of Will Ince & Elnor his wife* [18] in the Church of St Mary Magdalene in Himbleton on 29th September 1689. Somehow, William Ince in Elmley Lovett came courting thirteen miles and found himself a wife and a house in Shell. It may be that Dorothy Mowle, Elianor's mother, was connected to the Mowle family living in Elmley Lovett or the Moules of Snead Green on the edge of Elmley Lovett and he learnt of the death of Dorothy and her husband, John Eaton, through them. By marrying Elianor, William became the owner of the land in Shell, giving him the right to vote.

William and Elianor did not stay long in Shell. The next known baptism is for Elizabeth on 2nd January 1694, back in Elmley Lovett. The Parish Register entry reads *Eliz: ye daughter of Will: Ints (Junr) and Elinor his wife*, showing his father was still alive. William and Elianor had two other children, William and John. William was a wheelwright in Kidderminster who died in 1749, whose baptism has yet to be found. John was the glass-grinder in Covent Garden and father of William Ince the cabinet-

---

[18] Bishop's Transcript for St Mary's Himbleton.

maker. He was baptised on 10 April 1699 in St Mary the Virgin, Stone, showing the family had then moved about four miles north of Elmley Lovett.

They may have moved there on the recommendation of William's uncle, Thomas Ince. According to the parish records for Stone, Thomas Ince (Inch) buried two wives, Elenor in 1669 and Margrett in 1678. He then had six children baptised between 1681 and 1691. These children were probably the offspring of Ann Ince who died in 1720.

The parish records also revealed that William Ince (1667-1728) was a husbandman, this information being given at his burial with the confirmation that he was buried in wool[19]. He would also have received an income from renting out the land in Shell. He was buried in Stone on 28th May 1728 and Elianor was buried there on 6th January 1739[xxi].

Land Sale

In 1719, while his parents were still alive, William the wheelwright took charge of the land in Shell. In June, he bought a different piece of land and in October the original land was sold, together with the land in Feckenham.

An indenture dated 20th June 1719 said William Ince Junr paid five shillings[20] to William Chandler and his wife Mary for *half .. of one messuage or tenement house and barne together with one garden, one orchard …* The purchase included hempland, foldyards and arable land. He took the *freehold and inheritance thereof to him and his heirs for ever*. William and Mary Chandler had moved to the City of London. A further document states that the agreement for him to own the land was *in consideration of the sum of eighty pounds*.

> The Indentures themselves were made of parchment which has yellowed and hardened a little over time. Some were folded up into squares and it was unnerving unfolding them in case they cracked. The 1622 document was folded into twenty squares! All the Indentures had been cut with wavy lines, showing that there were two or more copies. The other copy would match the indentures exactly, proving they belonged together. Hence the name Indenture.
>
> The documents were very repetitive, the same thing being said in as many ways as possible eg one *messuage or dwelling house or tenement*. They gave a detailed description of the land by referring to other occupiers on the north, east, south and west sides of the property. This makes it very hard to work out exactly where they were as those markers are long gone.

---

[19] May 30th 1728 Mary wife of Richard Walker maketh oath that Wm Ince of the Parish of Stone, Husbandman was not buried in any materials contrary to ye Act of Parliament.
[20] Five shillings was the nominal sum stated on the indenture. There was another document showing the full amount paid. £80 was worth nearly 2½ years wages for a skilled tradesman.

An Indenture of 9th October 1719 showed that the land in Feckenham, inherited by Elianor from her uncle Humphrey Eaton, was sold to the mercers Thomas and Richard Roberts of Droitwich. The property included the dwelling house, *now in the possession of Thomas Baynes with the Barnes, stables buildings gardens orchards fouldyards and banksides… also all that eight Butts and a pyke of arable land.. in the wholle about two acres, … and (another) five butts of arable land.* The same indenture shows that the land in Shell, which was originally bought by William Mowle and given to John Eaton on his marriage, was also sold to Thomas and Richard Roberts by William Ince and Elianor Ince.

The most illuminating document was the deed dated 10th October 1719 which stated the agreement was between **William Ince the elder** of the Parish of Stone in the County of Worcester and **Elianor his wife** which Elianor is the only daughter and heir of **John Eaton** late of Shelve Glover and **Dorothy** his wife both died and which John was the late brother and heir of **Humphrey Eaton** late of Feckenham Glover Dorothy was one of the daughters and co-heirs of **William Mowle** late of Shelve now deceased of the first part, **William Ince the younger** of the Parish of Kidderminster.. Wheelwright of the second part and Thomas Roberts the younger Mercer and Richard Roberts Mercer both of Droitwich of the third part.

Signatures of William Ince and William Ince Junior and Mark of Elianor Ince 1719

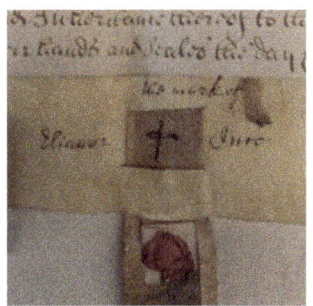

This confirmed the story as set out in the indentures, that Elianor inherited two properties, which became the property of her and her husband on their marriage. William Ince the younger was included as the heir of those properties. There was one small inaccuracy in the statement, and that was that according to Humphrey Eaton's will, he bequeathed his property directly to Elianor and her brother.

It is interesting to note that Elianor Eaton had equal status with William Ince and made her mark. Both William Ince the Elder and the Younger were able to sign their names. Mary Chandler signed the June 1719 indenture as well as her husband. On the earlier documents, William Mowle made his mark.

It seems likely that William Ince the Younger borrowed the eighty pounds needed to buy the Chandler's property, which was repaid when the other land had been sold. It also seems likely that the Chandler's property was of better quality and likely to bring in more rent. Both properties were near Shell Brook with the arable land in Millfield, which was presumably next to the Mill. On visiting the hamlet of Shell the most likely scenario is that William Mowle bought Shell Cottage, which was eventually inherited by Elianor Ince (nee Eaton) and was later sold to buy Shell Mill Farm, where William Chandler was living at the time of the 1664 Hearth Tax.

Shell Cottage is highlighted in *Worcestershire* by Nicholas Pevsner and Alan Brooks where it is described as a fifteenth century hall in miniature with later added fireplace and first floor. The solar and service rooms would have been extensions, the solar still existing at the front. Shell Mill Farm was probably late sixteenth century with a stone chimney with two star stacks.

A rent agreement of 25th March 1740 stated that William Ince of Franch was to receive rent of £3 10s a year on land in Shell to be paid by Thomas Barnet in half yearly payments. The renter was also to pay the Land Tax.

Will of William the Wheelwright

This William Ince died in 1749 and in his will made provision for his sister and his nephew and nieces living in London. He gave his sister Elizabeth *all that my Messuage Tenement or Dwelling House together with the Lands and premises thereunto belonging commonly called or known by the name of Shell… now in the tenure or Occupation of Richard Lewis*. On the decease of his sister, or the day of her marriage, the property would go to *my Nephew John Ince of the City of London Glass-Grinder*.

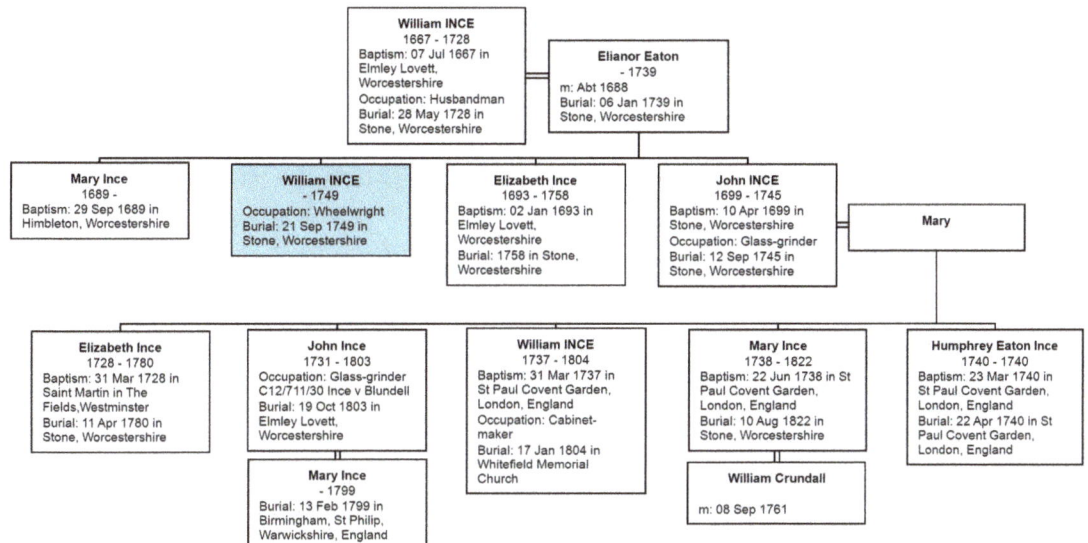

He also gave his sister the house *wherein I now dwell* in Kidderminster, which on her decease or marriage was to go to his nieces Mary and Elizabeth Ince, the daughters of his late brother, John Ince. He also gave his sister *the full and free use of all my Household Goods and Interest of my Money (Not Lessening the principal)* and after her decease or marriage his best bed was to go to John Ince and *my clock and case*. He gave his nephew William fifty pounds, together with *my Second best bed and my Silver Watch* on Elizabeth's decease or marriage, and everything else to be divided between his nieces Mary and Elizabeth. He suggested his executors should use his money to buy an *Estate of good title* leaving enough money to give William his fifty pounds. One of his executors was John King of the parish of Elmley Lovett.

William was buried on 21st September 1749 in the Parish of Stone, although he was no longer living there. It is possible he was buried in a family grave with his brother John (1699-1745) and both their parents.

John Ince and the sale of the land
To complete the story of the property in Shell we need to move to the mid- eighteenth century and William the cabinet-maker's brother John Ince, the nephew who would inherit the land after his aunt Elizabeth died or married.

Rather than wait for this to happen, John borrowed money in advance from the trustees of his uncle's will, and later persuaded his aunt to sell the Shell property.

A document dated 20th December 1756 revealed that John Ince *late of Saint Giles in the Fields.. Westminster now of .. Birmingham Glassgrinder..appoint Elizabeth Ince of Ffranch .. my true and lawful attorney for me and in my name to sell and dispose of all that ... given by late uncle William Ince... she the said Elizabeth Ince after deducting the forty pounds and interest borrowed by me of the trustees of my late Uncle*

An indenture dated 28th September 1757 showed that Elizabeth and John had sold the land in Shell to Edward Bearcroft of Droitwich. They received five shillings in hand *for the Manor or Lordship of Shell with all its rights, members and appurtenances thereunto belonging and all that messuage or tenement situate standing and being near Shell Brook .. garden and orchard… and parcel of arable land being in Millfield within the Manor.. in the occupation of Thomas Boughton together with all the Great and Small tythe.* A document dated 10th September 1757 mentions 89 guineas as further consideration for this transaction.

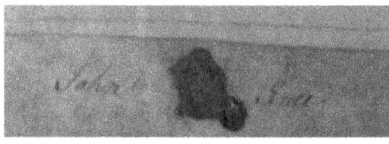

Signature of John Ince, brother of William the Cabinet Maker

It is curious that the property was now being described as a Manor. It was not the Manor of Shell, which was shared between two brothers and their descendants; one share was in the hands of the Pyncher/Fincher family from 1550 to 1755 and the other in the Lench family 1581-1671 and then the Foley family 1699-1737. Both portions were eventually owned by the Bearcroft family[xxii].

The property sold in 1757 would have been the land bought by William Ince (?-1749) the younger from William and Mary Chandler. He paid eighty pounds for it and Elizabeth and John raised eighty-nine guineas, reflecting 36 years of stable economy. Elizabeth Ince died in 1758 and her nephew, John, would then presumably have received the full amount, if he had not received it before.

The London Gazette dated 19th June 1761 reported that John Ince, glass-grinder, was in Marshalsea Prison for debt. His address then was given as late of Bedford Bury, Covent Garden, and now of Husband Street in the Parish of St Ann, Soho. It would appear that he had endeavoured to set up as a glass-grinder in Birmingham, but perhaps lacked the business acumen necessary so had to get all the money from the Shell property. Even then he failed in his business and returned to London. It may be that his brother William the cabinet-maker employed him to work on some of their plate glass mirrors after his release from prison.

Elizabeth Ince was buried in Stone with her siblings and parents in 1758. Her nieces, Mary and Elizabeth, William the cabinet-maker's sisters, would have inherited her property in Ffranch in accordance with the will of their uncle William.

Chapter 5 1699-1745

John Ince Glass-Grinder

John Ince, the father of William the cabinet-maker, was baptised in the village of Stone, Worcestershire on 10th April 1699. He was an enterprising young man as he left his home and went to London in his twenties while his parents were both alive. His father was a husbandman, a free tenant farmer or small landowner[21]. His older brother, William, was the wheelwright who worked in nearby Kidderminster. Their father died in 1728 and their mother in 1739, both buried in Stone. She was described as a pauper in the Burial Register, most surprising when viewed in the light of the wills of her two sons.

John lived through most of the first half of the eighteenth century. During most of this time England was not involved in any wars and the economy was stable. Living costs and wages remained much the same over this period, and the main problem was the irregularity of employment. The weather was cold, with a great frost from Christmas Day 1739 to mid-February 1740[22] and a Frost Fair was held on the river Thames, great fun for those involved but the cause of misery and distress for those unable to get any work, food or shelter.

John worked as a glass-grinder and according to the records of the Joiners' Company[23], he was apprenticed to James Welch for seven years from 26th July 1720. In this record he was described as the son of William Ince, husbandman of Stone. It is surprising that a twenty-one year old from Worcestershire would be apprenticed to someone in London but James Welch was the son of Henry Welch, a tailor in Stourbridge, Worcestershire which is only eight miles from Stone and it seems very likely that the families knew one another. James Welch had been apprenticed in 1699 to John Smalwell, who was a master joiner *of His Majesty's Works*[xxiii].

This apprenticeship was *turned over to John Wight Cit. & Haberdasher of London to learne the Art of a Joyner by consent.* James Welch was *Made free by servitude on 11 Nov 1718. On the report of Thomas Taxon Cit & Haberdasher of London and William Hayes Cit & Grocer of London the said Wight being out of Towne.* It is not clear how a haberdasher taught him how to be a joiner.

---

[21] A husbandman had lower social status than a yeoman.
[22] The mean temperature for January that year was -2.8°C
[23] In 1706 the Glass Sellers Guild refused to allow the Glass Grinders to have a separate charter.

St Paul's Covent Garden

Children of John & Mary Ince
Timothias Ince   Baptism: 06 Mar 1725   St Faith under St Paul, London
Elizabeth Ince   Baptism: 31 Mar 1728   Saint Martin in The Fields, Westminster
John Ince
William Ince   Baptism: 21 Oct 1733 St Paul, Covent Garden, London
Sally Jenney Ince   Baptism: 31 Oct 1735 St Paul, Covent Garden, London
William Ince   Baptism: 31 Mar 1737   St Paul Covent Garden, London, England   Burial: 17 Jan 1804 Whitefield Memorial Church
Ann Stephenson   Marr: 20 Feb 1762 St George, Hanover Square, Westminster, Middlesex   Burial: 04 Dec 1806 Whitefield Memorial Church
Mary Ince   Baptism: 22 Jun 1738 St Paul Covent Garden, London, England
Humphrey Eaton Ince   Baptism: 23 Mar 1740 St Paul Covent Garden, London, England   Burial: 22 Apr 1740 St Paul Covent Garden, London, England
George Ince   Baptism: 13 Nov 1741 St Paul Covent Garden, London, England   Burial: 12 Jan 1744 St Paul Covent Garden, London, England
Samuel Ince   Baptism: 21 Sep 1743 St Paul Covent Garden, London, England   Burial: 02 Oct 1743 St Paul Covent Garden, London, England

James Welch was at 'The Rose & Crown', Broadway in July 1724[24] when he advertised his ability to supply wholesale or retail a *great Variety of Peer, Chimney or Sconce Glasses, fine Dressing-Glasses, Coach, Chariot or Chair-Glasses, with Plate Sash-Glasses &c.* He also offered to clean and modernise old glasses. John Ince would have been working for him then, presumably as a glass-grinder.

John and Mary Ince's first child, Timothias, was baptised on 6th March 1726 in St Faith's Church, near St Paul's Cathedral so hopefully John was earning a wage by then, and able to support his family. The church was known as St Faiths under St Paul's as before the Great Fire in 1666 the congregation worshipped in the crypt of the Cathedral. After 1666, they shared St Augustine's church in Watling Street, just to the east of the Cathedral.

John's wife, named as the mother of their children in the Parish Registers, was called Mary, and it seems likely that her father was called Timothy as none of the earlier Inces bore that name. No other information about Mary's origins, or her marriage to John has yet been found.

Their second child Elizabeth was baptised in St Martin in the Fields in March 1728 and it seems likely that the family had then moved out of the City of London and John Ince had set up his own business. It is likely that the necessary money came from the land sales of his parents.

---

[24] Daily Courant, 29 July 1724

Another eight children were baptised between 1733 and 1743, most at St Paul's Covent Garden, including William the cabinet-maker on 31st March 1737. John was then running his business from Bow Street, Covent Garden where he was paying rates from at least 1736.

London was a rapidly growing city, with a population of about 575,000 in 1700 rising to 750,000 by 1750. It was the largest city in Europe and was a strong magnet for people from all over England as well as from overseas, not surprising when the next biggest city, Bristol, only had a population of around 30,000. The perceived opportunities for work and trade would have been huge. The growth in population was the result of people moving to London as there were very high infant and child mortality levels which kept down any natural increase. Only four of the ten Ince children baptised were still alive in 1745 when John made his will.

The city was very unhealthy. Human waste often ended up in the sewers instead of being carted away by the night-men and from there ended up in the Thames along with all the animal dung and carcasses; not to mention the swarms of rats. The best water was said to come from the Thames without filtration or settlement, hopefully from an area upstream of the sewers. Dirt, fog and smoke prevailed. Black carbon from the coal fires would have poisoned the air and killed many. At least no-one was more than a mile or two from open countryside and there were parks to be enjoyed[xxiv].

Covent Garden in the early eighteenth century had the fruit and vegetable market which by then was a thriving commercial activity with stalls, porters and hawkers. It was still a fashionable area with a few aristocratic residents as well as scientists, literary persons and artists. It also had two theatres, the Theatre Royal on Drury Lane and the Royal Opera on Bow Street which opened in 1732. These would have attracted droves of people in the evenings, with the accompanying prostitution. It was also the site of many coffee houses including Buttons in nearby Russell Street, which was where poets, playwrights and prominent wits gathered to discuss the events of the day and set the standards for public taste[xxv].

In 1720 Bow Street was described *as open and large, with very good Houses, well inhabited, and resorted unto by Gentry for Lodgings*[xxvi]. A few years later, however, the parish had a poor-house or nurses' house in the street, and 1739 saw the disappearance of the last private titled ratepayer. In the following year Sir Thomas De Veil appears in the rate books, at the site of No. 4, and the establishment of his magistrate's court here no doubt spoilt the street residentially. By 1743 there were eight licensed premises in Bow Street[xxvii].

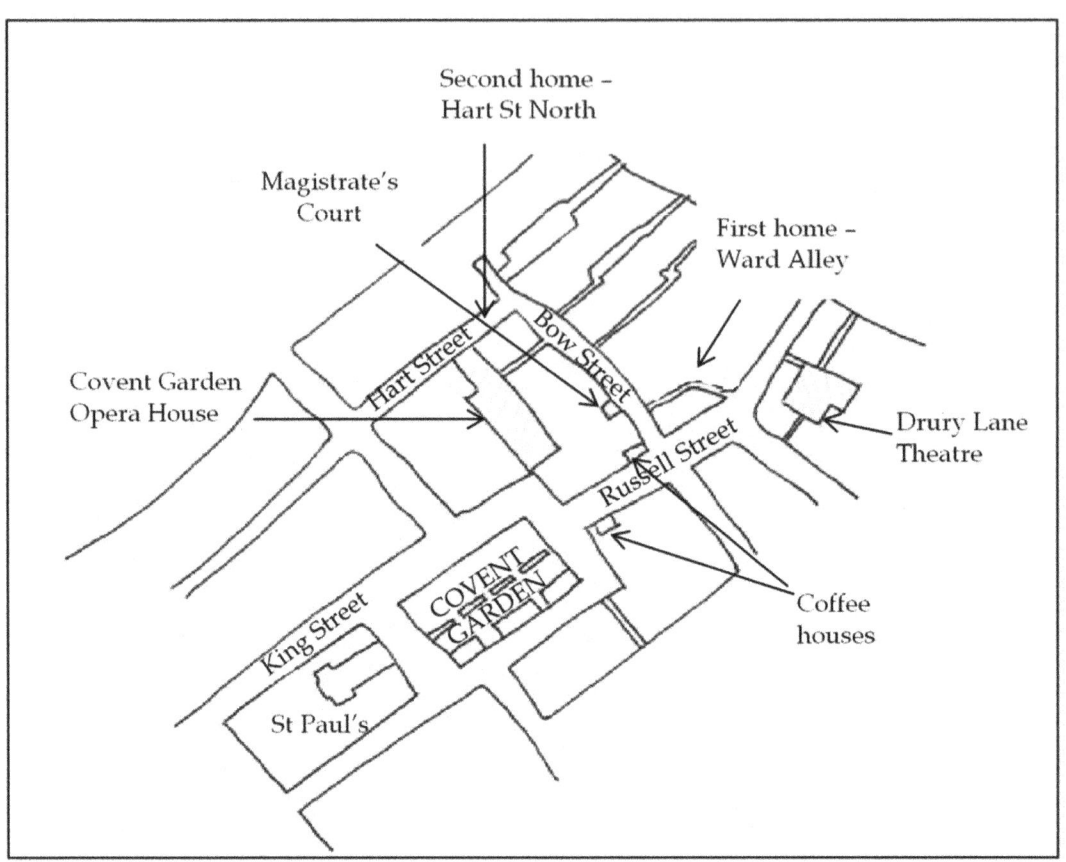

According to the Rates Books, the Ince family lived in Wards Alley off Bow Street from 1736 to 1742, and then moved round the corner to Hart Street North.

The Ince family would have been surrounded by a great deal of activity. Other occupations in the area included lawyers, engravers, booksellers, actors, poets, upholsterers and cabinet-makers, along with two coffee houses in Russell Street.

Glass-grinding was a tough occupation. A grinder would remove visible marks and excrescences from glass and polish it to give a shining surface. He *fixes plate glass horizontally and rubs it backwards and forwards upon a plane, upon which sand and water are constantly running. The glass being thus on both sides ground perfectly true is afterwards polished with emery and putty*[xxviii]. He would have used a spring-loaded wooden block for the polishing. The noise must have been horrendous. John Ince may also have been involved in finishing imported mirrors. This involved grinding, polishing, silvering and cutting to size. Silvering involved the use of mercury, which may have contributed to his early death. In his Universal Directory of 1763 Thomas Mortimer described the trade as follows: *These artists grind and polish Plate Glass aftr the Makrs, and then silver it for Looking Glasses, or leave it transparent for Coaches, Chairs, etc.*

In 1739 there was a report in the London Daily Post of one of John Ince's apprentices going missing. The reward for his return was 'six pounds of Broken Glass and no questions asked.'

John Ince died in September 1745. On the 3rd September he made a will[xxix] and on the 12th September he was buried back in Stone, with his parents. The will was witnessed by his sister Elizabeth who made her mark, revealing that he had returned to his family roots in Worcestershire and died there.

From his will it seems his main concern was that the glass-grinding business should be continued, first with his wife Mary in charge and then with his eldest son John to be admitted as a partner as soon as he reached the age of 21, with John and his mother sharing the profit equally. Their son William was only 8 when his father died, so the provision for him was to be bound apprentice with his mother when he reached the age of 14 and to become an equal partner on completion of the apprenticeship. Or, to be given twenty pounds to be apprenticed to a different trade and to receive a third part of his father's stocks and effects on completion. This payment would have helped William when setting up in business with John Mayhew.

John Ince left his two daughters, Elizabeth and Mary, the sum of sixty pounds each, with ten pounds of it to be used to apprentice them to a trade such as millinery[25]. He also left three watches: the chased gold to his wife, his best silver watch to the eldest son John and his other silver watch to William. He appointed four executors, including 'my loving brother William Ince' (the wheelwright) and requested that they accept *a gold ring a piece* to be bought out of his stocks and effects and also for them to be reimbursed for their *Trouble Travell Labour Costs Charges and Expenses*. He was not poor.

He allowed for his wife Mary to be paid £150 (or £120 if the business had suffered) should she re-marry to be taken as her share of the business, so long as her husband

---

[25] £60 was a good amount of money. According to the National Archives currency converter £60 in 1750 would have the spending worth of £7000 in 2017.

agreed to pay it back to the children on her death. If the new husband was not approved by the executors of his will, then John requested that the sum of £150/£120 be invested and the interest be paid direct to his wife for her own use.

Mary did remarry – on 21st January 1747 she married Hugh Lethard, a frame-maker but Hugh died and was buried on 12th April 1751 aged 31. This raises the question of whether Mary was fairly young when she married John Ince, who was 46 when he died.

On 31st March 1748 there was an advertisement in the General Advertiser *To be sold by auction Entire Household Goods Stock and Implements in Trade of Mr John Ince Glass grinder deceased by express Direction of his Will at his late Dwelling House the Upper End of Bow Street Covent Garden. The House to be Lett and Possession given immediately after the Sale.* The Rates Book for Westminster show that Mary Ince paid the rates in 1746, then Hugh Lethard took over for 1747 and 1748. The four children then aged around 20, 17, 11 and 10 years, would have been living with their mother and her second husband. They then left that area.

Chapter 6 1737-1804

William Ince Cabinet Maker – His Life

William Ince was my great great great great grandfather and I became fascinated with his life after seeing some of the furniture that has been loosely attributed to Ince & Mayhew at Clandon Park, a National Trust house in Surrey[26]. His wife, Ann Stephenson, was also an interesting character as she was the person who took John Mayhew to court within a month of William having died.

Unearthing the details of the court case has been challenging, but has also revealed information about the amount of property that the firm invested in, both in Soho and in Hornsey and Crouch End.

Finding information about the Ince Family Grave at Whitefield Chapel in Tottenham Court Road, a non-conformist church, where Ann's father was buried in 1759, suggested that William was willing to stand against the establishment, though the wealthy patrons of the firm over the years provided him and his family with a comfortable living.

Historical context

The latter half of the eighteenth century was a period of relative stability in England. George III came to the throne on 25th October 1760 and was there until 1820. William Pitt the younger became Prime Minister in 1783 and was in office to 1803. The American War of Independence took place but had little impact apart from its effect on trade. The Agricultural Revolution was taking place, with increasing enclosures and movement to the cities as the Industrial Revolution moved manufacturing away from the villages. There was a great improvement in the roads which facilitated trade between internal markets. There was an increase in wealth and leisure for land-owners and manufacturers, but an increase in poverty for those made landless.

The wealthy could afford art and the art was still hand-crafted and of quality. In mainstream religious life, there was a tolerant attitude though religion was abstract and impersonal while the Methodists were spreading their message of evangelism and philanthropy. The Grand Tour which Robert Adam undertook in the 1750s had been popular with the wealthy for some time but it has been suggested that it was the discovery of Herculaneum in 1738 and Pompeii in 1748 that was influential in the move to neoclassical design.

---

[26] These pieces were only loosely attributed to Ince & Mayhew as they had no documentation. They were sadly destroyed in the fire at Clandon Park in April 2015.

Childhood

William Ince was born in 1737, being baptised on 31st March 1737 in St Paul's Covent Garden[xxx], the son of John Ince and Mary. John's trade as a glass-grinder would have provided a steady income and William would not have gone without food or shelter. According to the Westminster Rate Books the family was living in Ward Alley from 1736-1742, then moved round the corner to Hart Street North.

Very little is known about William's mother, Mary, but it seems likely that she educated her children, perhaps teaching them to read and write. She may also have been artistic and encouraged William in his drawing.

William's father died in 1745 when William would have been 8 years old. In his will[xxxi] he left William his second best watch and the money for him to be apprenticed when he was of age. William's uncle, William the wheelwright in Kidderminster, died in 1749 and left William fifty pounds along with his second best bed and silver watch. William would have received this money in 1758 after his aunt died.

Font at St Paul's Covent Garden
Photo: John Salmon

His father also made provision for his wife in the event of her re-marrying, which she did in January 1747. William's step-father was a frame-maker called Hugh Lethard, who died 4 years after his marriage to Mary Ince. By this time there were four surviving children from her first marriage, John, William, Elizabeth and Mary, the other six of the ten baptised presumably having all died. In 1748 according to an advertisement in the General Advertiser of 31st March 1748, there was an auction at the house of the *Entire Household Goods Stock and Implements in Trade* and the house was to be let with immediate possession. It is not known exactly where they moved to though his brother was described as *of St Andrew, Holborn* in 1751 when this family became involved with the law.

Hugh Lethard, the step-father died in April 1751 and on 27th April, John, now aged 21, put in a Bill of Complaint to the Chancery Court[xxxii] against the executors of his father's will as he was *desirous of employing his share of his said father's efforts in setting him up for his way of trade.* John was described as a glass-grinder but may have been working for someone else. He was also complaining on behalf of William who was under age, but in need of his share of his father's estate to buy his apprenticeship.

By answer in May, it was reported that Mary had carried on the trade for 18 months on her own, and then another 18 months with her second husband – a slight exaggeration if the house and tools were being sold in March 1748. The three London executors, Messrs Bladwell, Shelton and Boggins had paid debts totalling £583 and had over £800 remaining. They were ready and willing to act but wanted reasonable costs and charges. Their mother Mary wanted her fair share of the business for herself and her two daughters.

She believed the complainants were entitled to all their father's effects and stock and utensils in trade after payment of debts and of the £150 to her and £60 a piece to the two daughters. The records of the case tell us that the two daughters, Mary and Elizabeth were too young to make their own answer, so a guardian was appointed for this purpose, named Elizabeth Ince who was from Franche a small village north of Kidderminster in Worcestershire where she made her oath. This is the person who inherited the house and property of her brother, William the wheelwright.

There was a notice in the London Gazette in July 1752: *Pursuant to a Decree of the High Court of Chancery the creditors of John Ince late of the Parish of Covent Garden Glass grinder deceased are peremptorily to come before Peter Holford Esq. one of the Masters of the said Court at this Chambers in Symond's Inn in Chancery Lane, London on or before 20th day of July instant and prove their Debts, or they will be excluded the Benefit of the said Decree.* According to a later decree[xxxiii], the residue of their father's personal estate belonged equally to the plaintiffs (John and William) and William's moiety *was ordered to be laid out in South Sea Annuitys.*

As described earlier, John Ince endeavoured to set up as a glass-grinder in Birmingham, but it would appear that he lacked the necessary business acumen and eventually ended up in Marshalsea Prison in 1761 for debt. His daughter, Mary Jane, was baptised in St Anne's, Soho on 21 May 1761 but no more is known of him, until he was buried on 19th October 1803 aged 74 in Elmley Lovett, back with his Worcestershire ancestors.

After Aunt Elizabeth died in 1758, the two nieces, Mary and Elizabeth inherited her property in Ffranch, near Kidderminster and in September 1761 Mary married William Crundall, no doubt related to Edward Crundall who had witnessed the will of Uncle William the wheelwright[27]. Her sister Elizabeth appears to have remained unmarried and was buried in Stone churchyard in 1780. Mary was also buried in Stone in 1822,

---

[27] Mary Ince married William Crundall on 8 Sep 1761 in Kidderminster and they had ten children. This information was provided by Daphne Ince's neighbour, whose own family tree included six people with the name Ince. Our common ancestor is John Ince the glass grinder.

and in her will was described as a widow of Ffranch. She owned considerable property in Ffranch and gave each of her surviving seven children £100 each, apart from her son William who received *the sum of one shilling only.*

Apprenticeship

William Ince was apprenticed to John West, a cabinet maker of King Street, Covent Garden on 10th August 1752[xxxiv]. He was 15 years old. In order to raise enough money for his apprenticeship, he had to go back to Court[xxxv].

In his father's will William was assigned £20 to be paid for an apprenticeship if he did not want to join the family glass-grinding business. He would have known John West's business as it was very near the family home, but John West refused to take him on for less than £40. The Master of the Court had to examine whether the £40 would be well spent, and reported in the November that *the said John West was a person of very good credit and reputation and carried on a very large and Extensive trade and Business.* As a result the Executors were told to pay the £40 to John West so William could start his apprenticeship.

John West had many commissions including Alscot Park, Warwickshire, Woburn Abbey and some for the Duke of Beaufort. He did upholstery work and furniture including gilt pier glasses. William would have been trained to a high standard of cabinet-making and would also have been made aware of the importance of contact with the nobility as part of business. William subscribed to Chippendale's *Director* in 1754, which would have been influential in his own design.

He finished his apprenticeship when John West died in May 1758 having only completed six years of the usual seven. John Mayhew was among the group of three men who took over John West's business in November 1758, but within a month Mayhew left that firm and he and William went into business together, taking over the business of Charles Smith, given as *opposite Broad Street, Carnaby Market*, in their advertisement in the Public Advertiser dated 27th January 1759. It is interesting to speculate on why those two men in their early twenties chose to work together. John Mayhew may have been impressed by William's skill and the contacts he had made and William may have seen a keen entrepreneur in John Mayhew, who had the capital to get them started in business on their own.

Family

The London Chronicle of 20-23rd February 1762 reported: *Last week were married at St George's Hanover-Square, Meff Mayhew and Ince to Miss Isabella and Miss Nancy Stephenson*[xxxvi], the *Nancy* lending an air of frivolity to Ann. According to the marriage licence, Ann

Interior of St George's Hanover Square – John Salmon

Stephenson was only nineteen years old, and her mother agreed to the marriage, Ann's father having died. Her mother signed herself as Jean Stephenson, though the licence refers to Jane Stephenson. She did not attend at Doctors Commons to testify her consent, because of *old age and infirmity*. All four signed the entries in the Parish Register, and the witnesses were John Mayhew's father and William Ince, for John and Isabella, and again John Mayhew's father and this time John Mayhew for William and Ann. The curate, Thomas Vincent, performed the service along with the other three marriages that took place that day.

In his will William referred to the furniture that had come from Ann's mother's house in James Street, Grosvenor Square. According to the Rates Books for the Parish[xxxvii], a George Stevenson, later Stephenson, lived in James Street from 1758, and in 1766 the name changes to Widow Stephenson. It would not be surprising if the husband's name was left in for a few years after his death. The only marriage for a George Stephenson to a Jane in the appropriate timespan took place in St Clement Danes, Westminster on 1733 when George married Jane Rayner. She was the daughter of Thomas and Eliza and was baptised at St James Clerkenwell on 31st March 1712. It is likely that they knew the Mayhew family as John Mayhew only lived a few streets away in Green Street and they would probably have all attended services in St George's Hanover Square. It has not yet been possible to find Ann's or Isabella's baptisms.

Ann's father George died in 1759 and was buried in Whitefield Memorial Church, as were William and Ann and other members of their family. Someone called Isabel Stephenson was buried there in 1777, aged 78 years from the parish of Hornsey. She may have been Ann's aunt, and living near or with her in Crouch End. The name Isabella is passed on in both families. Widow Stephenson is recorded in the Rates

Books for James Street until 1769 and she was buried at St Martin in the Fields on 20th March that year.

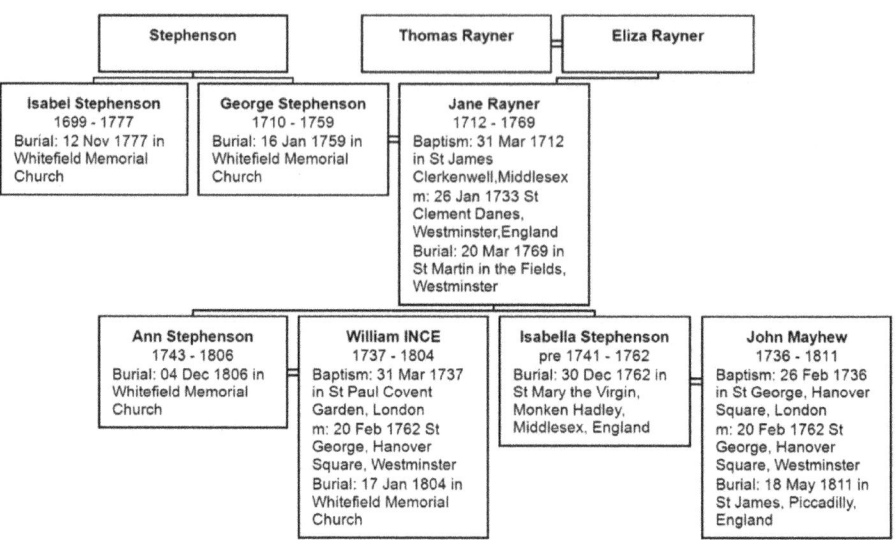

According to the Chancery records the two families initially lived in the same house It would have been a comfort for the sisters, Ann and Isabella, to live together, bearing in mind that Ann was only 19 when she married and the house had four stories and fourteen rooms and there would have been many workmen and apprentices around the place. Later on the Ince family lived in No. 49 Marshall Street, the Mayhews in No. 47 [28] and the business was run from No. 48.

Very sadly Isabella died after giving birth to twins at the end of the year of the wedding. Baby daughter Sarah died the following September, but Isabella survived to 1822. It's possible that the babies were nursed by Ann, who gave birth to the Ince's first child, Ann, three weeks later[xxxviii] and it would have been a difficult time.

John Mayhew remarried three years later. A marriage bond dated 23rd December 1765 shows John Mayhew married Bridget Winsley in St James Piccadilly, and according to his reply in the Chancery records dated 15th November 1806, the money he advanced to the firm between 1766 and 1769 *were actually and bona fide made by the Defendant out of his own separate property being what he derived from his wife on his marriage or chiefly arising from that.*

---

[28] Joshua Dorset Mayhew, solicitor son of John Mayhew, used the address 47 Marshall Street (Law Journal 1803)

The baptism records for St James Piccadilly record thirteen children being born to William and Ann Ince from 1763 to 1785 of whom 5 died in infancy and only six outlived their parents. The Timeline for William and Ann Ince gives the details.

Old Crouch Hall c.1885 Photograph by E.Scamell

The 1780 Land Tax records show that William had a property in Crouch End. It was the middle property of the three owned by William Smith, and was probably Linslade House, which was attached to Old Crouch Hall to the left. In 1788 William bought the estate of Old Crouch Hall from William Smith paying an annuity of £120 a year for it. In 1795 William Ince's house in Crouch End was destroyed by fire and he was paid £215 insurance money. It took 42 men to put out the fire[xxxix].

The estate included two cottages and land on which William paid tax in 1798 as well as paying tax on two houses owned by William Smith, ie Old Crouch Hall and Linslade House. Both the 1799 agreement and the Masters Account Books refer to William Ince's residence as separate to Old Crouch Hall itself, and by then he did not live there, but rented it out. According to his will written in 1800, the whole of the Crouch End estate had been brought into trade, being let out as furnished houses. His residence was sold on 2nd October 1823. The Smith family did well out of the annuity as the widow was paid a further £4000 when the estate was finally sold in 1827.

At that time there was a satirical print about businessmen retreating to Hornsey for their summer weekends but the Ince family seem to have settled in Crouch End. Both he and John Mayhew were surveyors for the parish, which involved making sure the road was in good repair. William was elected Church Warden of St Mary's Hornsey in 1793[xl] and in 1794 and in 1796 he was elected to the Committee to assist officers in regulating the Poor of the Parish, meeting on the first Monday of the month at six o'clock in the evening. Their daughter Isabella married George Cowell there on 24 December 1795, both William and Ann signing as witnesses. Isabella Mayhew, John Mayhew's daughter from his first marriage to Isabella Stephenson, (Ann's sister) had her first child baptised in St Mary's Hornsey in 1787. She was either living there, or went to her aunt's or her father's villa in Hornsey to have her first child. She was married to John Rush and he and their children were party to the 1825 Land Registry Document.

William was generous to his children. In his will[xli] he described how he had already helped them financially. He mentioned a letter from his oldest son, William, in which he said he had already had more from his father than he could expect and wished to be no obstacle to his parents' comfort. William had already given Charles some *furniture for a house in Kentish Town and a house in King Street, Portman Square and effects to a considerable amount.* Henry Robert had had furniture and effects for several houses. Frederick had had a house furnished for him near Saint Bartholomew's hospital and the fixtures of a Grocers Shop. William wished to give him the same as his brothers Charles and Henry Robert but advised his executors to buy Stocks and apportion the interest to Frederick. William furnished a house in America Square which he gave to his daughter Isabella on her marrying George Cowell. He wished to give Mary Ann who was not yet married, the same amount as Isabella, and desired £1500 of Government Security to be invested for her.

William wanted to divide his books equally among his sons and daughters which reveal an interesting collection for an eighteenth century cabinet-maker. He declared *an inclination to name some as in the manner following:*

Son William was bequeathed the three volume family Bible, Mortimer's History of England and two volumes of Geography, plus twenty volumes of the Encyclopaedia Britannica, and all the Universal magazines.

Charles received William's box of Drawing Instruments, all his architectural books and books of furniture and ornaments.

Frederick received his Dictionary of Arts and Sciences and such books as relate to Mechanics and Geometry and all his working tools.

Henry Robert received Salmons Herbal Philosophical Transactions abridged and all other books relating to Physic and Surgery.

Isabella received the rest of the music books and five volumes of Handel's Songs and Oratorys.

Mary Ann was bequeathed all the rest of the vocal and instrumental music and *all such others in my case as may be found proper for the instruction of a young woman.*

Music would have been an integral part of their life: the evidence being the two finger organs that are included in the later furniture sale, as well as the items of music bequeathed by William.

These bequests were thoughtfully linked to his children's chosen professions.

Ann Ince

Ann gave birth to eleven children in the twelve years from 1763 and 1775, eight boys and three girls. There was then a gap of seven years before Mary Ann was born in 1782 and Edward in 1785. Only six of their children outlived them and most of the children who died were still infants. It must have been an exhausting, sorrowful time.

Ann would have been in charge of 49 Marshall Street with the responsibility of nursing, feeding and clothing the every growing family, as well as providing food and fresh clothing for her husband and any live-in workmen or clerks. She would probably have been responsible for the household accounts. William did not take care of the firm's cash books for very long, so probably was not interested in the household bills and wages. So Ann would have paid any servants, the washer-woman, the butcher, the grocer, the tallow chandler etc. and kept the books. She would have had full responsibility for the household when William was away on business.

One of the reasons for having a house in Crouch End may have been to improve the children's health. The air would have been cleaner, and they may have had a garden there. In 1787 the youngest, Edward, died aged eighteen months, within a year of son, George John who had died in Hornsey at the age of 15. By that time the eldest William had joined the Regiment of Bombay Artillery (1782), Frederick had been apprenticed to a coach-maker (1786) and Henry Robert had been apprenticed to a surgeon (1788). Isabella married George Cowell in 1795, and Charles married Anna Maria Jones in 1797. By 1800 Mary Ann was the only surviving child still living with her parents.

They left Crouch End in order to rent it out and returned to Marshall Street to live, which must have been hard. William wrote his will in 1800 and may have had to be nursed for the remaining years of his life.

Ann's character came to the fore shortly after William died, when she took out the court case against John Mayhew, demanding a just settlement of the firm's affairs. She was supported in this by her son-in-law George Cowell. He was a merchant and probably more of a businessman than any of the immediate family. There is a sense of Ann as the driving force behind the court case, but the laborious system of the law took its toll and she died two years later. This would have been a week after the 15th November 1806 answer in court that John Mayhew was still pursuing his claim and the cash books had to be submitted. She probably despaired of receiving the justice she felt her family deserved.

Politics

William was entitled to vote in parliamentary elections in Westminster, which was the only parliamentary borough in Middlesex at that time, and had a 'scot and lot' franchise which qualified all men paying poor rates. 'Where two or more men are owners either as joint tenants, or as tenants in common of an estate in any land or tenement, one of such men, but not more than one shall ... be entitled to be registered as a voter.' Therefore, adult sons living at home or heads of households who shared houses were not eligible to vote. As a woman, Ann of course could not vote.

The Poll Books show that in 1774 William voted for Earl Percy and Lord Thomas Pelham-Clinton both described as non-partisan ie not Whig but supporters of Lord North. In 1780 he voted for Fox (Whig) and the Earl of Lincoln (Tory), and in 1784 he voted for Hood (Tory) and Wray (Whig) not Fox. This implies that he supported the status quo, probably because that was best for business although a number of their clients were of the Whig aristocracy[xlii].

William Ince and John Mayhew were both members of the Society for the Encouragement of Arts, Manufactures and Commerce (RSA) and they were also both Freemasons. William Ince was a member of the Lodge of Felicity, which included a number of their neighbours. John Mayhew was a member of the Lodge of Antiquity.

Faith and Burial

Both William and Ann appear to have held sincere religious beliefs. In his will William began with thanks to God: *first I commit my soul to that great good and Almighty God who has been always so gracious in protecting of me and by whose providence I enjoy those Things I now mean by this will to dispose of hoping his infinite Mercy will forgive all my offences as I do sincerely all those that have trespassed against me.* There was also a stipulation that his wife Ann should decide where he was to be buried. William died on 4th January 1804[xliii]. The cause for death was given as apoplexy. He was probably affected by the difficulties in ending the partnership, concerned about the debts and also affected by the death of his brother John in Worcestershire less than three months earlier.

Ann died on 21st November 1806[xliv]. In her will[xlv], she also gave thanks to God for her life, but revealingly there was no mention of forgiveness. She desired to be buried in the same vault as her *dear husband*.

It is likely that they both attended Whitefield Memorial Church in Tottenham Court Road, not far from Marshall Street. I have found an Ince Family Grave there with seven Ince burials and Ann's father George Stephenson was buried there in 1759.

Whitefield Tabernacle or Memorial Church was a popular non-conformist church set up in 1756 by George Whitefield, a contemporary of the Wesleys at Oxford. He was not a Methodist but a Calvinistic Dissenter and a populist preacher in the evangelical revival. He had the financial support of the Countess of Huntingdon. The Tabernacle was a large structure and was referred to as 'The Dissenters' Cathedral'. The church was enlarged in 1760 and included a vault below described as 'spacious catacombs'[xlvi]. Occasional visitors were William Pitt, the Duke of Grafton and Charles Fox.

Burials in the Ince Family Grave

Date of burial	Person	Age	Parish	Relation to William & Ann
July 29 1765	Mary Ince	4 years	St George Hanover Square	Niece
June 13 1786	George Ince	15 years	Hornseal (Hornsey)	Child
25 March 1787	Edward Ince	18 months	St James Westminster	Child
19 Jan 1803	Anna Maria Ince	16 months	St Mary le bone	Grandchild
18 Aug 1803	Wm John Ince	3 years 6 mo	St Mary le bone	Grandchild
17 Jan 1804	Ince	79 years	St James	Probably William
4 Dec 1806	Ince	50 years	St James Westminster	Probably Ann

The first Ince burial there was in July 1765 when the daughter of William's brother, John Ince the glass-grinder and his wife Mary, a little girl called Mary was buried at the age of 4[29]. Two of William and Ann's children were buried here, George who died in 1786 aged 15, and whose parish was given as Hornsey, and Edward in 1787, who was only eighteen months old. It seems likely William and Ann were worshipping there and they may have attended the memorial service for George Whitefield, who had died in America in 1770, when the preacher was John Wesley.

---

[29] Mary Ince daughter of John and Mary was baptised in St Anne's, Soho on 31st May 1761.

William was Church Warden at St Mary's in Hornsey in 1793, but that does not mean that he worshipped there. As Gebhard Wendeborn wrote in 1791[xlvii], *The troublesome duty of a church-warden falls upon every parishioner in rotation, who is obliged to serve two years, under a penalty of fifteen pounds, payable to the parish.* Dissenters were not only permitted, but compelled to serve when elected, just as they were required to pay their tithes and parish rates.

There were two other children in the vault, Anna Maria, buried in January 1803, and William John, buried in August 1803, both of St Mary le Bone parish, the children of William and Ann's son Charles and his wife Anna Maria[xlviii].

Five months later, in January 1804 there is a record for an Ince being buried, with no other details except for an age of 79 and of the parish of St James Westminster. Two years later there was another Ince burial in December 1806 with the age given as 50, again from St James Westminster. As these two last burials correspond extremely closely with the deaths of William and Ann, on 4th January 1804 and 23rd November 1806 respectively, it seems extremely likely that this was where they were buried, with their two children and two grandchildren. The ages given are incorrect: William would have been 67 when he died and Ann would have been 63. It is possible their children were unsure of their ages, or that false ages were given to hide their identities or the clerk may have misheard or written himself a note which he could not read correctly later. In any case, this was not their final resting place, as all the coffins at Whitefield Chapel were moved to Chingford Mount Cemetery in 1898[xlix].

It was for Ann to decide where William should be buried and the obvious option would have been St James Piccadilly. The parish records for this church and for St Mary's Hornsey have been checked, but he was not buried at either. At St James's John Mayhew was Church Warden in 1804 and they were battling with him to settle the closure of the partnership fairly, so one can understand why she would not have chosen that church. From William's account in his will that the Crouch End houses were being let, they would probably have already broken any connection with that church. Ann simply requested to be buried with 'her dear husband'.

John Mayhew was buried in the North Vault at St James Piccadilly in 1811 with his second wife, Bridget.

House Auction

Ann Ince, William's widow, died on 21st November 1806 and although various members of the family appear to have lived in the house in Marshall Street after this date[30], an auction would have been an opportunity for the family to raise some money, as all the money for the firm was tied up in Chancery. Accordingly a catalogue was produced with the title: *The property of the late William Ince Esq. Dec. at his late dwelling in Broad Street, Soho which will be sold by auction by Mr Christie on Monday 9th March 1807 and following day at twelve o'clock.*

The catalogue provides a fine description of the layout of their house as items are listed room by room. There were four floors. The ground floor had a hall, with a painted oil cloth to the inner hall and the stairs were carpeted. Amongst items in the hall were a pair of card tables and *a neat child's phaeton*. The kitchen and china closet contained a large quantity of pots, cutlery, coppers, including a chocolate pot and a coffee pot and 39 plates of pewter. The ground floor also had a Dark Room which contained various items of mahogany furniture, plus *a gun, a blunderbuss, 2 pistols and a globe.*

The Drawing Room and Dining Parlour were on the first floor, along with a further room and a dark room. The Drawing Room was beautifully fitted out with *eight very neat fancy chairs japanned… covered with green damask; a large sofa covered with green damask; a pair of small ditto; three sets of green damask festoon curtains lined and gilt cornices; a french plate pier glass 48 in. by 39½ in.. gilt frame; a ditto 48½ in by 43½ in.. gilt frame; a pair of elegant satin-wood pier tables, inlaid; an elegant inlaid commode; four gilt girandoles..; a two-flap lady's work table with a drawer made of yew, inlaid; a Parisian eight day clock, in an or-molu case; a neat inlaid chess board; a twelve in. terrestrial globe; a large blue and white China jar; a mahogany Pembroke table; a Wilton planned carpet 19 ft. 6 in. by 13 ft. 6 in..*

The Dining Parlour contained similar riches including *an excellent mahogany sideboard; an oval mahogany two-flap table; a set of mahogany dinner tables with circular ends 11 ft. by 4 ft.; a mahogany Pembroke table; a pair of neat mahogany dumb waiters; six neat square back chairs and two elbow ditto; a very neat mahogany chest of drawers;* a total of 48 knives and forks; *a Brussels carpet 12 ft. by 11 ft.; a French plate pier glass 44 in. by 33 in.; a fine Vauxhall plate 49 in. by 29 in,; an elegant eight day Parisian clock in a rich Or-molu case; two chair back skreens and a folding skreen.*

The two other rooms on the first floor also had carpets and items of furniture including a smaller pier glass, *a fine tuned harpsichord by Kirckman*, a loo table with a turn over top, a barometer, a large quantity of china including 24 Salopian meat plates, 69 pieces of Staffordshire china, and ornamental china and a large quantity of glass

---

[30] Martha Ince gave her address as Broad Street for the baptism of her son Percy on 28th November 1824.

and earthenware, including 132 large and small plates, 56 yellow dishes and 100 various other plates.

The second floor had the best bedroom which had a Wilton carpet, a 5'6" four-poster bed, *a very excellent mahogany dressing chest of drawers* and *a ditto to match* and a large quantity of furniture including two bird cages and a mahogany *bidett*[31]. The back chamber had a French canopy bedstead, two chests of drawers and *a washing stand, ewer and bason.* The middle room had a mahogany wardrobe, dressing glass, ladies dressing table with glass, a mahogany washing stand and six dyed chairs.

On the top floor there was a front attic containing two bedsteads and two deal chests of drawers, a deal table and 4 chairs, and a back room with a 5' four-post bedstead and various pieces of mahogany and deal furniture.

Also listed in the catalogue are some 130 books including books on gardening, Tomlins on Wills[32], Culpeper's Dispensatory, Description of Wilton House, Pilkington's Dictionary original edition[33], Ogilby's America, Ogilby's Persia[34], Maitland's History of London[35], a parcel of designs for ceilings, furniture etc, sundry maps on rollers, Arminius an opera by Handel, and Comus, also by Handel. The total amount raised from book sales was £39 11s 6d.

The ten lots of Prints included portraits and etchings and there were 63 lots of Pictures, which raised a total amount of £229 16s 6d. These include paintings by Sachtleven, Breughel, Teniers, School of Rembrandt, La Croix, Canaletti, and Moucheron. The latter's painting of a waterfall, went at the highest price of £18 7s 6d. Some paintings had been sold in an earlier auction by Christie's in 1805, under the

---

[31] Furniture listed: two oval glasses, two side tables, a two flap fly table and two hassocks, a mahogany *bidett*, a small book shelf, an easy chair, an elbow chair, 2 stools, a work table, two bird cages, six painted chairs and 4 stools.

[32] *A familiar, plain, and easy explanation of the law of wills and codicils, and of the law of executors and administrators. ... The whole written as much as possible without the use of law words or terms. By a Barrister, of the Inner Temple* Thomas Edlyne Tomlins, Sir, London, 1762-1841.

[33] *The gentleman's and connoisseur's dictionary of painters. Containing a complete collection, and account, of the most distinguished artists, who have flourished in the art of painting, ...*By the Rev. Matthew Pilkington, Vicar of Donabate, Dublin. London, 1770.

[34] *Asia, the first part : Being an accurate description of Persia, and the several provinces thereof. The vast empire of the Great Mogol, and other parts of India: and their several kingdoms and regions: with the denominations and descriptions of the cities, towns, and places of remark therein contain'd. illustrated with notes, and adorn'd with peculiar maps and proper sculptures* by John Ogilby 1600-1676. London Printed by the author 1673

[35] *The history of London from its foundation to the present time ... including the several parishes in Westminster, Middlesex, Southwark, &c., within the bills of mortality* by William Maitland, F.R.S.1693?-1757. London: J. Wilkie, 1775.

name Mrs William Ince. They also went at a low price. An 1804 auction included paintings with the seller listed as Mayhew & Ince, so may have belonged to the firm[l].

Some dozen items in the 1807 sale were bought by the Ince family themselves, including the *harpsichord by Kirckman with a mahogany case and stool* bought for £2 5s.; *a Wilton carpet; forty-nine piece of fluted tea and coffee China with blue sprig of old Worcester* for 10s 0d; *a pair of large figures of Milton and Shakespeare* for £2; *28 cut wine glasses, 12 engraved punch tumblers 2 cut salts, 2 pepper castors;* and from the Dining Parlour, the 2 flap table, a dumb waiter and the eight chairs.

Amongst the items bought by George Cowell, Isabella's husband and one of the orators in the Chancery case, was a *rifle barrel coach gun by Clarkson skrew barrel* for £3 3s. Stephen Habberton, principal clerk of the firm and one of William's executors bought one of the *French plate pier glass* for £11 and *a 5 ft. 6 in. four-post mahogany bedstead* for £8 16s. and a cheese toaster. James Bolton, one of the long term employees of the firm bought some furniture including the *set of mahogany dinner tables with circular ends* for £9 9s.; and a *four leaved map skreen*[36] for £3 3s. The grand total raised from the auction was £711 1s 6d (over £33,000 in 2017[li]) and it is to be hoped that the proceeds were distributed amongst all the family.

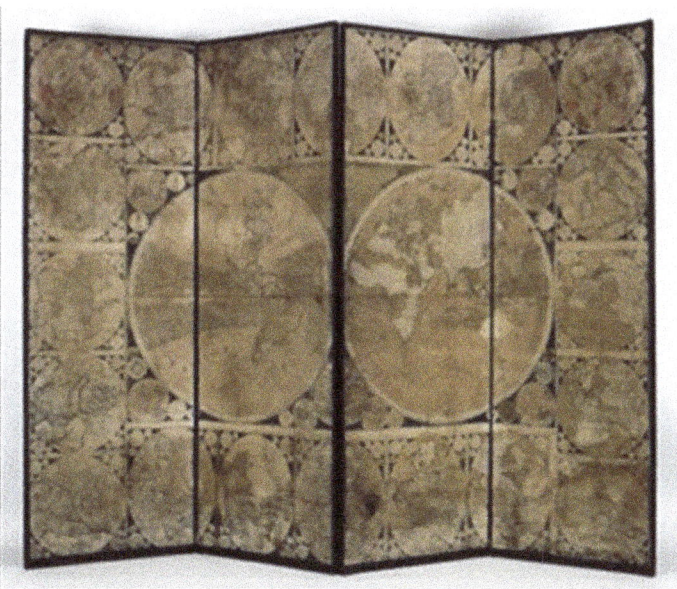

Four-fold map screen, with 21 engraved maps 6ft x 8ft
British Library Thomas Jefferys John Bowles c.1750

---

[36] A map screen was a simple wooden frame with a map glued to a canvas backing attached to the frame. Its main purpose would have been to reduce draughts, but it could also have been used as an educational tool, and to impress visitors.

Timeline for William and Ann Ince

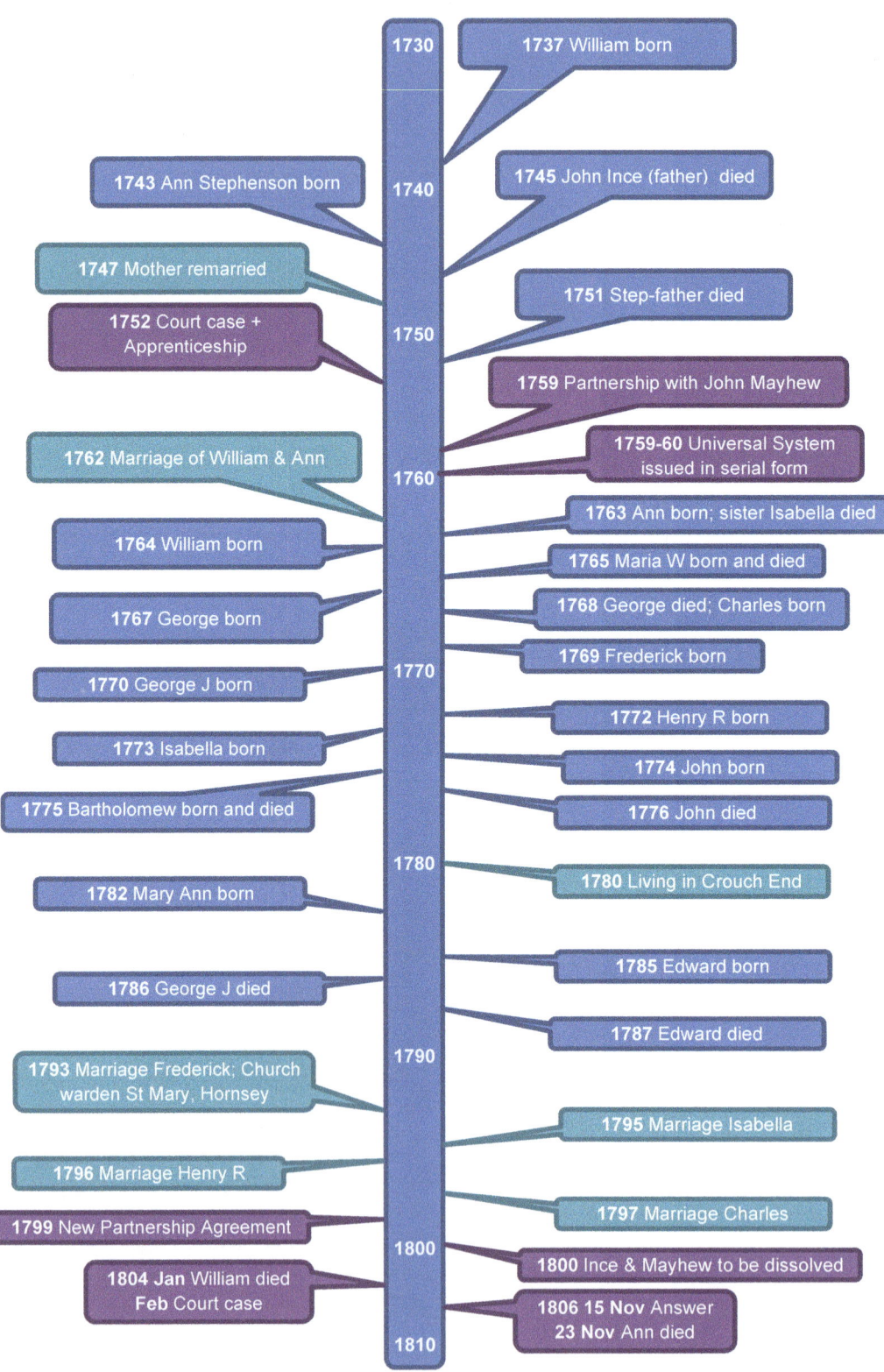

Chapter 7 Ince & Mayhew
William Ince Cabinet Maker – His Work

Ince & Mayhew was one of the most prestigious firms of cabinet-makers in eighteenth century England, producing furniture of high quality for their aristocratic clients. William Ince was the partner responsible for the cabinet-making side of the business and John Mayhew was the salesman who brought in the customers. He was probably also in charge of the Upholder side of the business.

The two partners set up a formal agreement on 16th January 1759, committing themselves to a partnership of 21 years from 25th December 1758 with the purchase of the property of Charles Smith, late of Marshall Street, including a dwelling house, a workshop behind and a stock of wood[lii]. They described themselves as Cabinet-makers and Upholders.

In 1747, Robert Campbell writing on apprenticeships in *The London Tradesman* described the trade of an Upholder as follows:

"*He is the man upon whose judgment I rely in the choice of goods; and I suppose he has not only Judgment in the Materials, but Taste in the Fashions, and Skill in the Workmanship. This Tradesman's Genius must be universal in every Branch of Furniture; though his proper Craft is to fit up Beds, Window-Curtains, Hangings, and to cover Chairs that have stuffed Bottoms: He was originally a Species of the Taylor; but, by degrees, has crept over his Head and set up as a Connoisseur in every article that belongs to a House. He employs a Journeymen in his own proper Calling, Cabinet-Makers, Glass-Grinders, Looking-Glass Frame-Carvers, Carvers for Chairs, Testers, and Posts of Bed, and the Woolen-Draper, the Mercer, the Linen-Draper, several Species of Smiths, and a vast many Tradesmen of the other mechanic Branches. The Upholder, according to this Description of his Business, must be no fool; and have a considerable Stock to set up with.*"

There is a full description of the firm's activities in the article in the Dictionary of English Furniture Makers 1660-1840 by Hugh Roberts and Charles Cator[liii], also available online[liv], so this is more a celebration of their work.

John Mayhew did more of the managerial work and William Ince was the designer and draughtsman, overseeing that side of the business.

In the letters exchanged with Boulton & Fothergill, who provided ormolu mountings for the firm, it was William Ince who they hoped to entertain in Birmingham with *a well-aired Bed wholesome Bread & Cheese, and a hearty welcome from B & F* and William who was asked to get a copy of Museum Florentinum for them in London[lv]. His interest in design was shown in his subscriptions to various books such as Thomas Malton's *Compleat Treatise on Perspective*, 1775.

The Universal System of Household Furniture

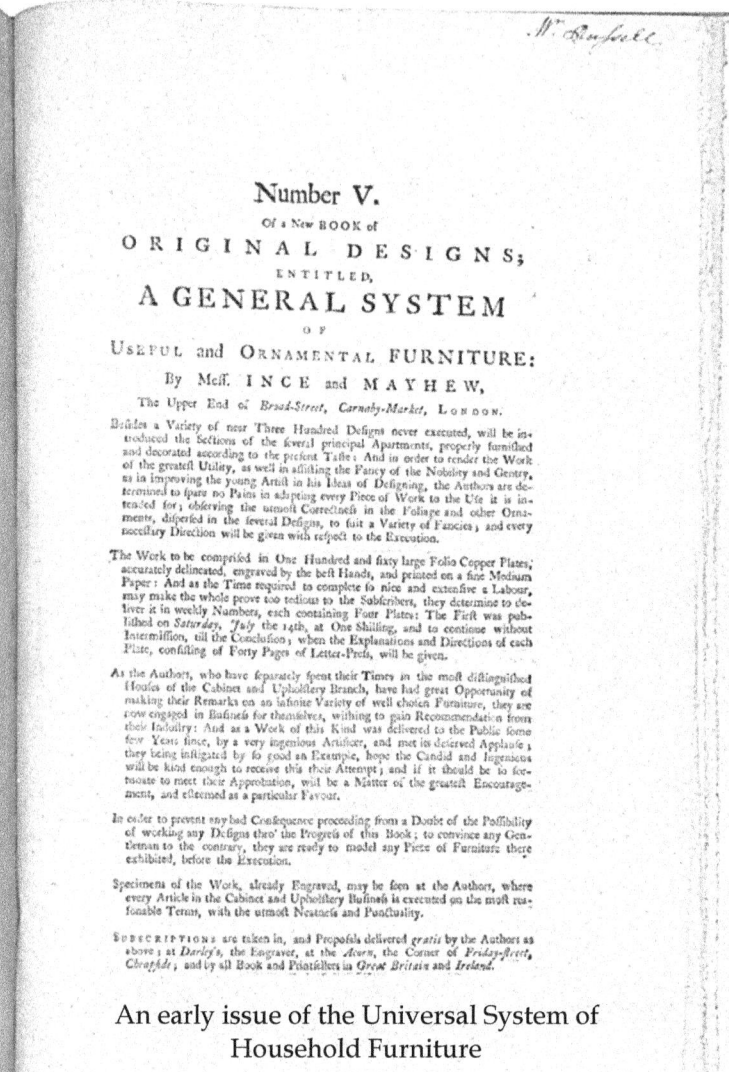

An early issue of the Universal System of Household Furniture

The firm produced a directory called '*The Universal System of Household Furniture*' over a series of issues between 1759 and 1760. The first issue was published on Saturday 14th July 1759 at one shilling. All the issues were published as a single volume in 1762, which consisted of 95 plates of '*elegant and practical furniture patterns*'. William Ince signed 75 of the designs, as well as the title page, ten were signed by John Mayhew, one by both and nine were unsigned[lvi]. The *Universal System* was an open imitation of Chippendale's *Director*, with an unnamed description of him in their forward as *a very ingenious Artificer*. The *Universal System* was not offered in America until 1766 but individual copies might have been brought over from England before then. An advertisement appeared in the South-Carolina & American General Gazette, Charleston on July 18, 1766 which read *Robert Wells, At the Great Stationary and Book Shop on the Bay, has imported for sale Chippendale's and Ince and Mayhew's designs of household furniture from London*[lvii].

In the 1870s and 1880s book dealers were advertising for old copies of furniture directories, and in 1894 The Universal System by Ince and Mayhew was sold at Sothebys for £25 (around £2000 today). The 1762 edition of the Universal System was *specially scarce* and a copy in perfect condition was priced by Batsfords in 1940 at £150[lviii]. In 1996, Christie's sold a copy of an intermediate issue, dated about 1765, for £6,325 and in 2011 they sold a copy for £8,125. An extremely fine copy of the Universal System of Household Furniture was recently for sale at £24,770. This copy had notes and drawings made by the cabinet maker who originally bought it[lix].

From an early issue of the Universal System of Household Furniture
W. Ince inv^t et delin

Chippendale produced a French version of his *Director* in 1762 and the *Universal System* has both English and French text. The French seems a very literal translation and some is quite amusing. The Claw Tables in Plate XIII are described in English as *Three very neat Designs for Claw-Tables* and in French as *Trois Desseins élégans de Tables- à -un-seul-pied.* In the drawings they only have two feet, but in French, just one! Plate LIV shows a design for an organ case, in which *at A B C, &c are the Stops*, translates as *et à A B C &c sont les ….*

William must have worked extremely hard to bring out the directory as it was initially produced at one copy every two weeks and by the time it was produced in book form they had already executed a number of the designs for their clients. The designs reflect something of William's education and training: one features the Greek god Phaeton showing some knowledge of the Classics.

Morrison H. Heckscher has written about *The Universal System* in some detail in the journal *Furniture History*[lx], and suggested that many of the designs would have come from books the two partners owned, and from other illustrations of the riches to be found on the Grand Tour. Most of the designs in their directory were in the rococo style which was going out of fashion. There are some existing pieces that can be linked to it, notably a mirror in the Metropolitan Museum of Art in New York.

Mirror in Met Museum New York: from Shillinglee Park, Sussex
Note the small squirrels in the top corners of the frame.

Peter Ward-Jackson[lxi] suggests they developed a 'peculiar ornament of their own…..the somewhat degenerate issue of a cross between rococo scrollwork and Gothic tracery'.

Work with Architects

Once they started working in the neo-classical style, they sometimes collaborated with architects such as Sir William Chambers and Robert Adam, when they would produce items to a specific design that was given to them.

The commodes at Osterley Park attributed to Ince & Mayhew have been compared with the Adam drawing for them and they correspond almost exactly. In 1775 Ince & Mayhew produced a commode for the Countess of Derby's Dressing room, part of the redesign of Lord Derby's house in Grosvenor Square by Robert Adam. The drawings for this commode are at the Soane Museum and the design was faithfully copied by William Ince as he interpreted the drawing into a solid piece of furniture. The only difference he made was to change the feet so the cabinet did not fall over when the central door was opened. The bill sent by Ince and Mayhew to the Earl of Derby dated 3rd November 1775 made it clear that the Commode was from a Design of Messrs. Adams.[lxii]

There was no particular 'house style' but the firm's furniture was noted for its *highly proficient and adventurous use of marquetry*[lxiii]. It is possible that they sometimes used marquetry panels made by Christopher Fuhrlogh, based on compositions by Angelica Kauffman[lxiv]. Christopher Fuhrlogh was a Swede who moved to London in 1768, and Angelica Kauffman, a Swiss-Austrian, arrived in 1766 and set up her studio in Golden Square, very near Broad Street. Other local artisans include the carvers Sefferin Alken and Sefferin Nelson who had workshops in Dufours Court off Broad Street. Sefferin Alken was responsible for some of the carvings at Croome Court where Ince & Mayhew had a commission in 1764.

The Earl of Coventry employed Ince & Mayhew for both his town house in Piccadilly and at Croome Court in Worcestershire for thirty years. As the Earl liked to employ local people at Croome Court it is possible that he knew William Ince had family in Worcestershire, so he was happy to keep on the firm although it was London based. There are twenty-three entries for Ince & Mayhew in the Earl's account books from 1764 to 1794 totalling the grand sum of £1359 15s 8d.

The Earl's first known commission for Ince & Mayhew was for marquetry commodes, which were made for Lady Coventry in 1764. Ince & Mayhew's bill describes them as *2 very fine Sattin wood & Holly Commodes, Neatly Grav'd & Inlaid with Flowers of Rosewood, the one with Drawers, the other with shelves to slide.*

They have small shelves in the top that pull out, designed to provide a flat surface for brushing clothes. These shelves are decorated with a meander or key pattern. The design for the urn on the front of the commodes and the pomegranate leaves on the ends are from a book *The Parallels of the Ancient Architecture with the Modern* written by a Frenchman Roland Fréart, and published in English in 1733.

They also contributed to the Tapestry Room[37], producing a pier glass designed by Robert Adam, which was 8'9" tall x 5'6" wide and carved with a shell on top, drops of husks and goats heads all *in the very best Double Burnish'd Gold.*[lxv] The Earl was billed £35 for this mirror in 1769. The firm also provided the chairs and settees for the Tapestry Room, the curtain cornices, the base for the marble top pier table and sent a crew to hang the tapestries and apply the seat covers.

In April 1768 a bill shows they went to Croome Court to mount a small tapestry, returning in September to see *about the tapestry*. The furniture for the tapestry room was sent in April 1770 though the bill for putting up the tapestries was not received until 1771. *Three Men's time at Croome putting up the Tapestry* — the men were Jones, Elwood and Bolton, at 44, 44 and 41 days each at 5s., 4s.6d. and 3s.6d. per day respectively, £28.1s.6d.[lxvi]

---

[37] The chairs, settees and a large pier mirror made by Ince & Mayhew for the Tapestry Room are now on display at The Metropolitan Museum of Art in New York in the new British Galleries.

They also carried out such tasks as *Lent sundrys for entertainment* (1772-3); dealing with problems of damp *in your Lordships Closet.* Brown paper was put on the walls, then *63 yards of fine stampt Elephant Paper put up with a thick interlining Paper under it... & colour'd fine green in verditure at 20d. a yard* £5.5s (1774); adding feathers and beating bed mattresses (1777); making *A very neat Sattinwood Cabinet for Curiosities* £31 10s (July 1781); 18 June 1792 for £13.4s.0d *a Large Walnutree Bookcase with glazed Doors & 12 Drawers.*[lxvii]

I & M curtain cornice

The house also contains a beautiful redwood stand by Ince & Mayhew made to display a Sevres porcelain basin and ewer. It was made from padoukwood which is bright red when cut, and the stand is beautifully carved with a ram's head at the top of each leg.

One of the best examples of the firm's work is the beautiful Kimbolton Cabinet, which was made in 1771-1776 by Ince & Mayhew to a design by Robert Adam. It is made of mahogany and oak with marquetry in satinwood and rosewood and was designed to display eleven Florentine pietra dura panels made by Baccio Cappelli. It has ormolu mounts made by Matthew Boulton in Birmingham. It is now on display in the Victoria and Albert Museum in London.

Hallmarks of Ince & Mayhew marquetry include tied ribbons, husk swags and Neo-Classical urns; the creation of a 3-D effect by looping ornamentation over and under objects, the use of yew and of ebonised mouldings and borders.

Serpentine Commodes

The Bull Cabinet, attributed to Ince & Mayhew, is an example of a serpentine commode, made of mahogany with veneers of kingwood, tulipwood, purplewood, harewood and other woods, with ivory for the bull's horns, eyes and hooves and ormolu mounts[lxviii]. The front medallion would have been purple when first made, with the bull depicted in light brown box or sycamore on a grassy plateau made of pearwood, olive and cedar. The door panels are at each end of the commode and depict urns on a pedestal using harewood and sycamore, box, plum, tulipwood and purplewood, with pear and padouk for the plateau. The colours would have been stunning.

Bull Cabinet LL4246 Lady Lever Art Gallery c.1780
Courtesy National Museums Liverpool

There is an example of a serpentine commode in the Metropolitan Museum of Art in New York, which has exquisite marquetry on its top in the shape of a violin with a bow and a sheet of music.

The commode, dated 1760-1770, is made of pine veneered with satinwood, mahogany, burl, yew, and purplewood and has gilt bronze ornamentation. At least eight other commodes have been identified, all with very similar shape and style. One is nearly identical to the one in the Metropolitan Museum but depicts a sheet of music draped over what is probably a recorder or a flute.

The Metropolitan Museum of Art, New York, Fletcher Fund, 1959 Accession No. 59.8

The serpentine commode below was made of padouk and mahogany and its distinctive shape and style enabled an attribution to Ince & Mayhew. The top has a beautiful centre piece, with a Tudor rose surrounded by what could be feathers amazingly executed to give a sense of depth. There is a shallow drawer at the top with a vitruvian frieze, which opens to reveal a mirror on a ratchet and a number of compartments, some lidded. The curved cupboard doors open to reveal three graduated drawers. The back of the cupboard doors have been strengthened with bands of mahogany, which look fresh as they have not been exposed to the light. The front of the commode is decorated with foliate marquetry depicting acorns and oak leaves tied with ribbon. It is not known who the commode was made for, but it has a curved back so was probably made to fit into a particular room.

Picture courtesy of Lennox Cato Antiques

Pictures courtesy of Lennox Cato Antiques

Other furniture

The Royal Collection includes a side table attributed to Ince & Mayhew, which is in the East Gallery of Buckingham Palace. It was acquired by Queen Mary in 1931 and is made of gilded walnut and pine with a marble top. The frieze has a crouching lion in the centre. This lion is similar to one on a medallion on a side table supplied to the Earl of Kerry by Ince & Mayhew, as well as one on a serpentine table at Kenwood.[lxix] The table in Buckingham Palace came from Woodhall Park in Hertfordshire and was made for Sir Thomas Rumbold who used Ince & Mayhew as his principal furniture suppliers.

Ince & Mayhew produced three round Loo tables for the Prince of Wales at Carlton House in 1788-89[lxx]. They were billed at £5, £9 and £9 9s and the most expensive had a central mahogany pool, five counterwells and a three branch adjustable light. The third Lord Monson hired card tables and chairs from Ince & Mayhew presumably for a party at his home, Burton Hall in Lincolnshire. Sir John Griffin Griffin Bt. paid for a neat Morroco Backgammon Table and Leather Boxes in 1774 at a cost of £2 for Audley End or his London residence 10 New Burlington Street. At Goodnestone Park, Kent there were a pair of Ince & Mayhew yew-wood card tables with ebonized borders inlaid with engraved flowersprays bought by Sir Brook Bridges. Sir Brook's daughter, Elizabeth, married Edward Austen, the brother of Jane Austen. Jane would visit them at Goodnestone and started writing Pride and Prejudice immediately after staying there in 1796[lxxi]. Did she perhaps play Speculation on an Ince & Mayhew card table?

These delightful corner commodes were commissioned by Archibald Douglas, 1st Baron Douglas around 1773 as companion pieces for a commode now at the Lady Lever Art Gallery, which has the same garlands and ribbons on the front but a lion medallion. They have a pine carcase, veneered with tulipwood, satinwood and amaranth, so would have been yellow and purple originally. The front medallions are of Bacchus and Ampelus, and A Domestic Sacrifice, both derived from plates in Sir William Hamilton's Collection of Etruscan Greek and Roman Antiquities published in 1766. The cupboards can be seen at the Museum of Fine Arts, Houston.

Museum of Fine Arts Houston part of the Rienzi Collection

Family Accounts

A striking fact about the firm was that they kept the same family account over many years. For example both the third and the fourth Earls of Darnley employed Ince & Mayhew at Cobham Hall for over forty years from 1761 to 1803 and the fourth Duke and Duchess of Bedford and the fifth Duke of Bedford used their services from 1767-1797. This indicates a high level of satisfaction from their customers. They also imported and sold French furniture and hired out furniture for entertainments.

Lady Shelburne was one of the customers who dealt directly with William Ince. In her diary for 1765 she wrote: *Saturday the 28th We all went to Ince the cabinet makers to see our furniture for the drawing room and my dressing room at Bowood. Gave Ince plans from Herculaneum and Palmyra for ornaments for a Comode of Yew tree wood inlaid with Holly and Ebony.*[lxxii] In 1768 she wrote *To Mayhew and Inch where is some beautiful cabinet work and two pretty cases for one of the rooms in my apartment, and which though they are only deal, and to be painted white, he charges £50 for.*

Lord Palmerston made reference to Ince in a letter to his wife about the sofa for their Hanover Square house written in 1795: *Ince has been altering it as to the stuffing and making cushions etc according to the directions you left him. The question now will be, will you have those eight chairs of his which will match very well with the sofa…*[lxxiii]

Lord Palmerston's account books reveal that he made a total of £1,959 9s 9d in payment to Ince & Mayhew between 1785 and 1798 for Broadlands and for their London home, 22 Hanover Square. Broadlands was remodelled by Lancelot Brown in the 1760s and 1770s when Ince & Mayhew provided the pier glasses and marble-topped tables in the Drawing Room, the hall chairs, the side tables in the Dining room and the bed in the Green Bedroom. Later, when Holland was making further improvements in the late 1780s and early 1790s they provided items such as the pier tables for the Wedgwood Room, and the desk for Lady Palmerston, which she mentioned in her inventory of 1797 as *secretary made by Ince (17)82*. There are also some lovely Ince & Mayhew commodes there, a pair in the Salon, along with a beautiful Pembroke table, and a pair of serpentine marquetry commodes in the Wedgwood Room[lxxiv].

Lord Digby gave many commissions to Ince & Mayhew for furniture at Sherborne Castle in Dorset and he used the firm for Lady Digby's funeral in 1765. After he married a second time, Ince & Mayhew were among those who provided furniture for his new wife. She may have used the Universal System of Household Furniture for some ideas, as there is still a copy in the library. There is some lovely bedroom furniture there, a metamorphic dressing-table made from yew and two wonderful marquetry inlaid mahogany commodes. There are no bills to indicate exactly which pieces of furniture came from the firm but from the accounts books a total of £1103 4s 9d was spent between 1763 and 1785, around £96,000 today.

In 1781 Ince & Mayhew undertook the funeral of the third Earl of Darnley, a magnificent affair on a royal scale. They designed the plaque for the Earl which can be found in St Mary Magdalene church in Cobham, Kent. They also introduced the widow of the third Earl of Darnley and her son, to the Westminster Fire Office, who insured Cobham Hall in Kent for £24,000 in 1789 and they provided a large amount of furniture.[38]

	From Coutts Bank books for John Bligh 3rd Earl of Darnley[lxxv]				
Both the third and the fourth Earls of Darnley employed Ince & Mayhew at Cobham Hall from 1761 to 1803.				£	s	d
	1761	July 14	To Will Ince	31	12	
	1762	July 24	To Will Ince	26	6	4
	1765	Aug 1	To Will Ince	80	--	--
	1765	Oct 11	To Will Ince	120	--	--
	1768	Apr 3	To Will. Ince	600	--	--
	1771	Aug 10	To Will Ince	210	--	--
	1773	Aug 6	To William Ince	109	--	--
	1773	Nov 24	To Willm Ince	200	--	--
	1774	July 6	To William Ince	72	--	--
From the accounts it would appear that William Ince had a personal relationship with the 3rd Earl of Darnley.	1776	Jan 20	To William Ince	500	--	--
	1776	Jul 24	To William Ince	800	--	--
	1777	Oct 8	To William Ince	500	--	--
	1778	Aug 28	To William Ince	150	--	--
	1780	Oct 30	To William Ince	580	--	--
	Bill presented for funeral of 3rd Earl of Darnley					
	1781	Sep	Ince & Mayhew	962	18	--
	July 1782 to July 1789 missing account books					
	From Coutts Bank books for John Bligh 4th Earl of Darnley					
	1789	Jul 8	Ince & Co	668	17	6
	1791	Feb 2	To W. Ince	1300	--	--
	1793	Aug 15	To Mr Ince	500	--	--
	1796	Aug 5	To Mr Ince	500	--	--
	1797	Feb 1	To Mr Ince	400	--	--
	1798	Jan 15	To Messrs Ince	200	--	--
	1803	Feb 9	To Mayhew & Ince	36	11	9
				8547	5	7

---

[38] Tester bed and day bed are still in Cobham Hall. Various other pieces are in store including a set of eight gilt side chairs and several pieces that may be *ensuit* with the bed - a sofa, a set of five arm chairs, a side chair, a fire screen and a pole screen.

UNDERNEATH IS DEPOSITED THE BODY
OF THE *RIGHT HON*
JOHN EARL of DARNLEY
HIS LORDSHIP DEPARTED THIS LIFE
ON THE 31ST DAY OF JULY 1781
IN THE 62ND YEAR OF HIS AGE

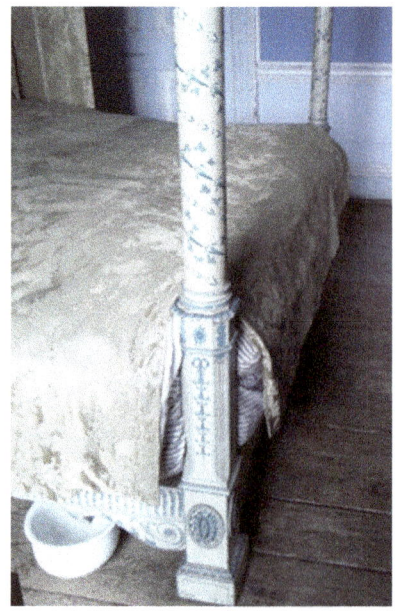

I & M furniture at Cobham Hall
Day Bed No. 88409358
Tester Bed No. 88409367

Over the years Ince & Mayhew received many other commissions from the nobility including the Duke of Marlborough, the Dowager Duchess of Bedford and the Earl of Kerry. There are bills to show Ince & Mayhew worked with Robert Adam to produce furniture for Sir John Griffin Griffin 1767 at Audley End or his London house, 10 New Burlington Street and for Lord Kerry in 1771 for his Portman Square residence as well as for Lady Shelburne's London house.

Not all their clients were aristocrats. In 2016 Christie's, London held a sale of items from Linley Hall, Shropshire, the property of the Late Sir Jasper & Lady More. This included a set of four George III giltwood open armchairs by Ince & Mayhew dated 1774. The chairs were part of a suite of seat-furniture supplied to Sir Thomas Edwardes (d. 1785) for the drawing room of his London mansion in Portman Square. The firm was responsible for the refurbishment of the principal rooms. The seat-furniture was recorded in an estimate and invoice dated 22 August 1774. Elizabeth Montagu, a bluestocking who wrote *An Essay on the Writings and Genius of Shakespeare* published in 1769 and hosted an important literary salon, paid *Mayhew, Ince & Co.* some £62 between 1796 and 1800 most likely for furnishings for her new property at 22 Portman Square[lxxvi].

Ince & Mayhew employed many people at the height of their success, at one time advertising for a *hundred workmen*, though they may never have had that many. They charged the highest premiums for recorded apprenticeships of all the West End firms, which emphasises their considerable reputation. Looking at the quality of the furniture that was produced, it would appear that the workmen were extremely highly trained, presumably thanks to William's skill. They would also have employed a large staff of both men and women to carry out some of their other services, such as the funerals they arranged, paper-hanging, carpet-laying and bed-cleaning.

Both partners mention workers in their wills. William asks that James Bolton and George Reynolds be given twenty pounds each and his servants ten pounds each for mourning. John mentions Ann Walls, one of his wife's servants, James Bolton and his wife, clerk George Reynolds, Joseph Higham and James Parker, cabinet-makers and two workwomen, Elizabeth Pasmore and Margaret Hall, who had all been with him for very many years. James Bolton was working at Croome Court in 1768.

Two men were sent to Burghley in 1768 to fix the bed and window curtains, mend four stools, mend bells and stuff the headboard, for which the Earl of Exeter was charged four shillings per day, including travel.

I&M bed at Burghley

23 days @ 4/-	£4-12-0
Paid the two mens coach hire there and back	£4-0-0
Paid there expenses, on the road and lodgings	£1-10-0
Paid porterage, mens tools and materials to the Inn	1s-6

Another bill item was for:

Mens time, taking down a large picture and packing ditto in strong case, sent to Burleigh, and afterwards return'd the use and loss of ditto, and mens time, unpacking and fixing the picture	£1-1-0

And:

Men's time at Grosvenor Street, mending a gerrondole	£0-2-0

An example of the variety of their activities is shown in their bill for the Earl of Exeter at Burghley for 1767 to 1768[lxxvii], which included:

Cleaning and repairing the tapestry refreshing the colours	£12-2-0
A large chimney glass and borders, in a rich frame, with festoons of flowers and other ornaments of carving, gilt in the best burnish'd gold	£110-0-0
Making up a very large window curtain, in drapery and covering the cornices	£3-10-0
Four tripods for the Hall, very richly carv'd and gilt with lamps to ditto gilt and varnish'd	£120-0-0
Two large plates of glass from France, each 42 inches by 92, cost at Paris sterling	£130-3-0
Customs, package, carriage to Calais – the English dutys, shipping, freight, & other expences	£130-0-0
Discount salvage and assurance	£32-10-0

I&M carved Bedpost at Burghley
By kind permission of
@fringefrogandtassel

The firm produced a number of urns which were placed in dining-rooms. They were lead-lined sometimes with a brazier at the bottom to keep food hot. Some had a tap and would have been filled with hot water. The top drawer in the pedestal would be opened and a cistern placed below so glasses or tableware could be washed under the hot water between courses. They could also be used for storing iced water for drinking.

When dealing with the aristocracy William was well aware of his status. Two letters still exist which were written by him to Richard Myddleton of Chirk Castle in 1782 and 1783[lxxviii]. The first one ends *I have the honour to be Sir Your very respectfull and Most Obedient humble Servant*; the second *I am Sir with great regard Your Most Obedient and very humble Servant at Command*.

Seal on letter in National Library of Wales

In the first letter he asked for the subject of the paintings on the *cieling… so the compartments over the Glass's in the piers might be correspondant with them*. In the second he mentioned repairs, but was also acting as intermediary for a property called Putney Lodge. William's handwriting was firm, large and clear, with flourishes on certain letters and under his signature. On the back of one is a seal, presumably that of the firm. When enlarged it is possible to make out M&I.

Marquetry

The marquetry in their furniture used woods from many parts of the world including East Indian satinwood, purplewood from northern South America, ebony from India and Ceylon, padouk from West Africa and Burma, kingwood and tulipwood from Brazil and rosewood from the East Indies as well as English woods such as box, holly, pear, plum and sycamore. They used mahogany, deal and oak for the carcases of their commodes[lxxix]. The firm was unusual in their use of yew for some of their veneers.

Ince & Mayhew commode with Siena marble slab top
Met Museum New York 1770-1780

This panel from the front of the commode would have been brightly coloured when it was originally made. The veneers are made from satinwood, kingwood, holly, rosewood and other woods so there would have been yellows, reddish browns, almost white and purplish browns.

Pictures courtesy of Lennox Cato Antiques

There is an interesting frieze on this corner washbasin stand including olive leaves and berries, very similar to the leaves and berries on a commode in the Lady Lever Art Gallery, No.26 in Lucy Wood's book Catalogue of Commodes. Inside the stand are two small wooden bowls and a space for a larger one and there are hooks on the tops to secure the stand to the wall when in use. Even the undersides of the lift-up panels are decorated. The front and top of the stand have ovals of amboyna and harewood veneer and the greens and browns would have been much stronger when it was made around 1780.

Native and Exotic Woods used in Ince & Mayhew furniture

Birch	Native Wood	Light golden brown	
Box	Native Wood	Light brown used for stringing lines	
Harewood	Native Wood	Sycamore stained greenish grey with oxide of iron, stripy	
Hornbeam	Native Wood	Dense, off-white	
Holly	Native Wood	Almost white	
Lime	Native Wood	For carving pale white to cream	
Pear	Native Wood	Pale to mid brown, takes stain well	
Pine / Deal	Native Wood	For carcases	
Plum	Native Wood	Yellowish brown	
Walnut	Native Wood	Soft brown to reddish brown	
Yew	Native Wood	Orangish brown	
Amaranth	Tropical America	Another name for Purplewood	
Amboyna	Amboyn Island, Indonesia	Burl wood of Ptercarpus sp. Including Padouk Rich reddish or yellowish brown	
Blue Mahoe	West Indies, Tropical America	Brownish grey with dark blue cast and regular fine rays	
Cedar	Middle East and Britain	Softwood with regular stripes	
Ebony	India and Sri Lanka	Mid-brown to black, very heavy Used for stringing lines Ebonised: Large areas of cheaper wood stained black	
Fustic	Tropical America	Golden to bright yellow darkening to brown Hard dense	
Kingwood (Rosewood)	Brazil	Reddish brown with black bands for cross-banded borders	
Mahogany	West Indies, Central and South America	Medium to deep red brown For veneers and carcases	
Makore	Ghana and Ivory Coast	Lustrous wood, pinkish to purplish brown	
Olivewood	Southern Europe	Yellowish brown with bands of white, brown or black	
Padouk	West Africa, the Andaman Islands, Burma	Golden brown to deep red, hard wood	
Purplewood	Northern South America	Bright purple when newly cut darkening to reddish brown	

Rosewood	Brazil and East Indies	Mid to dark purplish brown often blackish markings	
Sabicu	Central America	Chestnut brown with darker stripes, for banded borders Resembles mahogany	
Satinwood	West Indies / East Indies	Creamy to golden yellow usually straight-grained Used on its own and as ground for marquetry	
Snakewood	British Guiana	Nut brown mottled with black	
Tauroniro	Brazil and British Guiana	Lustrous reddish-orange	
Tulipwood	Brazil	Creamy yellow with pink stripes For cross-banded borders	
Wengi	Zaire	Dark brown with darker and lighter bands Blunts tool edges, splintery	

Fire!

Both Ince and Mayhew served as Directors of the Westminster Fire Office[lxxx], serving for two years each time. Mayhew was elected six times between 1763 and 1810 and Ince in 1771, 1780, 1789 and 1798. They would have attended the weekly board and carried out inspections of properties, writing up reports. This work would have provided useful business contacts, and they also introduced some of their customers such as the widow of the third Earl of Darnley and her son, who insured Cobham Hall in Kent for £24,000 in 1789. They insured their own property through the Westminster Office, receiving compensation when their house in Silver Street burnt down in 1782 (£375) and again when William Ince's house in Crouch End burnt down in 1795 (£215). William Ince designed a headpiece for the Westminster Fire Office policy documents in 1782 and the firm provided new chairs for the Fire Office in 1792 and other furniture when the Fire Office moved.

Ince & Mayhew owned a fire engine and were paid for the use of it. In January 1773 Ince received 4s 6d *being so much expended by him at the late ffire in Tylers Court* and in 1779 they were paid one guinea to be divided among the men as have at various times attended and worked their Engine at Fires.

The photo is of a 1785 fire engine in the Anne of Cleves House in Lewes, Sussex. It cost £65 5s 0d and was made by a company called Bristow which was based in Ratcliff Highway, Whitechapel, London.

Photo used by kind permission of
Sussex Archaeological Society, Anne of Cleves House Museum

> Instructions for Use: When you play the engine to its full length hold the Branch steady, let as many men work at the Handles as can stand and likewise upon ye Treadles and take Quick Strokes from top to Bottom, when you play by Suction Unscrew the Brass Cap which stands by a Chain and screw the suction pipe when you play water out of the Cistern turn ye handle in again, let the Cistern be half full of water when you play by suction and Always keep water in the Cistern in summer but none in Winter.

Ince & Mayhew was also the supplier for *Joachim Smith's new-invented Machine for the immediate and certain Safety of Lives (particularly adapted to the Care of Ladies and Infants) from the Distress of Fire* as advertised in The Public Advertiser in 1775. The chutes were made of sailcloth and could be stored in a case of wood or metal and kept in the recess of a window. They were priced from £10 from Mayhew and Ince[lxxxi].

As a fire rages in a house people are being helped to escape by means of chutes extended from the windows to the ground.
Etching. Credit: Wellcome Collection. Attribution 4.0 International (CC BY 4.0)

William in Worcestershire

As William had family connections in Worcestershire, it is not surprising that he was the partner who continued to sign receipts for the Earl of Coventry at Croome Court in Pershore. His two sisters, Mary and Elizabeth were under the guardianship of their aunt, Elizabeth, for the 1752 court case. She lived in Franche, near Kidderminster, and died in 1758. The two girls would then have inherited her property in accordance with the will of their uncle William. Sister Mary married a William Crundall in Kidderminster in 1761 and it is very likely that William the cabinet-maker stayed with her when in the area.

It would have been convenient for William to see them when on business for the firm. He visited Matthew Boulton in Soho, Birmingham which is less than twenty miles away and there are a number of houses in the region who either had Ince & Mayhew receipts or attributable surviving furniture which he may have had cause to visit. These include Sandwell Park (which was near Boulton's Soho Manufactory), Croome Court, Alscot Park, Compton Verney, Adderbury House, Warwick Castle and Daylesford House[lxxxii].

Coffee trees

Travel in eighteenth century England would have been slow and uncomfortable. He may have used the stage coach which took around nineteen hours from London to Birmingham or he may have travelled by horseback. Mail coaches were introduced in 1784 which carried a few passengers and were also faster. The Ince & Mayhew property sold in Marshall Street in 1825 included a coach house and there was a coach house at the property in Crouch End, so it is possible that the firm had its own coach.

It may also have been his connections in Worcestershire that led to William being the joint appraiser at Hartlebury Castle and the Bishop's Palace in Worcester in 1781[lxxxiii]. The author of *An Inventory of Hartlebury Castle*, P C Moore, expressed surprise that William was the appraiser as he was *the famous London cabinet maker* but acknowledges this gave a *guarantee of accuracy, both of description and value.*

Interesting items in the Castle include a *A Mahogany Marlbro Elboe Chair cover'd with Crimson Velvet & serge case (name probably given by Ince).. A Berometer.. 8 Pewter Ice Moulds* in the Dairy, *A Coffee & a Pepper Mill* in the kitchen, and *4 Coffee Trees* in the garden. The garden had a Hot House and a Green House. There were *4 Post Bedsteads* in all the rooms including the servants' quarters. Items in the Housekeepers Room included *3ct 39st & 3lb of Soap… 3ct 19st & 17lb Candles… 6ct & 26lbs of cheese… 5lb of Caster sugar… 37 lb of lump sugar.* The Bishop was never short of drink as he had a Brew House, an Ale Cellar, a Wine Cellar, a Small Beer Cellar and a Cyder Cellar. The appraisal for the castle concludes:
All the Articles of Furniture etc contain'd in this Inventory are Appraisd at the Sum of Twelve Hundred and Sixty four pounds twelve Shillings and Two pence by us
£1264 12s 2d (Sgd) Wm. Ince   (Sgd) Thos. Kent
July the 21st 1781
N.B. *if the Fire Engine in No. 70 was not purchased by the Bishop of Wincheser, five guineas to be deducted from this Valuation*
The fire engine was purchased by the Bishop. Nothing therefore deducted R.W. (Hurd)[39]

---

[39] In 1781 Brownlow North had moved to the See of Winchester, from Worcester, taking his fire engine with him. Richard Hurd had become Bishop of Worcester.

The Firm's Property

Using Horwood's Map of London 1813 it can be seen that Nos 47 to 49 were on the west side of Marshall Street, facing Broad Street. The partners gave Broad Street as their address and their advertisement when they opened for business used the words *opposite Broad Street* so it would seem this street had more cachet than Marshall Street.

The land detailed in the Land Registry document of 1825 gave further details about the property in the area. These included a tallow chandler and a cheese monger next to their houses, with a warehouse/workshop 80' x 50' behind. On the opposite side of Marshall Street there were two workshops, one 92' x 19' abutting a peruke maker and one 96' x 19' abutting premises in Silver Street. They also owned houses in Marlborough Row and Carnaby Street along with stables and coach-houses and various other brick buildings. In 1808 an advertisement appeared for the lease of one of the properties in Marlborough Row which had room for four carriages, a five stall stable and a capacious apartment.

The document also recorded a slaughter-house and a tripe-house sited fifty feet across from the yard of William Ince's house from 1786, a rather noxious neighbour. More pleasant neighbours would have been William Blake's family, who lived on the north corner of Broad Street and Marshall Street. William Blake, the painter and poet was born there in 1757 and his father was a hosier. After his marriage in 1782 William set up in business as a print seller next-door in No. 72 (then No. 27) Broad Street, but had moved to Poland Street by Christmas 1785; his partner, James Parker, remained at No. 72 until 1794[lxxxiv].

When Thomas Sheraton produced his Cabinet Dictionary in 1803, there were four other cabinet-makers in Broad Street: Hudson and Corney at Nos. 4 and 13, Jermain at No. 10 Broad Street, Lonsdale at No. 7 and Owen an upholsterer at No. 54. Thomas Sheraton was himself living at 8 Broad Street where copies of the Dictionary could be obtained. It would be very surprising if he and William Ince did not meet occasionally to discuss design and trade. Thomas Sheraton died in 1806 and the writer of his obituary in the Gentlemen's Magazine was concerned that he had left his family *in distressed circumstances* mainly because since 1793 he had been supporting himself as an author. He was described as *a very honest well-disposed man; of an acute and enterprising disposition*.

Broad Street also housed a number of instrument makers, including the harpsichord maker Jacob Kirckman who came to England in the 1730s, and had his business at No. 19. He was organist of St. George's, Hanover Square, and the author of several compositions for the organ and the pianoforte which he published himself at the sign of the King's Arms in Broad Street, Carnaby Market. He died in 1777 but the business was continued by his nephew, Abraham. There is record of a square piano inscribed Jacob and Abraham Kirchmann dated 1775 and a grand piano dated 1780 was also theirs[lxxxv]. William Ince owned a Kirkmann harpsichord which was sold at the house auction.

Frederick Beck the piano maker was at No. 4 Broad Street, producing square pianos between 1772 and 1788, with attributions to 1798. Thomas Beck, pianoforte maker was at the same address. Beck was also in business with George Corrie of 41, Broad Street about 1790[lxxxvi]. Christopher Ganer was a piano maker, inlayer, music publisher and seller initially at 22 Broad Street moving to 47 Broad Street, Soho and also at 48 Broad Street from the early 1780's. From 1779, he made very elegant inlaid square pianos on a *French* frame stand as well as plain examples[lxxxvii].

The two sculptors and carvers, Sefferin Alken and Sefferin Nelson were based in Dufours Place, a little alley off the north of Broad Street. According to Sun fire insurance records John Denson, an upholder, also lived in Dufours Place, and his widow, Elizabeth took over the business in 1786. Joseph Jackson was a cabinet maker in Carnaby Street in 1781.

A National School was established in Marshall Street in 1827, described as situated at the end of Broad-street, Golden Square – the exact site that Ince & Mayhew bought from Charles Smith in 1758, as shown on the map in the Victoria County History[lxxxviii]. Three school rooms were erected with apartments for the masters and mistresses plus a shop used as a depot for the Society for Promoting Christian Knowledge. There were two day-schools and two evening-schools, separate for boys and girls, and an infant-school. There were over 1000 pupils in total. The school closed in 1892.

The buildings belonging to Ince & Mayhew would have had to house all their business requirements. The plan for Chippendale's premises gives an idea of the sort of accommodation required: dwelling house, cabinet maker's shop, glass room, feather room, upholsterer's shop, veneering room, drying room, chair room, store room and warerooms with stacks for drying wood. Ince & Mayhew also bought a showroom in 1772 where they could exhibit *large glasses, fine pictures, superb furniture and inlaid work* and also display other articles to sell on commission.

In 1768 John Mayhew's father died and he inherited a number of *messuages or tenements … in the Parish of St George Hanover Square*[lxxxix]. The firm expanded their business by renting these houses and leasing more to rent. In 1770 they were advertising three houses to let including one in Hornsey and were asking for more property. The rents were £100-£300 pa in 1778 and rent for a house in Cavendish Square in 1790 was £150 pa. Some of the houses may

Examples of houses from Sackville Street, Grafton Street and Albemarle Street

only have been rented during 'The Season', with overheads to pay throughout the year and therefore not profitable in the long term. Sun Fire Insurance records tell us that Lady Charlotte Williams Wynn was renting a property in Wardour Street from 14th January 1794, with Ince & Mayhew given as the upholders. Come August she would probably have retired to her country house. In The Times of 6th April 1791 Mr Christie advertised a leasehold house for sale *on the west side of Argyl Buildings Hanover Square* where Messrs Mayhew and Ince were the tenants, paying £70 per annum with six years left on the lease and responsibility for the repairs to the property. Ince & Mayhew also acted as estate agents, advertising property for sale such as a house in Lincoln Inn Fields in 1765. In an advertisement in the Leeds Intelligencer on 17th May 1785 they were offering a property to be sold or let which was in Kendall in the County of Westmorland.

They also bought a substantial amount of land in Crouch End[xc], nearly 50 acres, using loans from others to do so. This was presumably as an investment with a view to building on the land or selling it later.

Some of the property was linked to the firm borrowing money including £1500 from Mrs Mary Cowell for warehouses, shops and premises in Marshall Street. According to the 1799 agreement, George Romney, the social portrait painter, loaned them £1200 in indentures dated 28th and 29th September 1792. George's father was a cabinet-maker and George lived near Marshall Street in Cavendish Square. This loan was still outstanding in 1825 as George Romney's executors are named in the Land Registry document.

In 1798 Ince & Mayhew paid Land Tax on 17 properties in Westminster: four in Albemarle Street, one in Grosvenor Street Lower, two in Grafton Street and one in Old Soho (probably Wardour Street), plus two houses and one workshop in Marlborough Row East, three houses and one workshop in Marshall Street West, and one house and a large workshop in Marshall Street East. In Hornsey, William Ince paid tax on two properties owned by William Smith, presumably Linslade House and Old Crouch Hall, plus two cottages and land in his own name. The Old Crouch Hall estate was four acres in size. Other property in the area included the villa in Hornsey belonging to John Mayhew which included twelve acres, the freehold land near the New River consisting of eight acres purchased from Mr Cooper and occupied by John Mayhew, the land known as nine acres to the north of the Old Crouch Hall estate and nine other areas of freehold land consisting of 17 acres of land between Middle Lane and Tottenham Lane sold to John Mayhew in 1791.

The London map shows when the property remaining at the dissolution of the partnership was sold off.

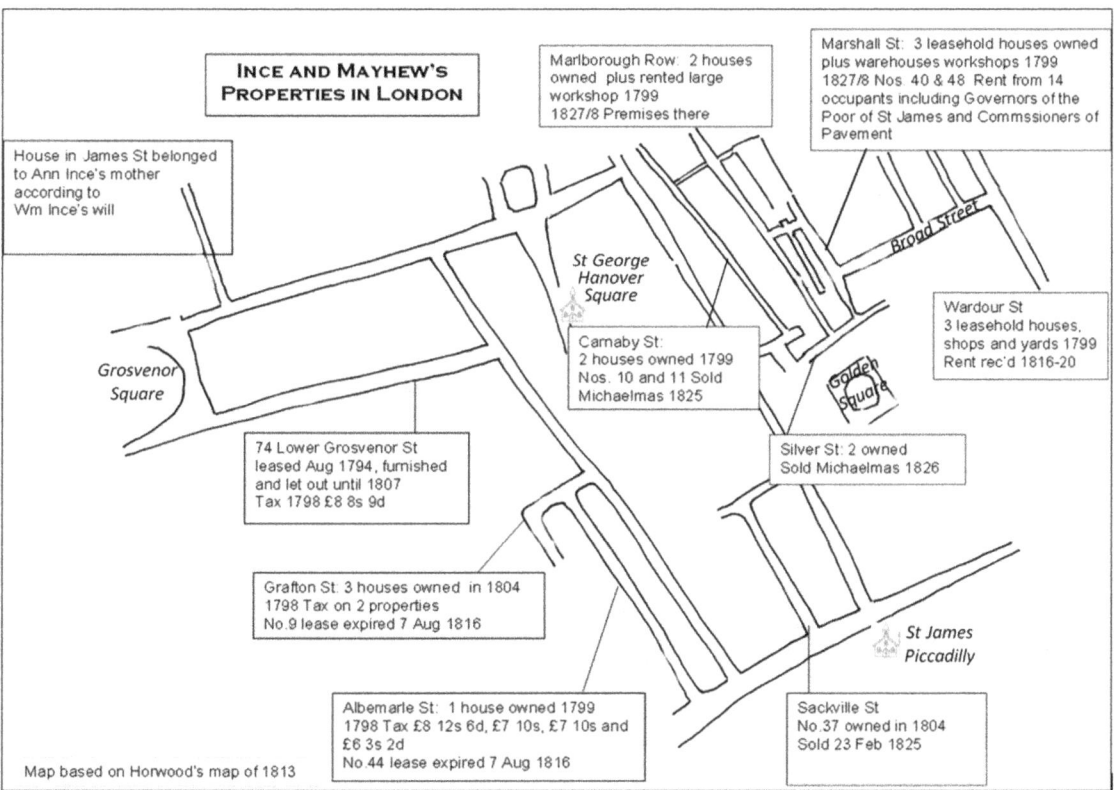

The Crouch End map gives an idea of where the property was and just how much of it there was – nearly 50 acres.

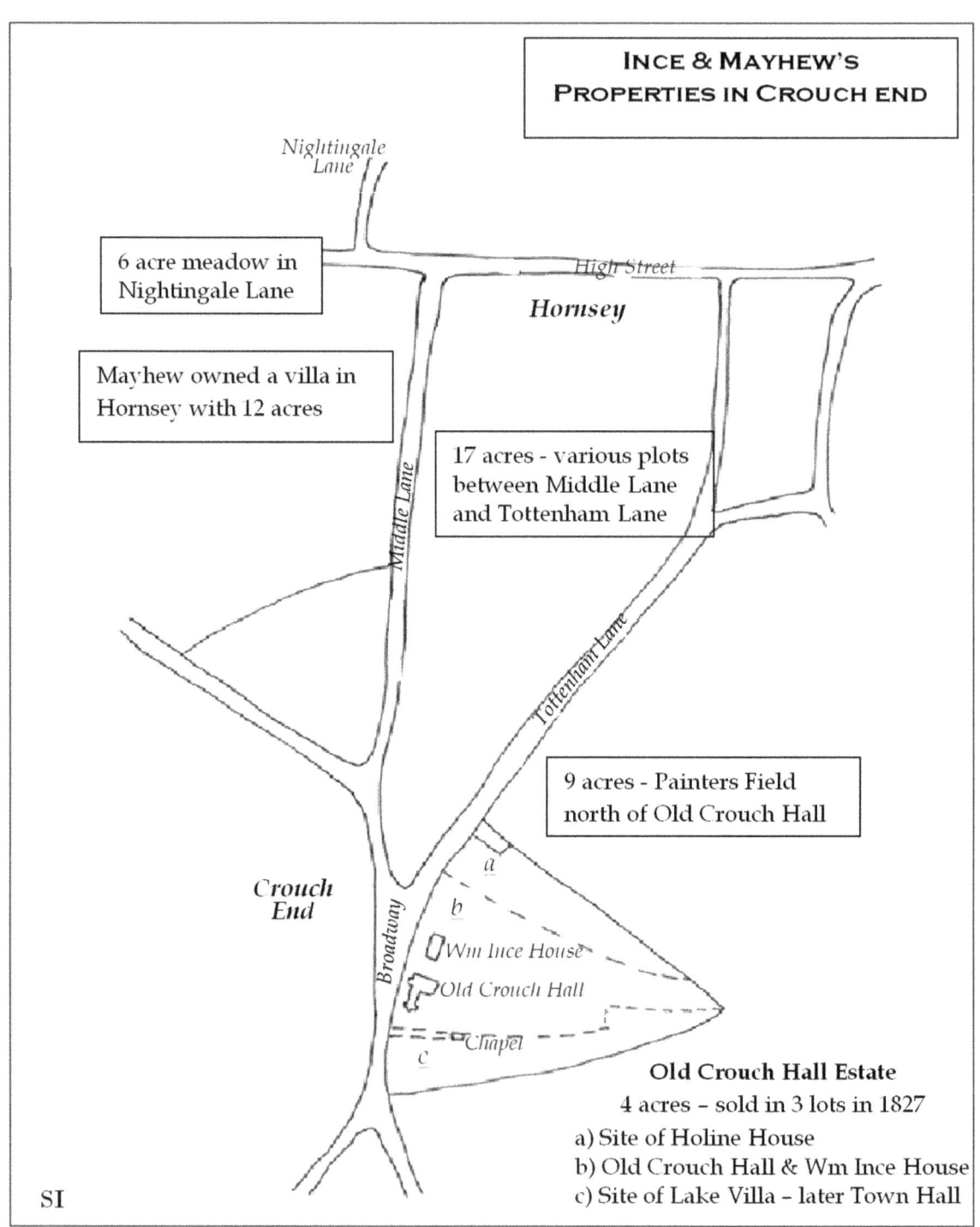

End of the Partnership

The firm was not good at keeping accounts, something that Lindsay Boynton noted in his article about the correspondence between Ince & Mayhew and Boulton & Fothergill[xci] and by the end of the 1790s they were in considerable debt. They were slow to produce their bills, and their clients may have been slow to pay. The firm may also have over-invested in property. The debts amounted to £7000 (roughly £300,000 today).

For whatever reasons, because William wanted to settle the accounts, they agreed to dissolve the partnership. They signed an agreement in 1799, detailing the arrangements and taking out a mortgage for £7000 to pay off their debts[xcii]. A notice about the ending of the partnership appeared in the London Gazette on 12th April 1800.

It is significant that William Ince made his will on 8 August 1800 implying his health may have been suffering. There was an auction by Christie's in May 1801 according to the Morning Chronicle when some of the furniture was sold. Included in the items for sale were a full-sized billiard table and two fine-toned finger organs. They also attempted to sell their property in the Broad Street area including *most capital Exhibition-rooms, Ware-rooms, Workshops, Accompting house and two eligible residences.*

Although Charles Ince, William's second son, was said to take over the business in an advertisement in the same issue of the London Gazette, it would seem that he moved the business to Holles Street, where he paid rates from 1801 to 1803. He was listed there in Thomas Sheraton's Cabinet Dictionary in the list of Master Cabinet-Makers, Upholsters and Chair Makers in 1803. However a notice in the Morning Post advertised an auction at the premises on 11th and 12th April 1804. *Excellent cabinet and upholstery stock* was to be sold by auctioneer Mr Squibb, including an *elegant rose-wood cabinet, mahogany secretaries* and *an excellent counting house desk*. The advertisement reported that *Mr Charles Ince* was *declining business.*

Chancery

William Ince died suddenly of apoplexy in January 1804 and on 14th February his widow, Ann Ince, put in a Bill of Complaint against John Mayhew in the Chancery Court[xciii] requesting an injunction on selling any property.

There was an answer on 11th June 1804 when Mayhew claimed he deserved a larger share of the assets (five times as much as Ince) as he had put more into the partnership when it was first set up, and a further answer on 15th November 1806 when all the cash books were submitted. In this answer William was described as *a man of very small property* who only put around £500 into the trade.

On 21st November 1806 Ann Ince died, but the court case continued to limp on for at least twenty years. Various bills were presented from the Ince side, and also from the younger Mayhew children against the executors of their father's will.

There appears to have been a dispute over unsettled accounts. We know that the accounts books were not kept up to date each year as originally outlined in their 1759 agreement. William Ince kept the books for a few years, but then left them to John Mayhew whose book-keeping appears to have been fairly haphazard. There was also a complaint against Mayhew that he had loaned money to the firm and then claimed unreasonable interest on those loans.

A Bill of June 1811[xciv] said that the delay had been caused by unsettled accounts not being signed by William Ince or his executors. The settlement was in the hands of Mr Campbell, one of the Masters of the Rolls. The Master was to enquire what the partnership property consisted of at the time of William's death and in whose hands or possession it then was. He was to examine all the books, papers and writings relating thereto and *to make unto the parties all just allowances*. The Master said he would not consider an account settled unless it was signed by William or someone on his behalf and in April 1811 reported that *there were not any such settled Accounts*. John Mayhew was dissatisfied with this report so there were still some 'Exceptions' in dispute when he died in May 1811, though in a codicil to his will, Mayhew begs his executors to come to a settlement. In the 1811 Bill, George Cowell, on behalf of the Ince family, requests that the case either be settled or continued against Mayhew's executors, George Tennant and Richard Harrison and this was so ordered by the court.

The Mayhew children then went to court, all except John Mayhew the eldest, with a complaint that they had received nothing from their father's will and that the executors, Tennant and Harrison, were saying there was nothing to pay out, though the children knew he had *a very large personal estate*. There were various bills and orders from the court[40] from 1812 onwards[xcv].

Finally in 1824 there was a Chancery Report[xcvi] showing that James Gray Mayhew, John's fourth son, had offered himself as Receiver and was duly appointed. He was the hero who was willing to step in and make something happen.

---

[40] There is an account dated July 1824 which shows J. Campbell was paid £973 17s 1d (about £67,000 today) in the cause of James G. Mayhew v George Tennant for orders dated 28th November 1818, 29th November 1819, 18th May 1820 and 4th December 1823.

Chancery Case Timetable
1804
14 Feb Bill of complaint by Ann Ince, John Cowell, George Cowell
10 Jun Plaintiffs not fully prepared
11 Jun Mayhew's answer £31,270 to JM £6,093 to WI
1806
15 Nov Answer and cash books
1809
Petition re unsettled accounts
1811
31 Mar Masters Report - not any settled accounts - JM dissatisfied
11 May In his will JM requested that his executors, Tennant and Harrison, take charge of all his property and sell it when they thought fit
18 Jun Cowell v Tennant - Mayhew's executors tasked to appear before court
1812-22
Two bills presented by younger Mayhew children v Tennant and oldest son John Mayhew
1818
Further Bill lodged by George Cowell
1823
William Ince's house in Crouch End sold
1824
14 Apr James Gray Mayhew proposes himself as Receiver and was so ordered by the Court
5 Aug Indenture of Lease and Release
25 Sep Money paid out from William Ince's Will
19 Oct Money paid out from Ann Ince's Will
1825
12th April Indenture of Lease and Release registered
23rd June Property in Crouch End, Hornsey and Carnaby Street advertised for sale
1827
Old Crouch Hall estate sold
School established on the site in Marshall Street
1829
Jane Mayhew's family received £21,659 linked to leasehold in Carnaby Street

There are two Masters Accounts books from this period which show the rent income from the properties owned by the firm and approved each year by the Master of the Rolls[xcvii]. They included the properties in and around Marshall Street and in Crouch End. The first book ran from 1816 to 1820 and was kept by William Glazier, the second ran from 1822 to 1829 and was kept by James Gray Mayhew. This Master's Accounts Book showed when the commercial property belonging to the firm was sold.

From the Land Registry records it appears all the remaining property was assigned to the solicitors Tennant and Harrison in 1825[xcviii].

The death duty registers for William and Ann Ince show that the six surviving Ince children, of thirteen baptised, received an allocation of the personal property as outlined in their parents' wills in 1824 and 1826[xcix]. The oldest son, William, a Captain in the Bombay Artillery of the East India Company, died in 1808.

William's estate was said to be worth less than £10,000. Ann Ince, John Cowell, George Cowell and Stephen Habberton are named as executors. The last three named received £100 each less tax on 25th September 1824. Mr Bolton and Mr Reynolds (two of the firm's employees) received £20 less tax.

Ann's estate was said to be under £300, then under £2000 in September 1824. The following allocations were made:

19 Oct 1824	William Ince	Son	£100
	Charles Ince	Son	£50
	Frederick Ince	Son	£50
	Henry Robert Ince	Son	£50
	Isabella Cowell	Daughter	£602 6s 7d (part of a moiety of Residue)
	Mary Ann Willson	Daughter	£602 6s 7d (part of a moiety of Residue)
12 May 1826	Isabella Cowell	Daughter	£84 14s 2d
	Mary Ann Willson	Daughter	£84 14s 2d
Total			**£1624 1s 6d**

Hopefully, the legacy for their son William, who had died before matters were settled, found its way to his *girl Fatima* in India, to whom he had assigned everything in his will[41].

The money referred to would have been from the personal property of William and Ann, including his house in Crouch End, not the property belonging to the firm.

According to the Land Registry Records[c], all the commercial property was assigned to the two lawyers George Tennant and Richard Harrison in April 1825. This is a ten page document, listing seventeen interested parties and various properties or pieces of land in Crouch End/Hornsey and in Soho.

---

[41] Fatima Bibu of Bombay was sworn in as Sole Legatee and Executrix of William Ince's will on 28th November 1808.

On 23 June 1825 an advertisement appeared in The Times and other papers for a Sale by Auction on 28th June in lots *by order of the executors*. The details of the sale are as follows: *"Three copyhold family residences with suitable offices, coachhouses and stabling and capital gardens with several dwelling houses etc situated at Crouch End. Also two freehold cottages with stabling, chaisehouse, gardens etc A field of excellent pasture land containing 9 acres of capital brick earth.* (ie the whole of Old Crouch Hall Estate) *The Villa residence of the late John Mayhew Esq with pleasure ground, gardens, coachhouse, stabling and offices and 12 acres of pasture land full of brick earth…* (Belonging to Mayhew) *Two Closes of freehold land on the north side of the road from Hornsey to … Muswell Hill containing 8 acres and abounding with brick earth and contiguous with the New River and land near the summit of Muswell Hill. … presenting many beauty spots for the erection of detached villas in a delightful and very healthy part of the country and only 6 miles from town. And two freehold houses nos 10 and 11 Carnaby Street"*.

The interested parties included all the living Ince children and Mayhew children, the executors of George Romney's estate, the living partners and executors of the Bank from whom the £7000 mortgage was taken and the people who took over the Bank when it went into receivership.

From W B Marcham's account of Crouch End[ci] we learn that the Old Crouch Hall Estate was sold in three lots in 1827: the plot that later contained Holine House, the plot including Linslade House and Old Crouch Hall and the plot that contained Lake Villa and later Crouch End Town Hall. The latter plot was bought by John Bumpstead, a plumber who had rented it previously. There was a chapel on the estate, used by a Baptist congregation in 1820, but it is not clear when it was built.

In Westminster, the Master Accounts Books show when the leases ran out on the properties in Lower Grosvenor Street, Grafton Street and Albemarle Street. The house in Sackville Street was sold in February 1825, the houses in Carnaby Street at Michaelmas 1825 and the houses in Silver Street at Michaelmas 1826. It is not clear what happened to the houses in Wardour Street, though rent was only recorded as being received up to 1820. The properties in Marshall Street and Marlborough Row appear to be still owned in 1827 as rent was still being received.

Final settlement

There is some confusion over how much money was eventually raised from the sale of all the properties owned by Ince & Mayhew and how the money was divided between the families.

According to the Death Duty Register, William Ince left £440. When Ann Ince died, she left a total of £1624 1s 6d. According to the deed sent from Edward Ince to his father Frederick in 1830, he was entitled to £143 10s 6d as his one sixth share in his father's inheritance, which had been invested by George Cowell as instructed in William's will[42]. If Edward's share is multiplied by six, the total allocated to Frederick would have been just over £900, as he was given £50 to release the executors from any further claim. In his will William considered he had already given sufficiently to William, Charles, Henry Robert and Isabella. He wanted money to be invested for Frederick to bring his share up to that of his brothers, and for £1500 to be invested for Mary Ann to make her share equal to that of Isabella. Adding those sums to the total Ann left makes £4024, but what happened to the money from selling the properties owned by the firm?

According to notes written in 1925 by Charles Frederick Ince (my great grandfather) a sum of under £1000 each was received by his father, Percy Ince (William's grandson through Frederick) and his father's five siblings, but it is more likely that Percy received the £143 that Edward his brother received. William's son Frederick was destitute in America in 1836, but according to his letters he dipped into the inheritance to pay for his passage and set up his farm in Virginia. According to C. F. Ince, Percy spent his bequest on a yacht on which to woo his future bride Sarah Winkworth and her sister, Mary Ann.

John Mayhew left a total of £36,855, which included a payment of £21,658 to his daughter Jane Normansell and family in 1829, linked to a leasehold in Carnaby Street according to the Death Duty register. The £7000 owed by the firm in 1799 would have been paid off by the sale of the land and properties.

Ince and Mayhew or Mayhew and Ince?

William Ince was the talented cabinet-maker who produced the majority of the drawings for *The Universal System of Household Furniture*. He was the man to whom Matthew Boulton offered *a hearty wellcome*. He would have overseen the production of the furniture, probably choosing the workmen, training the apprentices and checking on their output. He was the man who wrote to Lord Myddleton at Chirk Castle to check the paintings on the ceiling. It is fair to say that William Ince was responsible for the furniture produced by the firm.

John Mayhew was the man who supplied the money to keep the firm going. His father invested in it and his second wife brought a large sum to the business after they

---

[42] See page 154

married in 1765. He entertained the clients who called and he was probably in charge of the Upholder side of the business and the renting of property. He almost certainly was responsible for the firm investing in land.

Eighteenth century records almost always refer to the firm as Mayhew and Ince. In their 1759 agreement John Mayhew's name comes before William Ince's on the legal document. Mayhew and Ince is how it is written in the Land Tax returns for the houses they owned and rented; it is referred to as Mayhew & Ince in some directories and advertisements. Charles Ince, William's son, refers to the *Firm of Mayhew, Ince and Sons* in his advertisement in the London Gazette of 12th April 1800 when he said he was taking over the firm. Also many of the accounts sent to their clients were headed Mayhew & Ince. However, occasionally they advertised as Ince & Mayhew, such as in an advertisement for a Lease which appeared in The Times on 23rd May 1799 and sometimes in the Bank books for their clients the name of William Ince appears, or Ince and Mayhew, Ince and Co, *Inch and Mahew,* Messrs Ince.

It is also interesting to note how the name has been presented in the antiques world. Initially *The Universal System of Household Furniture* was the main focus of articles and as William Ince's name appears before that of John Mayhew, the firm is referred to as Ince and Mayhew. In 1904 R. S. Clouston wrote an article *called Minor English Furniture Makers of the Eighteenth Century Article III-Ince and Mayhew*[cii]. An item in The Times dated 8th June 1921 refers to some chairs for which *there is reason to think that they are the work of Ince and Mayhew* as they resemble an illustration of a chair in the Universal System.

An article written by Lieut-Colonel E. F. Strange, Late Keeper in the Victoria and Albert Museum, for The Illustrated London News in 1929 entitled *English Hanging Mirrors* also referred to *the publication of Ince and Mayhew-The Universal System.* This article had a reproduction of Plate LXXVIII from their Directory showing two designs for Oval Glass-Frames which is a delightful illustration by William Ince, with a hunter and dog, birds, squirrels and possibly a little lamb included in the carving.

Another article appeared in The Illustrated London News on 25th May 1940. This was entitled *The World of Art in Wartime, Furniture "Convenient to the Nobility and Gentry."* by Frank Davis. He included four illustrations from The Universal System, each time referring to the firm as Ince & Mayhew. The particular volume from which they were taken, the 1762 edition, was *specially scarce* and in perfect condition so was priced by Batsfords at £150; Chippendale's Director being priced at £25. In 1946 the furniture shop Heal's ran a series of advertisements using quotations from *The Universal System*, citing the firm as Ince & Mayhew.

In The Times in 1963 Edward Pinto, in an article about the Furniture Makers' Guild, wrote *Such great names in the eighteenth century as Thomas Chippendale, William Vile, Ince and Mayhew were proud to call themselves Upholders first and Cabinet-Makers second.* Pinto used the same name for the firm when writing about the Kimbolton Cabinet in another article for The Times in 1969.

Lindsay Boynton's article in 1966 was called *An Ince and Mayhew Correspondence*[ciii]. Colin Streeter consistently refers to Ince and Mayhew in his 1971 article *Marquetry Furniture by a Brilliant London Master*[civ] as does Morrisson Heckscher in 1974[cv]. In 1981 Hugh Roberts wrote articles about Broadlands, called *The Ince and Mayhew Connection*[cvi].

However in the 1990s the name changes to Mayhew and Ince as seen in articles by Hugh Roberts and Charles Cator, in Lucy Wood's Catalogue of Commodes, and almost always in Lot Notes produced by the major auction houses. It is very pleasing to note that in his more recent articles Hugh Roberts has started using Ince and Mayhew again and that Christie's have followed suit.[cvii]

Legacy

The status of the firm of Ince & Mayhew has increased over the years as more of their work has been identified and the quality of their work has been appreciated.

Photos courtesy of Reindeer Antiques

Lucy Wood has examined this beautiful commode in detail and confidently attributes it to Ince & Mayhew along with nine other linked items, including tables formerly at Mersham-le-Hatch, once thought to have been made by Chippendale.

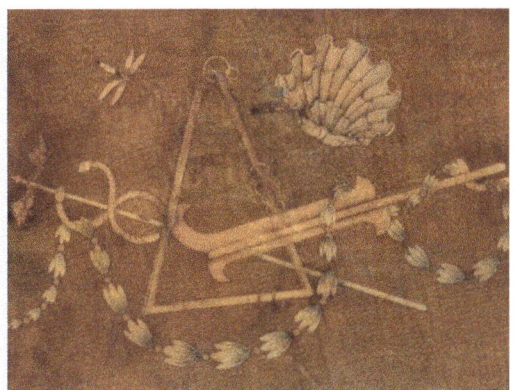 

The top of the commode has wonderful marquetry which would have been requested by the client and give some clues as to his or her interests and profession. There is a caduceus, which is a winged staff with two snakes entwined. This was an ancient symbol of commerce and negotiation and is associated with Hermes. It was also used as a symbol of printing, from the attributes of Hermes as Mercury the messenger. There is a triangle with rings, an instrument which had recently been accepted into the eighteenth century orchestra and another implement. These three items are interlinked with a chain of husks. Either side of the top of the triangle lie a dragonfly and a scallop shell. The latter is a symbol of a pilgrim to the Holy Land or one who has walked the Camino de Santiago. The firm Ince & Mayhew is described by the antique dealer as one of the finest cabinet-makers of the mid to late eighteenth century.

Not only can their furniture can be found at antiques dealers but also in auction house online catalogues, where it can be sold at a considerable price. For example two chairs made for the 3rd Earl of Darnley at Cobham Hall were sold by Christie's in New York in 2007 for $133,000 (£83,500). A pair of George III ormolu-mounted sycamore, satinwood and marquetry semi-elliptical commodes: attributed to Ince & Mayhew, circa 1775 were sold for £746,850 in 2012. A commode made from fustic, wenge and mahogany with ebonised borders was sold by Christie's in 2008 for £679,650.

It was made for George Finch, 9th Earl of Winchilsea and 4th Earl of Nottingham for Burley-on-the-Hill, Rutland. From his account book George Finch appeared to use Ince & Mayhew as his main suppliers of furniture when first modernising his mansion. He wrote to his mother in the winter of 1774 *I have got a number of things from*

Mayhew. I am sure the house will soon have a more furnished look. The commode was described as one of the firm's masterpieces of the 1770s, and later influenced the design of their work at houses such as Broadlands, Hampshire and Chevening, Kent. In July 2019 a pair of Ince & Mayhew serpentine yew-wood commodes with rosewood crossbanding and an ebonised moulded edge were sold by Sotheby's for £275,000.

In the 1940s the furniture company Heal's used quotations from Ince & Mayhew's *Universal System of Household Furniture* in their advertisements. *In furnishing , all should be with Propriety – Elegance should always be joined with a peculiar neatness through the whole house* and *any gentleman may furnish as neat at a small expence, as he can elegant and superb at a great one.*

The firm is mentioned in the Oxford Companion to the Romantic Age, interestingly in terms of their association with Sir William Chambers and Robert Adam as producers of *high quality furniture for aristocratic clients*[cviii].

It is a delight to spend time with the beautiful furniture which Ince & Mayhew created. It can be found at the Victoria and Albert Museum, London, The Lady Lever Art Gallery in Liverpool, Manchester Art Gallery, The Metropolitan Museum of Art in New York, The Museum of Fine Arts in Houston, as well as many other places including National Trust Houses and stately homes in the United Kingdom. A group of cousins descended from William Ince have made a series of trips to enjoy his artistry, including to Burghley House, the Lady Lever Art Gallery, Broadlands and Sherborne Castle.

Reflections on William's life

Researching the facts has revealed more of the lives of William and Ann Ince. The more I find out, the more I want to know about them, but because they were living in a completely different age to our own, what follows can only be conjecture, based on my own interpretation of human behaviour.

My sense of William is that although he was a very talented craftsman, he was a humble man with a genuine faith. His childhood was clouded by the death of his father at the age of 8, the re-marriage of his mother, then the death of his step-father. He went to court with his brother over the disputed inheritance and had to return to court to get sufficient money to pay for the apprenticeship he wanted – a sign of a determined young man.

When he and John Mayhew first met, there must have been a strong liking and respect for one another's skills: Mayhew appreciating William's craftsmanship and William aware of Mayhew's entrepreneurial skills. Mayhew had his own personal income and invested more cash in the firm, but also amassed a very large personal fortune. William Ince as the designer was an essential part of the success of the cabinet-making side of the business but he may not have had the same desire for financial success as he would have derived great satisfaction from the beautiful furniture the firm produced. It may be that he was not happy about the amount of money being invested in land and property, especially as he was worshipping at a non-conformist church. He made his will in 1800 and may not have been well for the last three years of his life.

It is very sad that the partnership ended so acrimoniously. Mayhew was obviously a very wealthy man and the 1759 agreement stated that they would share the profits equally, so he could perhaps have been more generous. It is interesting that it was not until after William had died that the court case was started. Could he not bear to go to court against someone he had worked with for so long? Or did he simply not have the physical strength to do so? Ann, his widow, had no doubt that she and her family deserved more than they were being offered and it was she who took out the Bill of Complaint within weeks of William's death. It would seem that William and Ann had a strong relationship. The deaths of seven of their children may have drawn them closer. William asked Ann to choose his burial place, and she wished to be buried with him, her *dear husband*.

Chapter 8 Colourful descendants of William Ince

The lives of the children of William Ince and Ann Stephenson were also colourful.

Baptisms for twelve of their children, all except Mary Ann, have been found at St James Piccadilly, London, the parish church for Marshall Street. The font at St James's is attributed to Grinling Gibbons, and was also used for the baptism of William Blake in 1757.

Font at St James, Piccadilly
Photo: John Salmon

Frederick Ince (1769-1836)

Frederick was the third son of William Ince the cabinet-maker and is my great, great, great grandfather. His greatest success was probably his marriage to Martha de Bar. His trade was in coach-making and he may have been a skilled craftsman, but he did not join his father's firm. In his will, William advised his executors to put Frederick's inheritance into stocks and just allow him the interest, which implied he was not very good with money.

On 2nd August 1786 Frederick was apprenticed to George Wellings of London in the trade 'Citizen Coach & Harness.' The business was based at 36 Camomile Street in Bishopsgate[cx]. Frederick was 17 years old when he took up this apprenticeship. The

Coach-Maker from 1800 Woodcuts by Thomas Bewick and his School[cix]

seven-year term would have ended in 1793 and he immediately married Martha de Bar on 31st August in St Botolph without Bishopsgate. Martha was only nineteen, so they married by licence, signed by her father Benedict de Bar to say he gave his consent. Frederick gave his parish as St James Westminster, so he may have been living with his family again. Martha and her family were living in Bishopsgate by this time.

According to Frederick's father's will written in 1800 he had *had a house furnished for him near St Bartholomew's Hospital in the City and the fixtures of a Grocers shop paid for by me.*

Their first child was baptised at St Marylebone but by the time of the third child, George, the family had moved south of the river as he was baptised at St Mary, Newington in 1800. Two years later Frederick was recorded as a Master taking an apprentice coach-maker with his address as Walworth, Surrey. The next four children were all baptised in Camberwell, Surrey, and Frederick was recorded as paying land tax there from 1803 to 1809. There is also a record of a Frederick Ince being granted a Victuallers licence in Lambeth in 1808. The eighth child, Alfred Horace Ince was baptised on 24th April 1816 in St Giles in the Fields, Middlesex and the family address is given as Broad Street, Golden Square, which was the old family home. Baptised at the same time was George Frederick Ince, their grandson from son Frederick (1796-1847). The occupation of both fathers is given as coachmaker.

Frederick and Martha's last child, Percy was born on 31st March 1818, but not baptised until 28th November 1824, after Frederick had left the country. The family address was still given as Broad Street. This time the baptism took place at the same time as that for son George's child, George Horace Ince who was born in 1824[43].

In 1819 Frederick wrote a letter to the War and Colonial Department and Colonial Office: Cape of Good Hope Colony, asking to become a settler at the Cape of Good Hope. His brother-in-law, Thomas Willson[44], who was married to his sister Mary Anne, had recently left to go there. Frederick's address on the letter heading was given as 28 Milk Street, Bristol. It is very likely that he was then working for Clark and Makepeace Coachmakers of Bristol who had a *Coach Manufactory* in Milk Street.

In the letter he states that he has six children, who would have been Frederick then 23, Isabella 21, George 19, Caroline 13, Edward Bret 10 and baby Percy, which implies that the other three baptised, William John (1794), Henry (1804) and Alfred Horace (1816) had all died.

In 1824, the Morning Chronicle reported that Henry Makepeace, coachmaker of Bristol, was bankrupt and in 1826 there was a sale at the Coach Manufactory in Milk Street of all his stock in trade.

The same year, according to the notes written by Charles Frederick Ince in 1925, *as entered in the Bible..(Frederick) set sail from Newport for New York on 18th September 1826 on board the Marothon, which may be known by applying to the American Consul, Small*

---

[43] George, the son of Frederick and Martha travelled to New York in 1829 and settled there. His son George Horace was a Captain in the American Civil War and died at the Battle of Gettysburg.

[44] Thomas Willson returned to England within a year and he became an architect. He drew up a design for a Pyramid Cemetery on Primrose Hill. See below under Mary Ann Ince.

Street Bristol near the Quay, settled I was told Wieling, America, and took up sheep farming and bought land at Wieling but my Grandmother refused (to go).

C. F. Ince's notes continue that Frederick *had overdone his ambition in sheep farming and land buying in Wieling and ended his life by shooting himself.*

His death date was given as 1836 at Fordridge Martin Mills, Orrave Creek, USA. There is no such place at Orrave Creek and by searching on an old map for the area around Wheeling it is likely he died on one of the farms on Fork Ridge, Grave Creek, Virginia either belonging to J B Martin or S Martin and possibly a few years later

A cousin who is descended from Frederick through his son Edward Bret Ince owns a series of letters which were written by Frederick when he was in America to his relations back in England. They tell a fascinating story which is related in the final chapter.

Martha de Bar (1774-1850)

According to Frederick and Martha's marriage licence she was nineteen years old in 1793, her father was Benedict de Bar and the other witness was James de Bar. The family may have had French origins but it is possible they came to England via Ireland.

Martha was born in Bristol and was baptised at St Augustine the Less on 15th May 1774. Her parents were Benedict and Martha de Bar and she had eight siblings, James the eldest being born in 1770, brother Benedict in 1778. The family lived in Limekiln Lane, Bristol, from where there were two burials for her sisters in 1776; Elizabeth born in 1771 and Mary born 1776. By 1783 the family had moved to Lambeth, Surrey where the baptisms of two more daughters were recorded. By 1789 they were living in Bishopsgate where George was baptised. There was an entry for a baptism in Jan 1792 at St George the Martyr, Queen Square for a child Mary Elizabeth d. of Debar born 23rd July 1791, but with no parent's forenames. No occupation was recorded for any of the baptisms for Benedict the father.

Frederick and Martha were both living in Bishopsgate, which is probably how they met[45]. Martha would appear to have had a strong influence on where they lived, as they moved to Camberwell, near Lambeth where she grew up, and later to Bristol where she was born.

---

[45] Apologies to those who prefer the romantic notion that Martha was rescued from Paris during the French Revolution.

It would appear that she remained with Frederick all through his coach-making days, bearing their nine children and shouldering the grief of the three who died.

Martha had a brother, Ben, who also lived in London and was an accountant, according to the baptism records of his children. Two of his children took to the stage and ended up in America. Ben de Bar (1813-1877) was immensely successful. He was an actor, manager, and theatre owner who, through his association with Ludow and Sol Smith, did much to help establish New Orleans and St Louis as leading theatre cities in America.

He made his American début in New Orleans in 1835 as Sir Benjamin Backbite in Sheridan's The School for Scandal, and acted there for the next 20 years except for a few visits to New York and London. In 1856 he moved to St Louis where he remained for the rest of his life, becoming owner of the influential Bates Theatre, renaming it De Bar's. Six years later he also acquired the St Louis Varieties Theatre and renamed it De Bar's Opera House. He had a fine comic gift and was highly praised as Shakespeare's Falstaff and Chanfrau's Mose the Fireman[cxi].

Sir John Fallstaff characterized by Mr Ben De Bar: F Welcker; G R Hall

His death in 1877 was mourned throughout St Louis. Many of the shops had a picture of Falstaff with crepe border in their show windows and some thirty-five thousand people went to view his body in the Masonic Building. Twenty-three leading citizens officiated as honorary pallbearers. The hearse drawn by four horses was followed by about seventy-five carriages and many private vehicles and there was a moving ceremony at the grave side in Bellefontaine Cemetery.

His sister, Clementina de Bar, was a dancer and appeared on the New York stage. She married Junius Brutus Booth Jr. and the de Bar house in St Louis was thoroughly searched after the assassination of Abraham Lincoln by Junius' brother John Wilkes Booth.

According to one of the obituaries of Ben de Bar the actor, his father was of French origin, but his mother was Welsh. There is a baptism for a Benedict de Bar in Dublin in 1746. The actor's family went to Ireland, and he danced on stage in Dublin, so there may have been connections there.

In 1826 when Frederick set sail for his new life in America, Martha refused to go. According to C F Ince's notes, she lived in Circencester then went to Earls Colne in Essex.

Their daughter Isabella married George Morse on 16th January 1833 at Earls Colne, with Martha acting as a witness.

Daphne Ince, great-great-granddaughter of Frederick and Martha, owns a sketch of Earls Colne Cottage entitled *Residence of Mrs Ince*.

By the 1841 census Martha had moved to live with Isabella, George and their two daughters in York House, Westgate Street, Gloucester. George was a linen draper and also living there were two assistants, two apprentices, and three servants. George appears to have had twins from a previous marriage, both aged 15, who were serving as an assistant and an apprentice.

Martha died at Westgate Street on 8th October 1850 and was buried at the church of St Michael in the City. The cause of death was given as spasmodic asthma. She was described on the death certificate as the widow of Frederick Ince, coach builder.

Other children of William Ince

William Ince (1765-1808) – the oldest surviving son was a Captain in the Bombay Artillery for the East India Company. He joined as a Cadet in 1782, possibly helped by his father's business connection with people in the East India Company such as James Alexander first Earl of Caledon, Warren Hastings and Robert Clive[cxii]. He was promoted to Lieutenant Fireworker in November 1783, but any further promotion was delayed by his appearance before a Court Martial in June 1786. He was suspended from rank pay and emoluments for six months. He was made Lieutenant in 1790, Captain Lieutenant in 1796 and Captain in 1797. He was appointed Major in September 1804.

William served in the Third Mysore War in 1791 and was present at the sieges of Dharwar, Simoga, Hooly Honore and Seringapatam. He was on Field Service in the Red Sea in 1800 and in the Ordnance Department from 1800-1803, serving in Gujerat. He took part in several battles including the taking of Broach (Bharuch) and Baroda (Vadodara). In 1807 he was the Officer Commanding for the Artillery *to the northward*[cxiii]. He died in Surat on 28th September 1808 aged 44. The causes are unknown, but it was not in battle.

Bombay: c.1731 by George Lambert (1710-1765), and Samuel Scott (1701-1772) East India Company warehouse in the centre, Bombay castle on the right with Union Jack flying.

In his will he left everything to *my girl Fatimah*. Fatima Bibu of Bombay was legally sworn in as his sole legatee and executor. In January 1809 there was a sale of William's effects which raised over 2000 rupees. Items included his uniform and boots, leather ghoggles, a sabre, all household goods, including 9½ dozen bottles of wine bought by the Colonel and a number of books including three volumes of the Universal Magazine which were presumably those bequeathed by his father. None of the other books left to him were in his possession, though he did own a map of Hindustan, Wales and Bailey's Astronomical Observations, *Lachies Mathematics* and *Elements of Fortification* amongst others. Articles of silver were sold privately raising over 1000 rupees.

Charles (b 1768) – In 1794 the name Mayhew, Ince & Sons occasionally appeared on their bills, and as Charles took over from his father in 1800 according to the advertisement in the London Gazette, he was presumably working there earlier. He paid rates for 23 Holles Street, Cavendish Square in 1801, and for 23 and 24 Holles Street in 1802 and 1803. He was listed in Thomas Sheraton's Cabinet Dictionary in 1803 in the list of Master Cabinet-Makers, Upholsters and Chair Makers. A notice in the Morning Post advertised an auction at the premises on 11th and 12th April 1804. *Excellent cabinet and upholstery stock* was to be sold at auction by Mr Squibb, including an *elegant rose-wood cabinet, mahogany secretaries..* and *an excellent counting house desk*. The advertisement reported that *Mr Charles Ince* was *declining business*. In his will, William wrote about Charles as *having left me and move*(d) *in Business for himself in such a way as to enable him to increase his fortune*. He gave Charles *My Box of Drawing Instruments, All my Architectural Books and Book of Furniture and Ornaments*, all appropriate for a cabinet-maker.

Charles married Anna Maria Jones, a widow, in 1797 and they had three children. Sadly two of them died in 1803 and were buried at Whitefield Memorial Church. The oldest, Charles Nigel Ince, married his cousin Isabella Cowell in 1828. Both George Cowell and Charles Ince were witnesses. The young couple had a child, Ada, who was born in Kingston, Jamaica in 1830, presumably when they had gone out to visit the estates that belonged to George Cowell and his brother John, as described below.

Charles and his wife Anna Maria moved to south Wales where his wife ran a school. She died in 1822 and according to the Land Registry document of 1825, Charles was late of *Lawnsea* (Swansea) *now of the City of Worcester*. He died in Claines, just outside Worcester in 1830.

Henry Robert (1772-1849) – He was apprenticed to William Hammond, Surgeon in 1788, aged 16 and joined the Berkshire Regiment as a surgeon in 1793. Later he was invited to be a GP in Presteigne. He was a surgeon in Presteigne, Radnor according to the 1825 document. He was paying land tax on a house in Grafton Street in 1800 and 1802, possibly one of the houses owned by Ince & Mayhew. His son was the renowned landscape painter **Joseph Murray Ince** (1806-1859). In his will, Henry made provision for three sons, Joseph Murray, Henry and Edward Ince Young, the child of his relationship with Mary Young.

Isabella (1773-1852) – She married George Cowell at Hornsey Parish Church in December 1795. William bought them a house in America Square. In 1825 they lived in Fitzroy Square. George was a brandy merchant in partnership with his brother John. They were both Executors of William's will and Ann's will, and supported Ann with the court case against John Mayhew, and took it on after she died. In his will George Cowell mentions the estates of William White and John Edwards in Jamaica. According to The Centre for the Study of the Legacies of British Slave-ownership at University College London[cxiv] in 1814 John Cowell had lent money to William White on the Hopewell estate in Hanover, Jamaica. The estate was assigned to George Cowell and Felix Booth as trustees, who *by their agents, entered into the possession and management of the Hopewell estate, and consigned the produce from it to [John] Cowell upon the trusts of the deed*. Sugar, rum and molasses were the main output of the estate.

Although the slave trade had been abolished in 1807 it was not until 1834 that slavery was abolished in in the British Caribbean, Mauritius and the Cape. When George Cowell applied for compensation for loss of the estate, he was unsuccessful and the money went to someone who had made an earlier loan to William White. The claim was granted on 19th October 1835 for £1652 7s 4d when there were 86 enslaved people on that estate. William White senior was a friend of John Cowell and asked him in his will of 1804 to close 'this whole business' by the sale of the Flat Point estate, where he owned 220 enslaved people. The Flat Point Estate was registered to White and Edwards and produced sugar and rum. In 1809 there were 490 enslaved people there, but this had reduced to 106 by 1832. In 1836 a claim of £2189 for the estate was granted to John's son, John Welsford Cowell, who had inherited from his father. He was also awarded £5058 for the Llandovery Estate, which had 232 enslaved people.

It seems shocking that the estate owners should be compensated, but the Centre explains that this was the negotiated settlement for the emancipation of the enslaved, with £20 million in compensation to be paid by British taxpayers to the former slave-owners. Instead of slavery, the newly freed men and women were bound into a system of apprenticeship, so they were still not at liberty.

George Cowell's sons failed to sort out their father's will after he died in 1845 and it was not administered until 1885 when his daughter Charlotte Dixon, the miniaturist painter (see below) was nominated a substitute Residuary Legatee and received the grand sum of £27 7s 3d.

Mary Ann (1782-1862) – She married Thomas Willson an architect in August 1808, at St Botolph's, Aldgate, where Mary Ann was resident. George Cowell was one of the witnesses, so she may have been living with her sister, Isabella. Thomas was then an architect, involved with the Chelsea Water Works.

In 1820 he led one of the parties promoted by the Government to settle in the Cape of Good Hope. He and his party of settlers, including Mary Ann and their children, Percy aged 9, Douglas aged 6 and Thomas aged 4, departed on 12th February 1820, arriving in Table Bay on 2nd May and Simon's Bay three days later. Thomas had tried to set up a scheme whereby he was treated as Lord of the Manor but the other settlers refused to comply and Thomas returned to Cape Town claiming that *the wretched-minded classes* had threatened to put a bullet through his head. In August he wrote to the Government, imploring to be sent back to England, and in December 1820, the family embarked at Port Elizabeth and came home.

In 1828 Thomas exhibited his designs for a Pyramid Cemetery for London, to be called the Metropolitan Sepulchre. He envisioned a honeycomb of catacombs, with room for a total of five million bodies. The whole structure would have occupied eighteen acres at its base which he proposed should be on Primrose Hill. At a height of 1500 feet, it would have been nearly four times the height of St Paul's Cathedral. Unsurprisingly it was never built[cxv]. However Thomas remained on the Committee to raise support and funding for the General Cemetery Company.

The family were then living in New Cavendish Street, Portland Place, and in 1829 he wrote a letter from there asking for appointment to the district surveyorship of Clerkenwell[cxvi]. By the 1861 census Thomas and Mary Ann were living in Acton with their unmarried daughter. Mary Ann died in 1862 and Thomas in 1866. No trace of a gravestone has been found, though a small pyramid would have been most fitting!

Other notable descendants of William Ince

Descendants of George Ince
George Horace Ince 1824-1863 son of George, who came to America in search of his father Frederick

George Horace was born on 5th August 1824 and baptised at St Pancras church, London on 28th November at the same time as his uncle Percy was baptised, shortly after Frederick, his grandfather, emigrated to America. George Horace appears in the New York census of 18 March 1830 with his parents and 3 sisters. By the 1840 census the family is living in Southwark Ward 4, Philadelphia. This would be after they came to Wheeling and disrupted life for Frederick.

George became the agent for his actress sister Annette and also toured with her and his other sisters, playing the piano. They were all in Hawaii in 1858 and 1859.

A few months after the start of the Civil War on November 12, 1861, George joined the 66th New York Volunteers aged 37. He steadily climbed the chain of command and became Captain of Company A on March 8, 1863. He was involved in the Battle of Gettysburg and on July 2, 1863, he received a wound to his arm, then a mortal wound to his chest. The report of the battle by Major Nelson explains how the regiment was moved around the battlefield once the rebels opened fire, but then pursued the retreating troops.

Very soon we were under fire of musketry, but, nothing daunted, we pressed steadily forward through wheat-fields, woods, over rail fences 10 feet high, stone walls, ditches, deep ravines, rocks, and all sorts of obstructions, every one of which had served as cover for the enemy, and from which a murderous fire was poured upon us as we advanced, but without avail, as nothing could stop the impetuosity of our men, who, without waiting to lead or even fix bayonets, rushed eagerly forward at a run, their cry being constantly: Forward! Charge! We passed large numbers of rebels in our advance, of whom, however, we took but little notice, so interested were we in our pursuit of the retreating foe.

Arrived at a rocky ridge about 300 yards from where we commenced our victorious advance, we halted, taking the movement from the right, and engaged the enemy at short range. Here fell many noble men. Capt. G. H. Ince was killed. He died from his wounds four days after the battle.

George Horace was buried with his father George in Green-Wood Cemetery in Brooklyn, New York. His mother received a pension from the army of $20 a month as George had contributed regularly to her support.

Annette Ince 1834-1892 Daughter of George Ince

According to various newspaper reports, Annette made her debut as an actress in 1850 with Junius Brutus and John Wilkes Booth - related to her through Ben de Bar, whose sister Clementina married Junius Brutus Booth Jr. She travelled all over America, including Philadelphia in 1853, where the family were living, Nashville in 1854, Virginia in 1855, San Francisco in 1857, where she apparently tried to raise the tone of the theatre, and Hawaii in 1858 and 1859. She starred at the Theatre Royal, Victoria, Australia, where the critics found her acting lacked spontaneity but she received many curtain calls, and in Washington in 1862 and 1863 when she played Juliet to John Wilkes Booth's Romeo. In 1864 she and Julia Deane Hayne took over the Metropolitan Theatre in San Francisco. In 1868 she played Salt Lake City, taking many parts. She was described as 4'6" tall with red hair. In 1868 she was proposed to by Brigham Young of Utah, but refused him. She may have known of the other 55 wives. In 1876 she went to London where the advanced notices of her appearance described her as *universally acknowledged the Reigning Queen of the American Stage*. She was also described as *a talented tragedienne*. She died in 1892 in San Francisco. In her obituary she was described as *among the leading actresses of her day*.

Other members of the family were also professional players. Annette's sister, Emma danced and Fanny and Caroline sang to the accompaniment of brother George on the piano. They were all in Honolulu in 1858 and 1859 en route to Australia.

Descendants of Frederick Ince[46]
Edward Bret Ince 1808-1886 Son of Frederick

Edward Bret Ince published The Law Journal from 1832, having taken over from J W Paget. The company was based at 5 Quality Court, Chancery Lane, London.

Francis Ince 1841-1920 Grandson of Frederick Ince, son of Edward Bret

Francis Ince one of William Ince's great grandsons, was an energetic man. He was the founder of the law firm Ince & Co in London where he developed a practice specialising in shipping and commercial law. He was there until 1919. He was also

1,000 LIGHT DYNAMO BY FERRANTI, THOMPSON & INCE

passionately interested in electrical science and played an important role in the introduction of electricity to the domestic home.

According to his daughter's book[cxvii], Francis was a practical man of business, by temperament excitable, impetuous and impatient of quick results. A lawyer by profession he was a passionate amateur scientist with a great interest in the technicalities of electrical science.

In 1881 he met Sebastian de Ferranti[cxviii], then aged 17, but already an ingenious inventor, who was then working for Siemens. Francis Ince recognised Ferranti's talent and set him up in business with the company Ferranti, Thompson and Ince.

---

[46] Family tree on page 133

Ferranti was a pioneer in electrical engineering, having grasped that electricity could be made on a large scale in one place and then distributed to all those who needed it. One of his aims was to use electricity to help women with their domestic chores. He was appointed to the London Electric Supply Corporation with Francis Ince on the Board of Directors. At the age of 24 he helped establish the world's first high voltage AC power station at Deptford with the ability to create 10,000 volts. He also invented cables to carry high voltage electricity; the transformer to reduce the voltage for use and the voltmeter to measure use. This is much the same system that is still in use all over the world today.

The London Electric Supply Corporations Works at Deptford 1889

By 1893 Francis Ince was a Member of the Institution of Electrical Engineers, Director of the London Electric Supply Corporation and Chairman of S. Z. de Ferranti. In 1889 he had been amongst the party to meet Thomas Edison when he visited the Deptford works. Francis left Ferranti's company in 1899, but they remained firm friends. Ferranti had married his daughter, Gertrude, in 1888 and was a support to Francis during his final illness.

Henry Bret Ince 1829-1889 Grandson of Frederick Ince, son of Edward Bret Ince

Henry Bret was the older brother of Francis Ince, both great-grandsons of William Ince, cabinet maker. Henry initially worked in shipping until he suffered an accident which limited his mobility and he was forced to change his career. He learnt shorthand and started work as a reporter, becoming a leader writer for the *Daily News*. He then decided to study law, entering the Inner Temple in 1852. He was called to the bar in 1855 and reported the proceedings in Vice-Chancellor Wood's court for *The*

Jurist. In 1858, he published a legal commentary, "A systematic treatment of the Trustee Act, 1850, and the Extension Act of 1852". He migrated to Lincoln's Inn *ad eundem* in 1859. On 28th June 1875, he took silk, and he was made a bencher of Lincoln's Inn on 4th November 1878. He was elected Liberal Member of Parliament for Hastings in 1883. When that constituency was reduced by a member in 1885, he was returned for Islington East, but was defeated in 1886. In 1866 he was elected a Fellow of the Statistical Society and in 1882 he was elected a member of The Royal Geographical Society. He died suddenly from a brain aneurysm at his chambers in Lincoln's Inn in May 1889[cxix].

Charles Percy Ince RBA RI 1875-1952 descended from Frederick Ince and son Percy

To Ethel on her Wedding 1935
Charles Percy Ince

Charles Percy Ince was a prolific landscape painter and cartoonist as well as a Director of the law printing and publishing firm Chas F. Ince and Sons. He was educated at King's College, London and studied art under Henry Moon. He contributed humorous illustrations to Bystander and Tatler magazines (1900-10) and a few cartoons to Punch. He was a member of the Royal Institute of Painters and the Royal Society of British Artists. He lived in Purbrook House, Purbrook and was buried in St Mary's Church, Porchester.

Descendant of Henry Robert Ince
Joseph Murray Ince (1806-1859) Son of Henry Robert

Joseph Murray Ince was the son of Henry Robert Ince, sixth-born son of William and Ann. He was a successful artist, best known for his watercolour landscapes. He was born in London on 7th April 1806 but moved with his parents to the Presteigne area (then Radnorshire, now Powys, Wales) when he was around 6 years old. In 1823 he started to receive private tuition in Hereford under the famous English watercolour artist David Cox. He moved to London in 1826, exhibiting his landscapes of Wales and of Herefordshire at the Royal Academy when he was only 19. He returned to Presteigne in 1830 and produced several drawings, paintings, and lithographs of local scenes, including large country houses and beauty spots, around this time. He also produced many drawings and watercolour paintings of Cambridge colleges as he was a drawing master there in the 1830s. He married in 1834, but sadly his wife Sarah Phillips died shortly after childbirth the following year.

Joseph Murray Ince: King's College Chapel, Cambridge, 1843

Around 1835 he returned to Presteigne, and painted many maritime and rural scenes which often feature castles and ruins, rural activities such as woodcutting and harvesting, as well as figures and animals. It appears he had addresses in London and in Presteigne for much of his life. He died in London on 24th September 1859 at the age of 53 and was buried in Kensal Green cemetery. There are examples of his drawings and watercolours at the Victoria and Albert museum and Tate Britain in London, The Fitzwilliam in Cambridge, Hereford Museum and Art Gallery, and a dozen in the print room at the British Museum.

He has a blue plaque on his former house in Powys and there is a memorial to him in Presteigne parish church.

Descendant of Isabella Ince
Charlotte Grace Cowell 1811- 1901 Daughter of Isabella Ince

Charlotte Grace Cowell, grand-daughter of William Ince, was a miniaturist painter. She was born on the 13th October 1811, daughter of George Cowell and Isabella Ince, who had married in St Mary's Hornsey in 1795 when William Ince was Church Warden. Charlotte was the youngest of their six children.

In 1834-1835 she won the Silver Isis medal for an original miniature from the Royal Society of Arts. She exhibited at the Royal Academy in 1851, two portraits being listed against her name; the late Levi Ames, Esq. and the daughter of J. O. Hanson, Esq. She was described as *Cowell Miss Grace Charlotte (afterwards Mrs F. Dixon) miniature painter of 12 Upper Gloucester Street.* She married Frederick Henry Dixon on 11th October 1851, two days short of her 40th birthday, at St Martin's in the Fields. Frederick was also a portrait painter. They had a daughter in 1853, born in Brighton, but baptised in Westminster.

According to The Dictionary of British Women Artists[cxx] Charlotte was active between 1851 and 1875 having been instructed by Frederick Crucikshank a portrait painter and miniaturist and François Théodore Rochard (French, 1798-1858) who also produced portrait miniatures and watercolours.

Bonhams sold a painting of hers in 2003. It was described as *A bearded and bespectacled Gentleman, wearing black coat over white shirt and blue cravat signed on obverse and dated G Dixon 1873, and on the reverse, Mrs. F. Dixon/ Miniature Painter/ 1873, fitted red leather case Oval, 108mm. (4 ¼ ins.) high.*

Another surviving painting is a miniature portrait described as *Oil on Ivory Portrait of a Toddler Holding a Rose, unsigned, but by Charlotte Dixon.* On the obverse it is inscribed *by Cowell Writing Painter Gilder No.16 Little New Street Shoe Lane Fleet Street.*

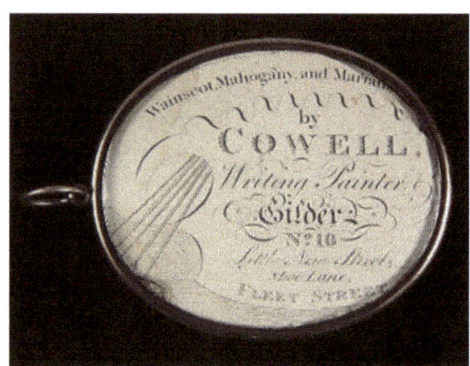

Images by kind permission of Thomaston Place Auction Galleries, Maine

According to the Dictionary of British Women Artists, Charlotte Grace Cowell visited Paris, but travelled mostly around Britain, producing portraits in miniature, and large portrait heads in black and white chalk. Her portraits apparently included such subjects as the Madonna, Caesar Borgia and Richard Bethel, the Lord Chancellor.

It was interesting to see in the 1841 census that her older unmarried sister was with their parents in Devon, but Charlotte Grace is not there. She may have been out of the country. It seems likely that her father gave her financial support; he was a wealthy city merchant. In his will, he left everything to his wife, Isabella, to be divided between the children on her death (apart from daughter Isabella who had received financial support on her marriage). Their mother died in the summer of 1852, but George Cowell's will was not administered until 1885, when Charlotte was a widow, living in Budleigh Salterton, Devon, with her daughter, Constance. According to George Cowell's probate record she was nominated a substitute Residuary Legatee and received the grand sum of £27 7s 3d. Her husband, Frederick Dixon had died the previous year in Bournemouth.

In the 1901 census she and her daughter were living in Bath with a servant, describing her occupation as living on independent means. Both Charlotte and Constance gave their ages as ten years less than they actually were. Charlotte died a couple of years later and was buried in Bathampton parish church, seemingly squeezed into plot 418a, the age on her death certificate given as 80 when she was in fact 91 years old.

Chapter 9 John Mayhew's Life and Family

John Mayhew, the partner of William Ince, lived in London all his life. He enjoyed a high standard of living in Marshall Street, with a villa in Hornsey and he even commissioned portraits of two of his children. He probably aspired to the life that his aristocratic clients enjoyed. However his life also had its hardships. His mother died when he was twenty and his first wife, Isabella, died in childbirth within a year of their marriage. He married again, to someone able to bring a substantial amount of money into the business, but she died five years before he did. Of the ten children from this second marriage, only five outlived him, of whom the eldest son had gone bankrupt.

His children lived varied lives. One was a surveyor and architect, another a lawyer and one of his daughters married a royal dentist. Some of the grandchildren were writers, including social journalist Henry Mayhew. The wealth that John Mayhew amassed enabled his children to live comfortably, but some of his grandchildren were imprisoned for debt while others worked for social justice.

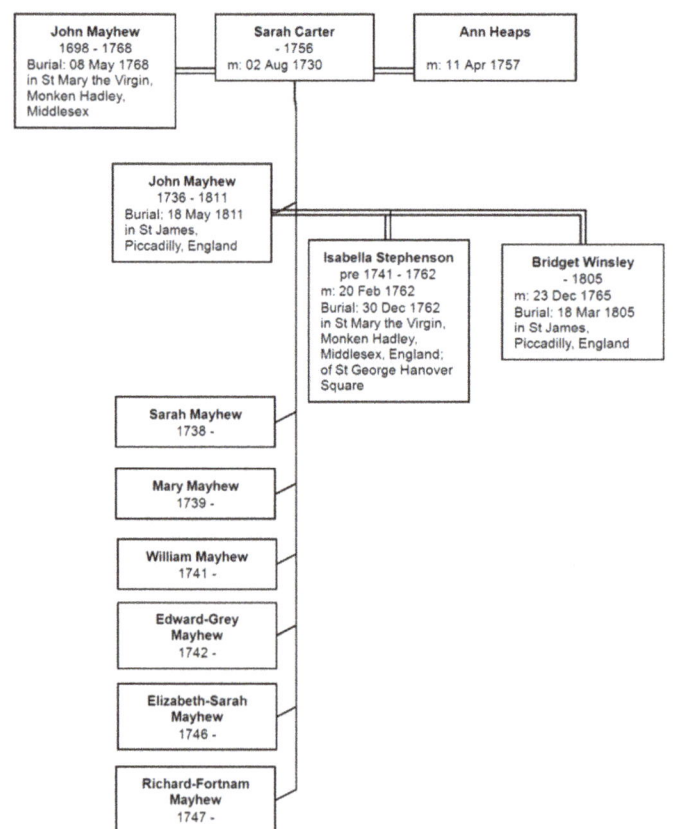

John Mayhew 1736-1811

John Mayhew was born on 21st February 1736 and baptised in St George Hanover Square on 26th February[cxxi]. He was the son of a builder of the same name, who lived in Green Street[47], Grosvenor Square, London and had seven siblings. He was apprenticed to William Bradshaw, Upholsterer, of Soho Square[cxxii]. His mother died in 1756 and was buried in St Mary the Virgin Monken Hadley, when he would have been twenty. His father remarried in 1757. In 1758

---

[47] John Mayhew Senior paid rates on Green Street in the parish of St George Hanover Square.

John the son went into partnership with James Whittle and Samuel Norman as a cabinet maker and upholsterer, taking over the premises of the late John West in King Street, where William Ince was serving his apprenticeship. By the end of that year he had gone into business with William in Broad Street.

John married Isabella Stephenson in the joint marriage with William Ince and Isabella's sister Nancy (Ann) in February 1762 at St George's Church, Hanover Square. Isabella sadly died in childbirth ten months later, and one of the twins she was carrying, called Sarah lived for less than nine months, being buried with her mother in September 1763 in St Mary the Virgin Monken Hadley. John's father was also buried there in 1768 as were John's infant children by his second wife: Theophilus William in 1767, Bridget in 1768, Edward in 1769, Sarah Christianna in 1773 and Michael Richard in 1774.

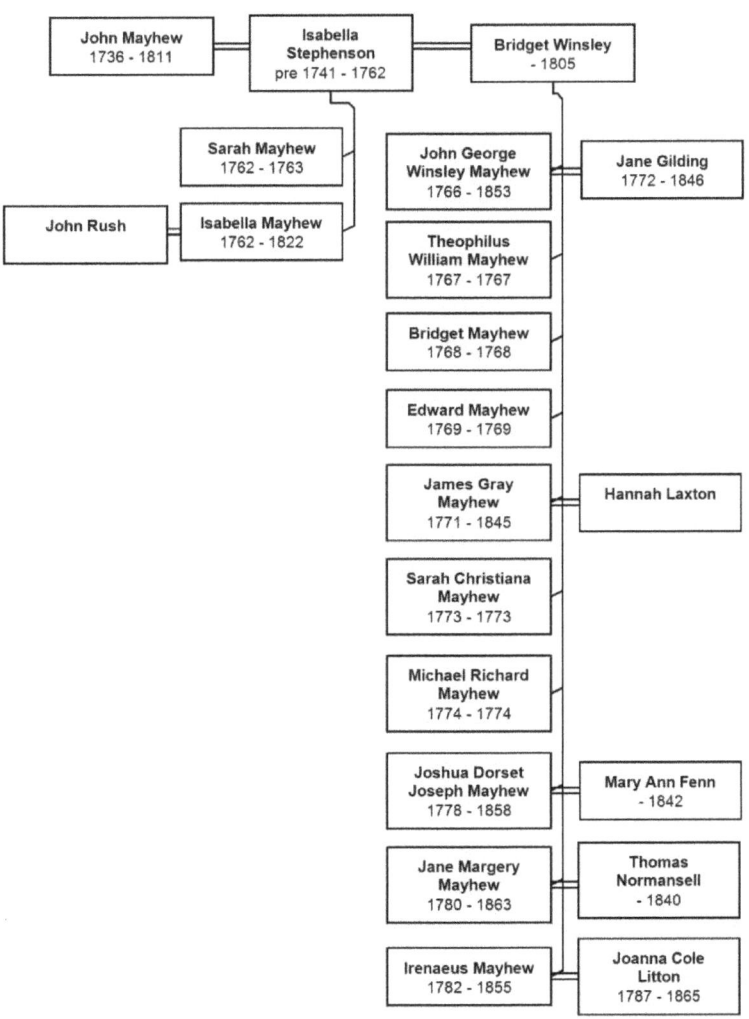

John remarried in 1765 and the settlement of 1799 records that his second wife, Bridget Winsley, brought £3000 to the business, which would be worth around £260,000 now. John and Bridget had ten children of whom five survived them. When his father died in 1768 he left John some property in Westminster which the firm may well have used to rent out. In a codicil to his will his father changed his mind about giving his second wife, Anne, £400, leaving that instead to John, and making her an annuity of £30 pa. It may be that John and his family took her in to live with them. Anne Mayhew was paying rates in Green Street up to 1770. John's father had earlier invested in the firm's business as mentioned in the 1799 agreement, one of the bones of contention being that William Ince had not repaid his share of the loans John's father had made.

John Mayhew enjoyed collecting art and his name appeared as both buyer and seller at Christie's auctions between the 1770s and 1790s[cxxiii]. The firm was advertising fine pictures for sale in 1772 so some would have been sold on. Two portraits of his children still exist. Both Isabella and James Gray were painted by Charles Ansell in 1780. He started selling his art collection after the Partnership Agreement of 1799 and his pictures are listed in auctions by Christie's in 1804, 1805 and 1812. They were mostly sold at low prices, the most expensive being a *View in Norway with a waterfall* by Ruisdael which sold for £42.

In 1786 John appeared before the Parliamentary Committee of Trade to be asked about the merits of French and British plate glass. He reported that the glass he had seen in Paris was as bad as that in England, from which it is clear he had travelled to France, and the firm is known to have imported French glass and furniture. Ince & Mayhew had lent £100 to the British Plate Glass Company in 1782.

John Mayhew owned a villa in Hornsey, which was burgled in 1786. A number of items of silver were stolen, worth around £55, including a marrow fat spoon, two pounds of tea and a quart of brandy. The silver was engraved with a mermaid or the character M. A reward of ten guineas was offered for information leading to conviction, with a further reward of ten guineas for *recovery of the above-mentioned plate*[cxxiv]. Thomas Wells was convicted of the burglary as his fence admitted to having received the items and gave evidence against him, and no doubt promptly received his reward. Apparently Thomas Wells poisoned a large dog with arsenic in order to get in. He was sentenced to death.

John Mayhew was surveyor and overseer of the highways for Hornsey in various years from 1782 to 1788, and attended church meetings there. In 1792 the Vestry Minutes record that Mr Mayhew's Seven Acre Field was to be *rated at 54s an acre which amounts to £101*. He must have been in arrears or the field was larger than its name. In late 1793 both he and William Ince were on a committee to look at repairs and alterations needed to the church. In 1798 he paid £7 15s 3d tax on land he owned in Hornsey, plus £2 7s 11d on land owned by Lady Gosling. William Ince paid £2 17s 6d on land he owned in Crouch End and £5 15s to William Smith who owned the Old Crouch Hall Estate. These taxes were well above the average. In 1804 John Mayhew was a church warden at St James Piccadilly. He was a director of the Westminster Fire Office between 1763 and 1810[cxxv], serving six two-year terms.

In the 1794 book on State Trials for High Treason[cxxvi], John Mayhew Esq. of Hornsey, upholder, is listed as having been summoned to serve on the Petty Jury for the trial of Thomas Hardy, a political reformer and one of the founders of the London Corresponding Society. This organisation was of and for the workers, mostly artisans, *mechanics*, and small tradesmen, and at its peak had over 100,000 people attending meetings in London with groups in over a hundred other cities and towns. The Treason Trials were an attempt by the government to stamp out any radical reform following the French Revolution. Thomas Hardy was acquitted after a nine-day trial, as were two fellow members of the LCS, with the other cases being dropped[cxxvii]. John Mayhew was not called to serve but it is fascinating to note that he was summoned as a property owner, while only a few decades later two of his grandsons aligned themselves with the workers movement.

William Ince and John Mayhew were both members of the Society for the Encouragement of Arts, Manufactures and Commerce (RSA)[cxxviii] and they were also both Freemasons[cxxix]. John Mayhew was a member of the Lodge of Antiquity.

The European Magazine And London Review issued by The Philological Society of London dated 1797 includes an overview of Hornsey and its pleasant residences, including *John Mayhew Esq. a delightful cottage and pleasure grounds.*

From his will it would appear that the last few years of John Mayhew's life were miserable. His wife had died in March 1805; his son John had been declared bankrupt and the case that Ann Ince had brought against him in 1804 was limping along. He wrote that he was waiting for God to relieve him *from this troublesome life,* describing his *unhappy daughter Isabella* and her brother John *whose imprudence was the*

origin of my sorrows. He begged his executors to come to an agreement with the Ince family *without waiting the ultimate decision of Chancery*. He died on 11th May 1811 and was buried in St James Piccadilly on 18th May. The details for the memorial plaque were set out in his will to be inscribed on a *tablet of plain white marble upon the pilaster supporting the Gallery nearest my pew*. The actual plaque is not as elaborate as the drawing in his will and is on the west wall of the church.

He made generous provision for his children, and for his old servants and workers in his will. The two eldest children, Isabella and John Winsley were both bequeathed an annuity of £60 pa (roughly £5000 pa in today's money) plus shares for their children 1/20 for Isabella's two sons, 1/20 for her four daughters, 1/20 for John's son and 1/20 for his two daughters. Daughter Jane received 1/20 as did her husband Thomas Normansell. Son Joshua received 4/20, James 3/20 and Ireneas 6/20, The other 1/20 went to the executors for the legatees in trust. Various monies were paid out at different times and the total after death duty had been paid came to £36,855, worth around £2,500,000 today. Irenaeus was appointed the Residuary Legatee and inherited his father's interest and property in the Basingstoke Canal Company[48], two houses in Queen Street, Cheapside, the best plate and linen or his father's books, and the remaining stock of the wine cellar.

John Mayhew was generous to his servants. He was distressed that Ann Walls, who had been his wife's servant, had left, although she had said she would stay while he was still alive, but he still bequeathed her an annuity of £30 pa in acknowledgement of her continual attention particularly during times of severe illness and asked his sons to be friendly towards her. He gave his *good old servant* James Bolton the house he lived in after payment of the lease, £100 to put the house in good repair and £20 pa for James and his wife. He left £50 to his clerk George Reynolds. To Joseph Higham and James Parker, cabinet-makers and his two workwomen, Elizabeth Pasmore and Margaret Hall, who had all been with him for very many years, he left £20 each for mourning apparel. He wanted the house to be kept up for two months after his death to give his servants time to find good places. His old friend Dr Bland received 20 guineas for a mourning ring.

---

[48] The Basingstoke Canal Company never paid any dividends and went bankrupt in 1866.

Looking at the Death Duty Registers[cxxx] the sums, rounded up, received over various years between 1818 and 1852 by the children of John Mayhew were as follows:

					Total	
Isabella Rush and family	£1,770		£100		£1,870	Isabella died in 1822
John Winsley and family	£2,150				£2,150	
Jane and family	£460	£2,610	£21,660	£1,930	£26,660	linked to leasehold in Carnaby Street
Joshua	£600	£500	£800		£1,900	
James	£450	£375	£600		£1,425	
Ireneas	£1,650	£1,200			£2,850	
					£ 36,855	

He appointed George Tennant and Richard Harrison as his executors and wanted them to take charge of all his landed property, freehold, copyhold and leasehold, *to be sold when they think fit and proper.* He gave them both £100 and left to Mrs Tennant *the Great Glass and the Table under it in my drawing room to be put in perfect order and the frame new Gilt.* Had she perhaps hinted how much she admired them when on a visit?

Isabella Mayhew 1762-1822

Isabella, the daughter of John's first wife, was baptised in St James Piccadilly on 26th December 1762 with her twin sister, Sarah. She married John Rush in St Clement Danes on 27th December 1786 and as recorded in the settlement document they had the use of one of the firm's properties for free in 1788-89. The partnership had a ready furnished house in New Burlington Street usually let by the week for £162. When it was empty in 1788 William Ince offered it to Mr Rush who took it for 6 months but no rent was ever received for it.

Their first child, John, was baptised in St Mary's Hornsey in 1787 and two other daughters, Mary and Fanny were baptised there in 1791 and 1793 respectively. Isabella had eight children altogether, 5 girls and 3 boys. Under John Mayhew's will Isabella received an income for life but sadly she did not live long after this was available as she died in 1822 and was buried in St James Piccadilly on 27th August 1822 aged 59. Her widower and children received their shares according to the death duty register.

There is a portrait of Isabella Mayhew by Charles Ansell in the Huntingdon Arts Museum in San Marino, California[cxxxi].

John George Winsley Mayhew 1766-1853

John was baptised at St James Piccadilly in October 1766 and married Jane Gilding in 1793. He was paying rates in Broad Street North in 1798[cxxxii], so living separately to his family but probably helping in the business. A letter of 9th July 1798 records that Mrs Mayhew of Broad Street took in a *penitent prostitute* called Elizabeth Greville, to work as a nursery maid[cxxxiii]. This would have been for William Gilding Mayhew, who was born in 1798. John and Jane had four children altogether of whom three were living at the time of the 1825 land registry document. John set up in business at 45 Wigmore Street, Cavendish Square, London as a cabinet-maker, upholder and house agent in 1801. He received a commission of bankruptcy on 19th January 1805 with the certificate of bankruptcy being issued on 15 November 1806[cxxxiv]. In the bankruptcy notice he is described as a cabinet-maker, dealer and chapman, or merchant. It seems possible that he invested too much in his merchant business before he was established. At some time John and his family moved to the Midlands as he is listed in the Post Office Directory of Birmingham of 1849 as a wine merchant. In the 1841 census he is described as Independent, and by the 1851 census, when he is living with his grandson, he is down as a Gentleman. His son, William Gilding Mayhew also settled in the Birmingham area and was a wine merchant. Both the daughters, Jane and Ellen died in the 1830s and his wife Jane died in 1846. John died in 1853 aged 89 and was buried in Edgbaston, Birmingham.

James Gray Mayhew 1771-1845

James was baptised at St James Piccadilly in March 1771. His father had a brother called Edward Grey which is likely be where the name came from. James married Hannah Laxton by licence at St Martin's in the Fields in March 1807. They had five children.

James was a surveyor and architect for Paddington. He was also a surveyor for the Westminster Fire Office. In 1824 he was appointed receiver for Ince & Mayhew, which led to the resolution of the law case. In 1832 he was the District Surveyor for the parish of St James Piccadilly[cxxxv]. He lived and ran his business at 14 Argyll Street, St James. By the time he died he was living in Cambridge Terrace near Hyde Park. The

Yale School of British Art has a drawing by him of A Project for a Triumphal Archway with Classical Figures in Foreground.

A Project for a Triumphal Archway by James Gray Mayhew

His son Charles Mayhew joined the business and was made FRIBA in November 1846. Son George was also an architect and took over the business in Argyll Street when Charles retired. George was responsible for the development and building of part of a group of fourteen shop houses in Leman Street and Hooper Street, London in 1845-46[cxxxvi]. He was also involved in a higher-status development at Ennismore Gardens near Knightsbridge. James' son Frederick was a solicitor and had a practice in Great Marlborough Street, London.

James died in 1845 and was buried in Kensal Green cemetery, the first of the seven garden style cemeteries for London. In his will he left an annuity of £60pa for his son Arthur Robert, who spent much of his life in and out of lunatic asylums. There is a portrait of James Gray Mayhew as a boy sailor by Charles Ansell dated 1780 in the Huntingdon Arts Museum in San Marino in California[cxxxvii].

Joshua Dorset Joseph Mayhew 1778-1858

Joshua Dorset Joseph Mayhew was baptised at St James Piccadilly in December 1778. He was an attorney and solicitor. His articles of clerkship were filed on 7th September 1796 to Thomas Greene and George Tennant, his father's friend and executor[cxxxviii], of Grays Inn, and he was admitted an attorney of the Court of Kings Bench in 1802. He married Mary Ann Fenn in 1806 and they had at least fourteen children. He and his family lived at 16 Fitzroy Square, London from 1828 to 1858 and his practice was at 26 Carey Street, Lincoln's Inn. He is depicted by his son Henry in a poem of 1848 as a tyrant with power over his family, using the allowance he granted them as a means of control[cxxxix].

In 1824 he supported and gave legal advice to his friend Henry Fauntleroy, who was a banker accused of forging a power of attorney, which defrauded the Bank of England of £265,000. Found guilty and condemned to death, Fauntleroy was hanged outside Newgate Prison on 30th November 1824[cxl]. Joshua was a victim of crime himself in 1846 when he hired a servant who stole £26 of goods including 8 forks, value £7, a salad-fork, £2 and a wine-strainer, £2. The servant was found guilty and also guilty of stealing a watch. He was sentenced to transportation[cxli].

Joshua died in 1858 aged 79 and was buried in All Souls cemetery, Kensal Green.

Joshua's son, Thomas, was articled to him in 1825, but left the law and went into radical journalism. He was one of the editors for "The Poor Man's Guardian: a Weekly Newspaper for the people" which was the best known illegal newspaper of the period with a peak circulation of 16,000. According to the Law Journal of 1834[49] Thomas tried to escape his debtors by pleading that he had been enrolled as an attorney in 1830 and was practising law. One of his claimants was J. Dixon an engineer and printing-press maker who was seeking recompense for a bill for £159 from Thomas Mayhew of the Penny National Library. The judges refused to believe he was an attorney as well as a publisher and printer so dismissed his plea. Thomas was sent to Fleet Prison and sadly took his life in October 1834 in Barnard's Inn using prussic acid and fumes of charcoal. He was buried at St James Piccadilly. In his obituary[cxlii] his father is referred to as Francis Mayhew, which is a sad reflection on how Joshua viewed his son. Uncle Irenaeus appeared to have supported Thomas as a partner in the publishing business. A notice in the London Gazette in March 1834 said that Thomas Mayhew, Irenaeus Mayhew and George Frederick Isaac had dissolved their partnership.

Joshua's son Edward was discharged from the Fleet Prison in 1836 and by the 1851 census is calling himself a veterinary surgeon, which changes to an author on equestrian subjects in the 1861 census. His story *Midnight Mishaps* appeared in Bentley's Miscellany in 1837[cxliii]. He also wrote for the Morning Post. Son Alfred was articled to his father's partner in 1834 and later went into partnership with his father as a solicitor in Carey Street. Daughter Rosalie married an East India merchant, Parke Pittar, who had been born in Rio de Janeiro. Daughter Emily's second marriage was to the widower Arthur Pittar, half-brother of Rosalie's husband and twenty years older than Emily, who had worked for the East India Company in India. Emily left over £80,000 in her will in 1903, over £6m in today's currency. Daughter Clarissa married a

---

[49] The Law Journal was published by J. W. Paget of Quality Court, Chancery Lane, and Edward Ince, grandson of William Ince, was working there in 1834.

hop merchant and lived with her sister Emily in Nutfield, Surrey when they were both widows. Daughter Lauretta also married a merchant.

The remaining sons were authors, and part of the Bohemian set in London that included Charles Dickens. The most famous was Henry Mayhew, who wrote London Labour and the London Poor described in the Wordsworth Edition of 2008 as *a masterpiece of personal inquiry and social observation*[cxliv]. He was educated at Westminster School, but ran away as the headmaster was going to flog him for revising his Greek grammar in the Abbey Service[cxlv]. His father sent him to sea on the tea-service to Calcutta and on his return he was articled to his father, but soon gave up the law. He wrote plays and collaborated with his brother Augustus on novels. Having edited a weekly periodical *Figaro in London* between 1831 and 1839, he was one of the originators of Punch in 1841. In 1846 he was declared bankrupt. After writing some light novels with brother Augustus, in 1849 he was invited by the Morning Chronicle to act as a correspondent for its investigation into labour and the poor, leading eventually to the publication of his book in 1851, a book that remains a landmark work of social journalism. He later spent some time in Germany and wrote about the Rhine and about Martin Luther. Henry left £90 10s when he died in 1897.

Joshua's son Augustus Septimus, yes, the seventh son, wrote many popular works of fiction including books and plays, and worked with Henry. Son Horace wrote farces and tales and worked with George Cruickshank. He was a sub-editor on Punch and wrote for Lloyds Weekly News. He was described in the Dictionary of National Biography as *a handsome and captivating man, a brilliant talker and raconteur and was very popular in society*[cxlvi]. Son Julius was either living on independent means or a merchant's clerk in the censuses, until 1881 when he said he was an architect. He designed the Pavilion Theatre in Whitby in 1878. In 1872 he and Augustus were defendants in a case taken out by Emily Sarah Mayhew widow of brother Horace.

Jane Margery Mayhew 1780-1863

Jane was baptised in May 1780 at St James Piccadilly. She married Thomas Normansell in 1806, when Mary Ann Ince, William's youngest child was a witness. According to the 1825 Land Registry document Thomas Normansell was a dentist and both his father and his son were also dentists. Mr Normansell (Senior) of South Moulton Street is listed as a dentist in the Medical Yearbook for 1783, which is very early for this profession. He is listed as operating in London from 1790 to 1799 when he had been appointed to the Royal Household[cxlvii]. He was a member of the

Corporation of Surgeons. Thomas the father died in 1815 leaving the rent from twelve houses, various stables and a coach house in the Portman Square area to his wife then his six children in equal shares. In 1818 Thomas Normansell appeared as a *Surgeon dentist* at 50 Portman Square and in a listing of the Royal Household for that year he is one of two Dentists Extraordinary. So John Mayhew's daughter Jane was married to one of the Royal Dentists! Thomas, Jane's husband, died in 1840 and left his one sixth share of the rents worth £200 (around £12,000 today) to his wife and then his four children in equal shares. Jane died in 1863. Thomas and Jane's son Frederick was also a surgeon dentist, and was listed at 1 Gloucester Street, Portman Square. Frederick was named as one of the executors for two of his uncles, James Gray and Irenaeus, as well as his mother. When he died in 1881 he left over £31,000, worth around £2,000,000 today. Jane's son Henry was a surgeon and went to Sri Lanka where he died in 1843. Her unmarried daughter, Mary, died in the Hotel Vittoria, Florence in 1890 aged 74.

Irenaeus Mayhew 1782-1855

Irenaeus was baptised at St James Piccadilly in January 1782. He was admitted to the Middle Temple on 13th June 1803, but does not appear to have been called to the bar. At the time of the 1825 Land Registry Document he was in Presteigne, and was probably visiting Henry Robert Ince, William's son, who lived there. In 1825 when he was 43, he married Joanna Litton Cole in Dawlish, Devon. Joanna was the widow of a lieutenant in the Royal Navy, William Matterface. Irenaeus and Joanna then settled in Devon and in Pigot's Directory of 1830 Ireneas is listed as a Gentleman of Whitehill House in Wolborough which is near Newton Abbott.

In 1834 Irenaeus dissolved his partnership with Thomas Mayhew, his nephew, and G. F. Isaac as printers and publishers of Henrietta Street, Covent Garden and in 1835 he sold his *valuable library* through B. Wheatley auctioneer[cxlviii], perhaps to pay off the debts incurred by the partnership. Presumably the library contained books from his father. In 1838 he was a witness to his brother-in-law Thomas Normansell's will and then had to sign an affidavit about the trustees in 1842 before the will could be proved. Under the Tithe Apportionment of Chudleigh he was listed as the landowner of four plots of land, two arable and two pasture, occupied by others. The total amount of land he owned came to over 15 acres. In the 1851 census he was described as a land proprietor living in Highweek Village, Newton Bushell. He died in 1855 and having no children was generous to his nephews and nieces, for example his brilliant diamond ring was to go to Mary Normansell on his wife's death; there were rings for Charles, son of James Gray Mayhew, and his fishing tackle and rifles went to Frederick Normansell.

Ince and Mayhew children

It is interesting to see how the Ince children and Mayhew children continued to interact after their parents died. They had grown up in close proximity to each other in Marshall Street, and though they would have lived further apart when at the country villas in Crouch End and Hornsey, they would have attended the same church.

George Cowell and Isabella Ince were living in Fitzroy Square, when Joshua Mayhew moved there with his very large family in 1828. The Cowells lived at No.36 and the Mayhews at No.16, directly opposite each other. They may have seen each other on a regular basis. Irenaeus Mayhew visited Henry Robert Ince in Presteigne and Mary Ann Ince was a witness at Jane Mayhew's wedding.

Summing up

William Ince the Cabinet-Maker was a superb craftsman and the research into his ancestors has revealed some of the people who would have had an effect on him either directly or through his genes. He would also have been influenced by his upbringing in Covent Garden.

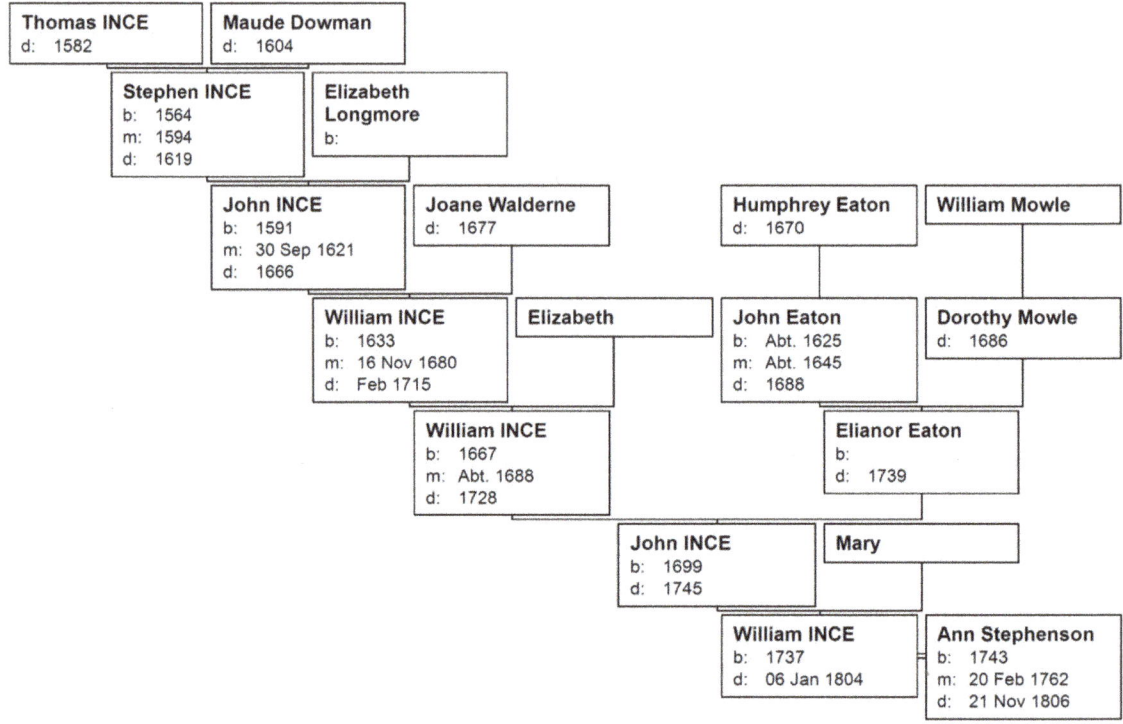

Other craftsmen in his family include his fourth great-grandfather, Thomas, who was a weaver; his great-great- and great-grandfathers, Humphrey and John Eaton who were glovers and his uncle who was a wheelwright. His father had the resourcefulness to move to London and set up business there as a glass-grinder.

There was also sufficient money within the family to support such endeavours and the Ince family appears to have had a good enough role within their community to give succeeding generations something to aspire to.

It is very likely that the women in the family also brought talent as well as good nurturing and upbringing to those children that survived the many hardships of their lives.

Elianor Eaton was important as the provider of the property in Shell and Feckenham, the rent and the subsequent sale of which enabled her children to live well and for her son John to make his way in London. The generosity of Uncle William's will may have provided the money needed for William to start his apprenticeship with John West. It may also be that his brother, John, could see what talent young William had and wanted to help him as much as possible.

Living in the vibrant area of Covent Garden as a child, William would have seen many craftsmen at work. Chippendale lived in the area from 1749 and had set up in St Martin's Lane in 1754, when William was apprenticed in nearby King Street. William would also have gained valuable knowledge and expertise from his apprenticeship as it was a large and busy workshop, with some aristocratic customers.

William was a very good artist and some of his designs suggest a degree of classical learning. Would all this have happened during his apprenticeship or was his mother a talented woman who gave him a basic education and passed on some of her own skills? What schooling would he have had in London? Whatever his learning, he undoubtedly had a great gift for working in wood.

He was also very industrious. When producing the *Universal System* he would have worked long hours, which would have continued as the firm evolved, including visits to customers to ensure his designs would fit in situ and careful checking of the final work before despatch. He produced a great many delightful objects in a wide range of furniture that reflect years of careful study and a profound understanding of the nature of different woods.

There is always more to learn and hopefully future generations of the Ince family will be able to build on the information so far provided.

Postscript:
The story of Frederick Ince in Virginia and Martha, his long-suffering wife

Preface

This story is based on the letters written by Fredrick Ince, my great-great-great-grandfather, which were sent from America between 1826 and 1836. Further information has come from my research into the family left behind in England, using records such as baptisms, marriage banns, burials, apprenticehip records, newspaper reports, law reports, etc.

The interpretation of the information is very much my own. There is a considerable amount of conjecture, but there are solid facts behind the story. Sometimes I have simply made a choice as to what might have happened. Everything in italics is taken directly from original sources, mostly Frederick's letters. I have improved the punctuation and moved sentences around in order to give a more coherent account of his activities.

My cousin Nigel Ince owns these letters, which are a wonderful resource. I have listed details of when the letters were written and to whom at the end.

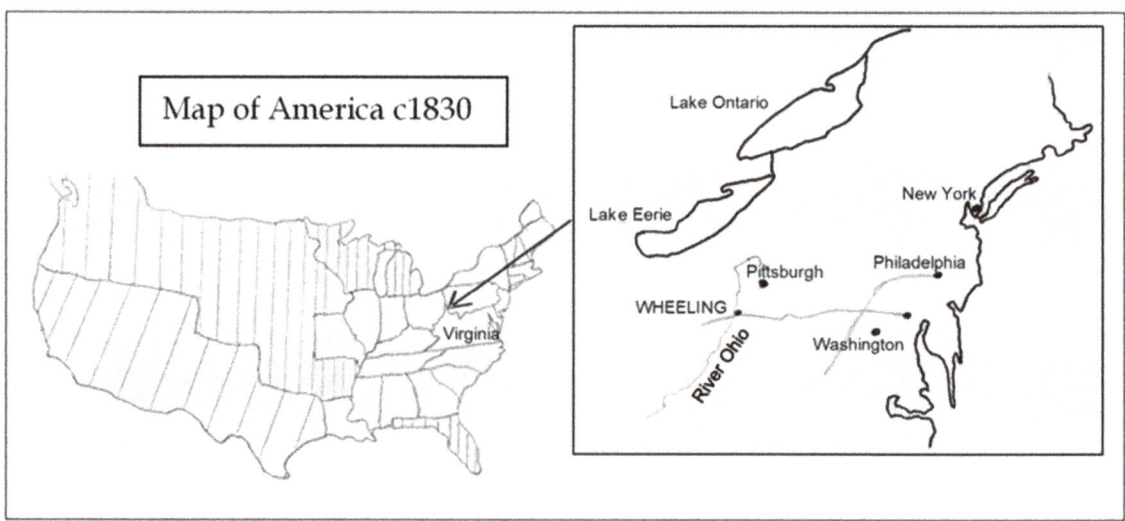

Children of Frederick and Martha Ince

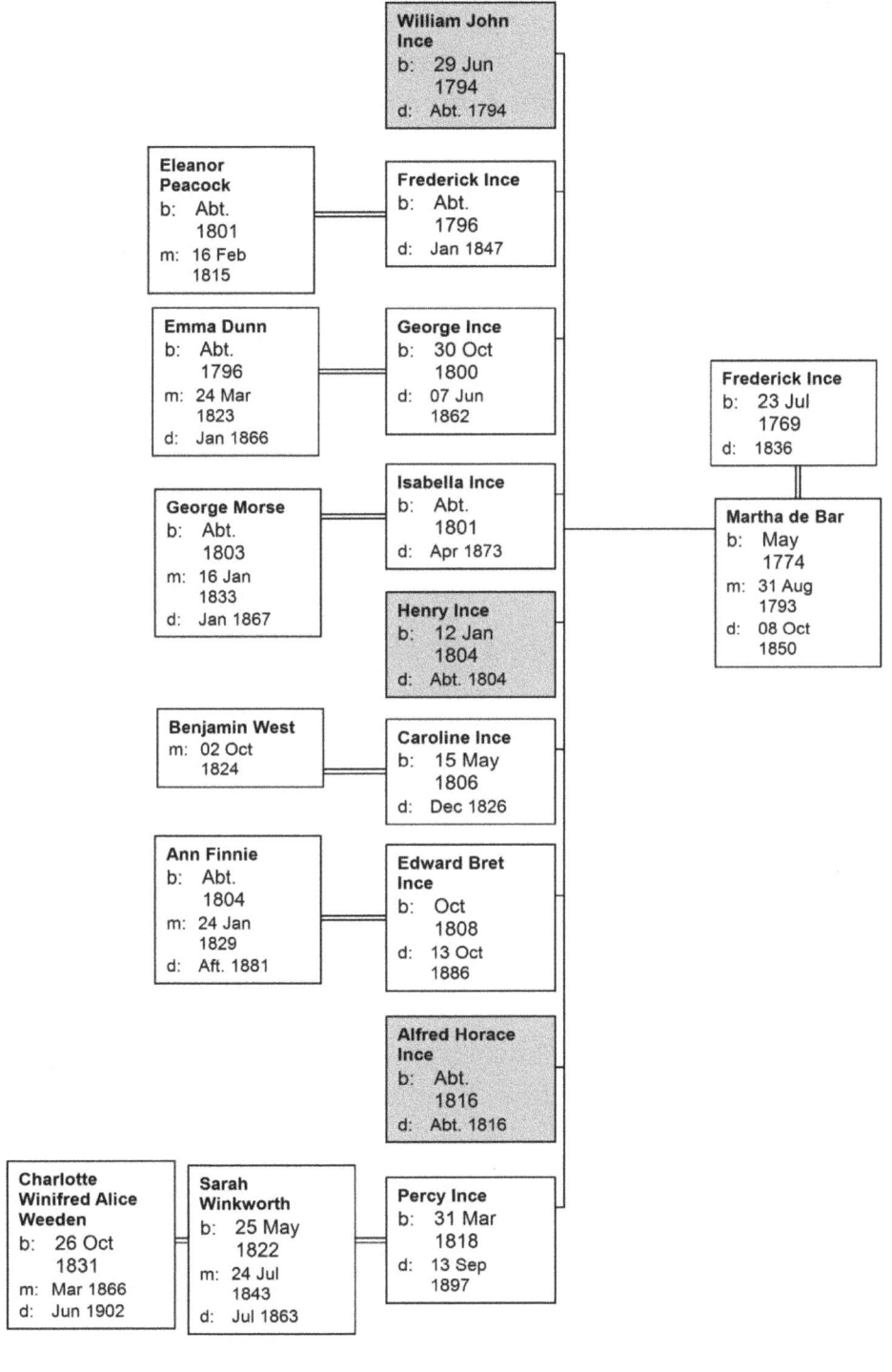

133

Frederick travels to Wheeling, Virginia 1824-1825

My name is Frederick Ince and my emigration story begins in 1819 when I heard that my sister, Mary Ann, was going to go to the Cape of Good Hope with her husband, Thomas Willson and their three boys. I wrote to the Colonial Office in December that year asking if I and my family could become settlers as well saying *I should have no objection should it meet your Lordship's approbation to accept of a similar charge whenever any other settlers may be sent thither… I could much wish to know how soon such an event may probably take place also the terms and responsibility attached to whatever situation your Lordship may think me capable of undertaking for the benefit of any part of the new colony.* It may be that I should not have mentioned that I was a mechanic, as although they may have needed such skills, there was a law prohibiting the emigration of mechanics at the time, which may be why we were not chosen to go.

I really hoped Thomas would have helped me, but he may have been too busy organising his own party of settlers. He had set up some sort of arrangement whereby they all had to pay him to help with supplies and their deposits for settlement, which was not something I could afford. In any case, it didn't work out for him and Mary Ann and they were back in England a year after they left. But their expedition really helped me see that it could be possible to escape England, that dreary country where living costs were so high and debts never seemed to go away.

I have worked hard all my life. When I was seventeen in 1786 I was apprenticed to George Wellings of London in the trade 'Citizen Coach & Harness.' The business was based at 36 Camomile Street in Bishopsgate[cxlix] and I served the full seven years. While in Bishopsgate I met the most wonderful girl and we were married at St Botolph's, Aldgate, in 1793. She was only nineteen at the time, and her father and brother had to sign the licence. Her name was Martha de Bar and although she was born in Bristol, the family had French blood.

I really wanted to keep her in style. I was used to a good life as my father was William Ince, an important cabinet-maker who made furniture for people such as the Earl of Darnley and Lord Palmerston. When I was growing up we had two houses, one in Marshall Street near Golden Square and one in Crouch End in the country. We had beautiful furniture and fittings and many paintings on the walls. My father's partner was John Mayhew, and unfortunately he and my father fell out when they decided to bring the business relationship to an end. They could not agree on what the share of the proceeds should be. My mother was really angry as the cabinet-making side of the business would never have been so successful without the talent and hard work of my father.

There was a long case in the Chancery court which dragged on and on for about twenty years. That was so frustrating as I needed the money I was entitled to under my father's will. Martha and I had nine children altogether, though sadly three of them died very young[50] and it was hard work providing for everyone.

When we first married, my father *had a house furnished for [me] near St Bartholomew's Hospital in the City and the fixtures of a Grocers shop paid for by him*. Unfortunately this did not make us much money. We later moved south of the river to Walworth as Martha had lived in the area when she was younger and I worked as a Master Coachmaker taking on an apprentice. I even tried selling liquor for which I had to get a licence in Lambeth[51].

It was hard work being a coach-maker. There was a lot of competition and it wasn't easy to keep up with all the improvements being made: elliptical springs, under-springs, two seaters. Although there was a demand for coaches there was tax to be paid on them[52] and the money never seemed to quite add up. I could never make enough to keep us in the manner I wanted, so eventually we went down to Bristol[53], where Martha had been born, and I took up work with Clark and Makepeace in Milk Street, still making coaches, but not with the responsibility.

Even down in Bristol my debts followed me. I really could not afford to stay in England. The only prospect I could foresee for old age was the workhouse and I simply could not bear to let that happen. As I wrote to my son Edward[54] *It seems as if some Malevolent Planet was hanging over the destiny of the whole connexion but probably that was not to be of long duration, and I certainly must have been under the same influence, had I remained in a country where I had never experienced any other than misfortune and misery, these were powerful motives for leaving it.* But Martha, my wife, she could not understand, or would not understand. She was *bent on staying in it, I therefore had no*

---

[50]When Frederick wrote to the Colonial Office he only mentioned six children. There are three others who were baptised with the parents Frederick and Martha: William John in St Marylebone 1794, Henry in Camberwell 1804 and Alfred Horace in St Giles in the Field, Holborn 1816.
[51]Rates paid: East Street, Walworth 5s 3d 1799; George bap 1800 St Mary's Newington; Rates 1803 and 1804 Camberwell 14s value Assessment 11s 8d; Caroline 1806 bap St Giles Camberwell; Edward bap 1808 Lambeth, 1808/9 Rates Camberwell 16s value Assmt 8s.
[52]In 1814 there were 23,400 four-wheel vehicles paying duty to the government, 27,300 two wheel and 18,500 tax-carts, totalling 69,200 carriages in Great Britain. History of Coaches 1877.
[53] Bristol was the second port after London, full of sailing ships of all sizes and rig, going out to the Caribbean, Canada and round the British coast. There were factories for sugar, brass and glass production, and they had started lighting some of the streets with gas lamps, though the streets themselves were mostly just dirt, with only the main ones being cobbled.
[54]Letter 1, 28 February 1826.

other alternative but taking these steps.... I have LONG lamented that your Mother would not enter into my views, particularly on the question of emigration. What in the name of God was I to do in England on such a trifling means, and over head and ears in debt, by heavens I could not do better than I have.

Struggling on in Bristol I was in despair, but finally the court case came to an end and I received the legacy from my father at last, over twenty years after he died. Thank God for James Mayhew who agreed to be the Receiver for the firm Ince and Mayhew. That was in April of 1824 and after that the wheels slowly turned as we signed away all the land to the two lawyers, Tennant and Harrison, and then the money was released. The dispute with the Mayhew family was not our doing, nor our desire. They were our old friends and we had grown up together in Marshall Street. The problem was their father John, and his second wife, Bridget, who wanted more than their fair share of the partnership's money at the end. Our poor mother. The law case sent her to an early grave and I'm sure contributed to our father's sudden death too.

All the money was released to George Cowell, the husband of my sister Isabella, a good businessman who led our side of the court case after our mother died. Because of the wording in my father's will, my share was invested by George so I could receive the interest. That was after a payment to my three oldest children, who had reached the age of twenty-one, that's Frederick, George and Isabella. The rest of the money would eventually go to the other three, Caroline, Edward and Percy.

I needed some money to buy my passage and to get started in America, so I dipped a little into the principle. That reduced the amount of interest I was paid, but I could never have gone without some financial backing.

So, having made the decision, I kept an eye on the papers for a ship sailing for New York, and made the acquaintance of a Captain Robinson, who would be sailing in September from Liverpool.[55] He saw no problem in getting me into America, suggesting I use an alias and say I was a farmer. *I assumed the name J.S. [John Smith] to enable me to clear out of Bristol, as a farmer the law being in force against mechanics leaving England, and it has hither to travelled with me owing to unavoidable circumstances, not having yet an opportunity to resume my own [name], but should I leave this place I certainly will.*

---

[55] The image is of the Charles W. Morgan, an American whaler, the most likely sort of ship Frederick would have travelled in. Photo: Mystic Seaport

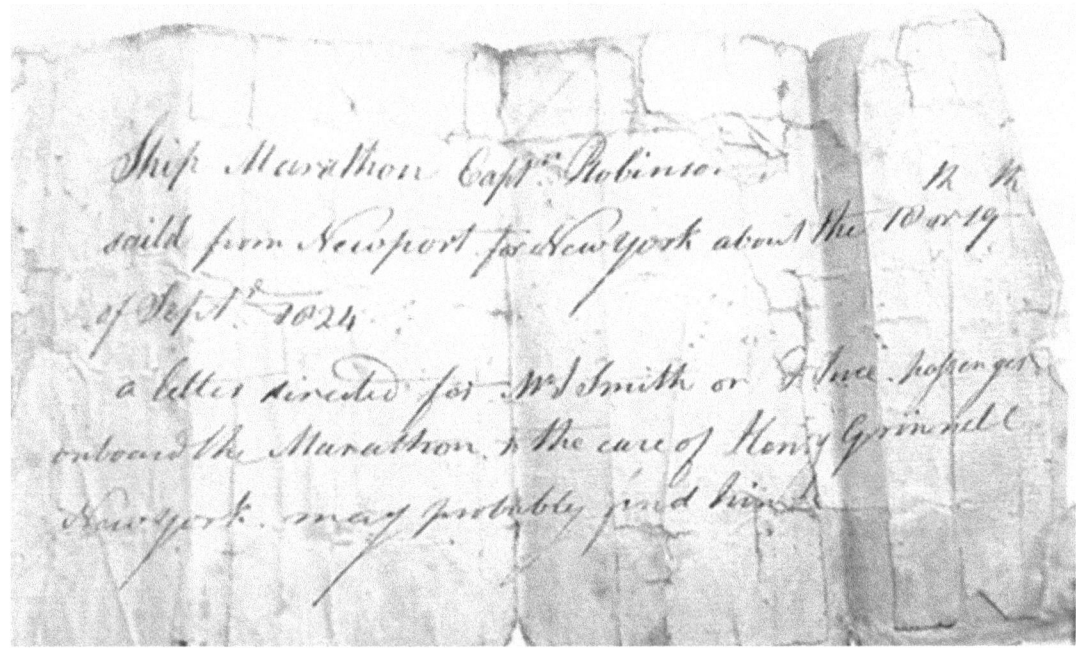

Ship Marathon Captain Robinson saild from Newport for New York about the 18th or 19th Sept. 1824.

A letter directed for Mr J. Smith or F. Ince passenger onboard the Marathon in the care of Henry Grimmell New York may probably find him.

Ship & date F. Ince (father of E. B. Ince) saild from England to America in and never returnd.

Passenger List for the Marathon 11th November 1824

I'm not sure how it happened but after I had bought my cabin room, I discovered that a young friend of mine was very keen to come with me, and as the Captain didn't see any problems, I changed the booking to the Captain's berth and we travelled together. As I wrote to Isabella, *I engaged with the captain first for myself as I then intended to come alone for £18 and take cabin fare, for my partner I paid £12 and the captains berth.* I haven't regretted that for one moment. Without her encouragement, I may not have made the journey at all.

On the 18th September 1824 we took a coach to Newport from Bristol and boarded the Marathon on her journey from Liverpool to New York[56]. We were the only passengers and *we were as comfortable as it was possible to be on board ship, there are a great many come cheaper but perhaps not so comfortable.* It took 54 days to make the crossing and we arrived in New York on 11th November[57].

Someone we met in New York told us there was good farming land to be had in Virginia. It had already been cultivated so for an old man like me, I'm 56 now, the work would not be too back-breaking, not like going into the frontier. So we made the long journey along the dirt roads and turnpikes by stagecoach and horse-drawn wagon. We travelled from New York to Philadelphia, nearly 100 miles, and then along the National Road to Wheeling, Virginia another 350 miles[58].

It was a most unpleasant journey. A foreign visitor who travelled by stagecoach from New York to Philadelphia wrote that the passengers were ill for an hour or more after being slammed about on a particularly rough stretch of road. Other travellers described clouds of choking dust and vain efforts to defend themselves against the hordes of mosquitoes. It took us ten days to get from New York to the town of Wheeling[59].

---

[56] According to Lloyd's Register, the Marathon was an American built and owned vessel with two decks, sheathed with copper and with *proved iron* cables. Her tonnage was 375 and she had a 15 foot draught.

[57] When the steam ship the Great Western sailed from Bristol in April 1838 it only took 14 days and 12 hours to cross the Atlantic and arrive in New York.

[58] If they had come a year later they could have used the Erie Canal, which was connected to the Hudson River in October 1825.

[59] Maps from the 1932 Atlas of the Historical Geography of the United States show rates of travel in different years. All the maps use New York City as a starting point on the East Coast, and show how long it would take to move westward across the country. In 1800 it would have taken around 2 weeks to travel from New York to Wheeling, and 5 days in 1830, so probably around 10 days in 1824.

The National Road at Willis Creek, just west of Cumberland by Carl Rakeman, an artist with the U.S. Bureau of Public Roads. It shows a stagecoach and two Conestoga wagons.[60]

---

[60] Picture courtesy of Federal Highway Administration, United States Department of Transportation.

In 1818 the National Road to Wheeling was completed. It was built by the Federal Government from Cumberland, Maryland and almost immediately there were many more travellers, as well as new taverns every few miles all along its 130 miles. Wheeling became an important commercial centre. Immigrants from the east would often end their long trip over the Allegheny mountains there and either stay or push on by boat down the Ohio. The town became a trading centre where horses were bought and sold; grain and whiskey were shipped; and where one could buy clothing or supplies of the sort needed in the backwoods.

According to the History of the Northern West Virginia Pan-handle[1] in 1810 the city had a population of 914; in 1815 about 300 houses 1500 people; by 1820 it had increased to 1,567; in 1830 it was 5,221. As many as 12 passenger coaches were going east and west each day to and from Wheeling; along with 40 road wagons carrying boxes and crates. In the 1820s the town had three churches, one Methodist, one Protestant Episcopal and one Presbyterian. There was a courthouse and several hotels. Dry goods, groceries and country produce was usually sold at the hotels. The leading men of society were highly aristocratic in their bearing, but affable and courteous in their manner, when they saw fit. Wheeling later had a Market House where *the citizens and watermen of every class upon the river were supplied, sometimes to overflowing, with meats of all kinds, wild and domestic, vegetables, fruits and all the substantials in rich profusion, by the country folks attending the markets*. There was also another smaller market.[cl]

We spent several weeks in the town, staying at one of the hotels. I made some good acquaintances and was helped to buy a little farm about twelve miles away. I could see it had great potential, so I put some money down on it. I wish I had brought more money over with me. I had enough to buy my passage, but not really enough to set up over here how I would wish.

Martha in London – 1824-1825

That man, that man! How selfish and irresponsible can anyone be? He decided he was going to go to America, and nothing I could say would make him change his mind. What a hopeless husband. Poor little Percy is only six years old. Six! And his father simply walked out and left him with me and his sisters and Edward. How am I supposed to bring him up and what am I supposed to bring him up on. There is hardly any money left. We had to leave Bristol and come up to London to be near my two eldest boys Frederick and George. It was no hardship to leave the city with all the tittle tattle going on behind my back. People were saying that Frederick had gone off with a younger woman and taken all the children's money. I can't believe he would do that.

My oldest son Fred has two children now. Sweet things. But there's no room for us there. He barely makes enough to keep his family. He was working for Dickie Taylor in London as a coach-maker and then he went to Bristol after his father left to work for

Henry Makepeace. He has now received some money from his grandfather's will and he's talking about setting up in business with someone in Dudley, still working as a coach-maker. But I don't know that he'll do any better than his father. He's a hard worker, but not a great businessman, and his inheritance won't go very far.

St Pancras, London

As for George, he's a great charmer, but he doesn't seem to understand the meaning of work. So far he's just lived off his father, and now off his grandfather's money. He seems to think he can live like a gentleman, but he'll soon find out sitting around writing songs does not pay the rent. His first-born, George Horace, was born in September 1824, just before Frederick left, and he and Emma decided to have the boy baptised. I thought it was a good opportunity to get young Percy baptised as well, so we had a joint baptism at St Pancras church in London on 20th November. It was very strange being there without Frederick, and having to fill the form in on his behalf. We had had a joint baptism before, some eight years earlier. That time we bought our dear son Alfred Horace to be baptised with our son Frederick's boy called George Frederick[61]. Sadly little Alfie did not live long. Then Percy was born two years later.

Isabella is the next in line after George. She's a dear girl and very concerned to look after me and help with Percy. Caroline, foolish girl, decided to run off and get married. I can only think it was a reaction to her father leaving. She went up to London soon after he left and we heard that she had had a ceremony at St Pancras Chapel at the beginning of October. She was only eighteen and I don't much like the fellow she chose, Benjamin West. He doesn't treat her very well. I so hope she didn't think she had to leave the family so I didn't have to support her. Edward has been living with her for a while. He's a great source of strength to me, although he's only seventeen and he's started working in an attorney's office in the City so he is bringing in a little money. I really don't know what we shall do.

Frederick has been impossible. Ever since his sister went off to the Cape of Good Hope he has been awful to live with. So dissatisfied. What I don't understand is that as it didn't work out for MaryAnn in the Cape, why did he think he could be successful in America. Not to mention the shame. There really was no choice for me and my family but to leave my home town of Bristol. The Lord alone knows where we will end up. I

---

[61] 24th April 1816 St Giles in the Fields, baptism Alfred Horace son of Frederick (Snr) and Martha Ince with George Frederick son of Frederick (Jnr) and Eleanor Ince.

have a brother, John de Bar, in Gloucester. He might help me. He's another coachmaker, but he was declared bankrupt a few years ago[62]. It seems only the most talented coachmakers manage to make a reasonable living. I know John will take us in if he can even if it's only for a little while. It will just be me, Isabella and little Percy. I suppose I may eventually have to find some way of supporting us myself, though what sort of work a woman of my age could find, I am not too sure. We have to eat though.

Frederick in Turkey Run 1826

We went out to the farm in the summer last year and it was even better than I had expected. The apples were just ripening when we arrived, and I was impressed by the amount we were able to sell.

The farm is *a pretty place, everything seems to thrive on it.* It's 133 acres in size but needs a great deal of work. I wasn't at all well for about three months in the autumn *with illness and distemper in my eyes from which I was obliged to have them both bound up…..I shall never have my sight very good again, nor yet my health, for I am most terribly afflicted with the Rheumatics, and much reduced in flesh.*

I thought farming would be a fine occupation, spending the day outside in the fresh air and knowing the satisfaction of hard labour. However, the *work there is to do on a farm exceeds everything I had any idea of and I believe is the sole cause of all my illness… It is always confined to the left side shoulder and arm and takes away the use of it for several days.*

I can't afford to pay anyone to come and help me as *the price of labour is vastly too high for a farmer to make a living* and prices for produce are so low there is little profit to be made eg *Indian wheat fetches on the average only 25 cents a bushel, a full grown chicken sixteen for a dollar. Eggs 6 cents a dozen, butter 72 cents a lb, butchers meat 3 to 4 cents a lb, turkeys at Christmas 25 cents each, as you will have perceived the profits of that farmer must be very small, besides the trouble of taking them any distance to market.* The only way I will be able make a success of this farm is if some of the family come out to help me. *I am much in want of society.*

The people round here live simple lives. *All farmers weave their own apparel both woollen and linen and the women universally spin and knit, indeed when a farmer's daughter gets married, the parents, that is their Daddy and Mummy for they never make use of the term Father or Mother, always however poor, give them a new spinning wheel and a bed, and I believe a cow, this is their fortune. No farmer in this part of the world ever thinks of saving*

---

[62]John de Bar, coachmaker of Gloucester was declared bankrupt on 17th September 1822 according to the Bankrupt Directory.

money, it is quite enough to raise sufficient necessaries for their consumption, and they only take enough to market to buy them tea, coffee, etc.

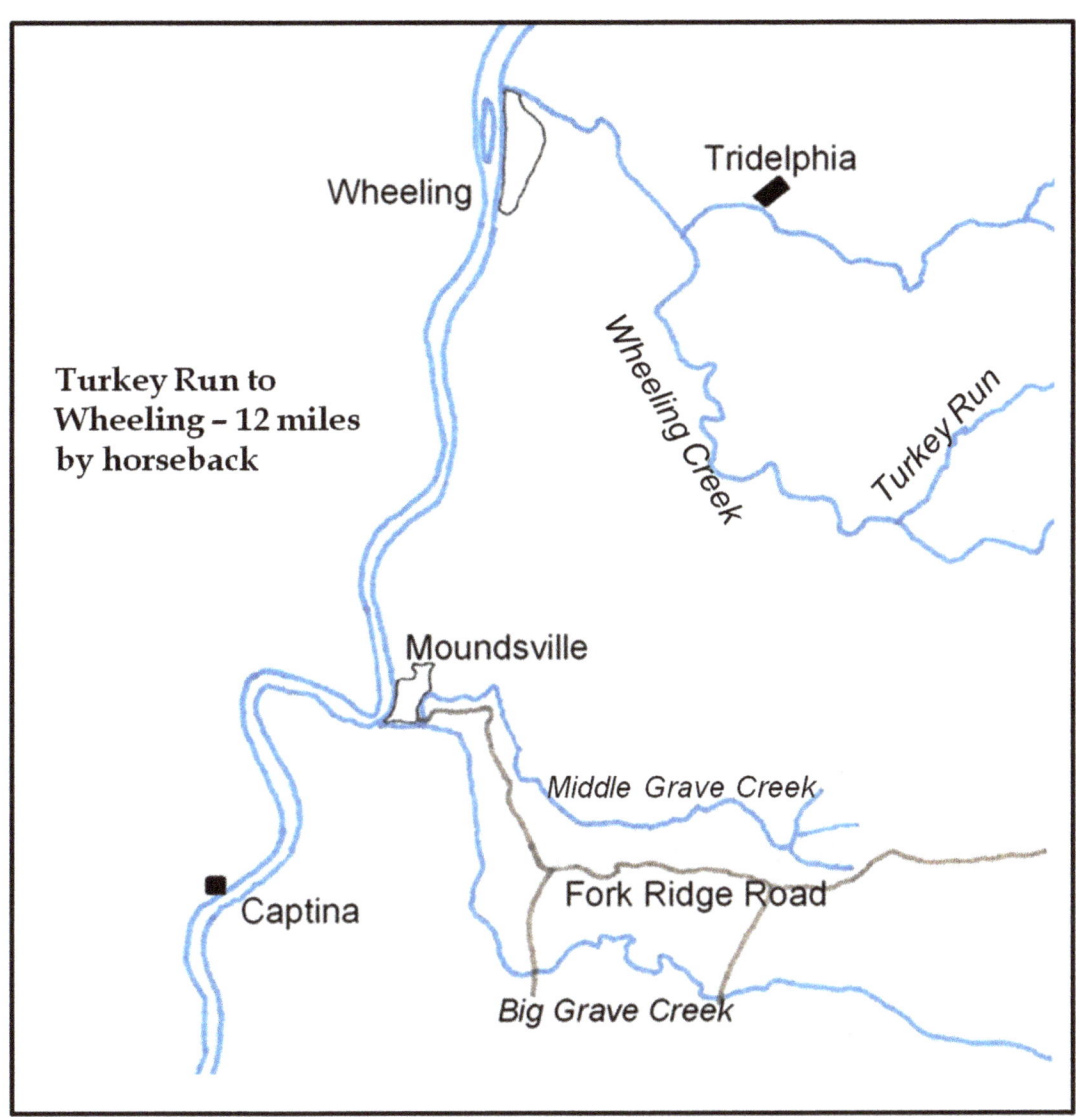

The people in the towns are widely different, the women go very gay, and the men wear good things, but are rather slovenly and very idle. Plaid cloaks are all the fashion and even the mechanic must put on his cloak only to cross the street. We have had two large fires in this part of the country, one at Pittsburgh which burnt down a very large brewery and a whole square, the other at Wheeling which burnt down 12 to fourteen houses.

It is not more than 30 years since the first settlers came to these hills, they were then annoyed by the Indians, since which period they have been driven more than 500 miles to the westward; 20 years ago there was but one solitary log house in Wheeling occupied by Noah Zane's Father a poor man. At present Noah is the richest man in Wheeling and lives in a splendid mansion about the middle of the town, there are now a number of very wealthy people in Wheeling.

I wrote to my sister Mrs Cowell because I needed more money to pay for the farm and for the stock having only enough to put down the deposit. I have to pay another three hundred dollars (about £60) or I will lose it all along with the deposit I paid last year.

My son Edward wrote to me. I was really pleased to hear from him after so long, but it wasn't a very agreeable letter. It was all about money and how his mother doesn't have enough to live on. He seemed to think all the interest from my father's inheritance should go to his mother but I have no recollection of having agreed to that. I can't understand why she has run out of money so soon. I had agreed that she could have the inheritance from my mother, plus the money from selling my tools, as well as Isabella's share of the inheritance from my father. *I lament that my funds are so small that I could not make that provision for herself and young Percy which Nature required but I hope it will [improve] in the course of a little time, in the [interim it is the] duty of Fred and George [to] do as much for her as is in their power.*

I perceive Caroline is of age in May next at which time she may receive her share if so minded it can be done, it would enable me to pay off all my debts and ease my mind considerably, and to devote a part to enable [Edward] to come over.

I do like the independence and simplicity of life that farming provides but it can be a hazardous occupation. *I very lately had a narrow escape of my life in going to Wheeling by my Mare taking fright of the mail coach, and plunging away with me down a very steep hill, but was not hurt.*

The distress of the old country is bringing a number of people over, but I expect a great many of them not very rich and as you say no money no friends; my little farm consisting of 133 acres would be a valuable acquisition in the old country as it contains besides a great quantity of fine timber coals of the best quality, Iron ore in great abundance, lime stone, sand stone and plenty of fine yellow clay beside blue clay, well watered with several good streams all running into Turkey Farm, upon which stands a saw mill, which was part of the property but I had not the means to purchase it, tho it might be had very cheap! All these advantages perhaps in a hundred years hence may be of some account, but at present is thought but little of.

The seasons here are much the same as in England except that the summers are much hotter and the winter at times extremely cold, the silver was down the bowl several nights last winter… I can have no enjoyments of the winter exercises such as shooting or hunting for the Rheumatism, at least I could not last winter, and I have no reason to suppose I shall be much better this. I had an abundance of apples in my orchard last year and have a still great abundance this[63].

Realising how much hard work the farm involved, and how poor my health had become, I did try to sell the farm. *I have had a visit here [in May] from an elderly Gentleman and son and son-in-law, who was looking about with an idea of purchasing a farm, he seemed much pleased with mine and I was in hopes I should have sold it to him, but he seems to wish to be nearer Philadelphia where he expects his two daughters will settle.* The old man came over on a month's fast passage from Liverpool and has brought over 12 thousand dollars. *I became acquainted with his son Joseph and his sister Mrs Ball soon after my arrival in Wheeling. They had been residents in this country about six years. He has travelled.. beyond Maurice Birkbicks and Mrs Fullers and down to New Orleans. He was obliged to return back to Wheeling on account of his health. It appears this is the healthiest part of the western country, and the further you go down river the more sickly it becomes, but even this I find is not as healthy as the old country.*

There are no letters not even to the residents of this town delivered in this country. Everyone must call or send to the Post Office in Wheeling, they are all advertised once a month at least all that remains there.

Martha 1826

My husband's behaviour is unbelievable. As soon as his inheritance came through, he left us to go to another country, leaving all his debts behind. He took some of the principle to pay for his passage and now he won't let us have the interest from the remaining money because he has had the stupidity to buy a farm that he cannot afford. He has no experience of farming and he says in his letter that there is no chance of any profit from what he produces. Why does he always do this? Why does he let other people take advantage of him? He would never have found this farm without someone telling him all about it, and no doubt they talked him into believing it was the answer to all his dreams and was too good an opportunity to miss. All the time we were together, he never really grasped the concept of money and the fact that it wasn't in endless supply.

I really do not understand why he had to buy such a large farm. Why did he even think he could manage it with no previous experience? Edward tells me that he tried to sell it this summer but had no joy.

---

[63] Apples are in season in West Virginia from July-October, so he was on the farm by mid 1825.

I also do not understand why he is living out there as Mr John Smith. It must cause so much confusion with the post. I am quite worried about whether Edward's letters will get through and we so need him to agree to let us have some more money. It is impossible to manage on what we have received so far, and there is no money coming in.

My sister-in-law, Isabella, says Frederick has written to her and wants George, her husband to start sending the interest from his inheritance out to America. That is not right. He has to support his family. I will get Edward to write to him again and tell him he must let us have some more money. And as for him having Caroline's money. Really! Doesn't he realise that now she's married it will go to her husband. The only happy news is that George and Emma had a little girl in June called Fanny.

I wish I could ask my brother Ben for help, but he has misfortunes of his own. He is living in Ireland now having left London after his trouble, but he has had to leave Hilsborough.

I received terrible news from Edward just after Christmas. Dear Caroline has died. I cannot believe that my dear daughter should be taken from me. We have been through so much already, I'm not sure I can bear it. She was only twenty. I am so sorry that she ran away and married. Her husband, Benjamin West, did not treat her properly and even when Edward was living with them, there was trouble and unpleasantness. We don't know exactly how she died but I have told my sons that we must make sure she has a proper funeral. I want it at St James, Piccadilly if possible, where the Ince family were all baptised[64]. George is dreadfully upset. He was very close to Caroline and he is absolutely furious at his father who he sees as causing her to leave home and make such an unsatisfactory marriage.

St James Piccadilly 1814

Turkey Run 1827 and 1828

I read of the unexpected demise of my dear daughter Caroline, a dear girl on whom I had placed my fondest hopes for her future welfare and happiness – but however if as you say her domestic affairs were far from being of a tranquil and happy turn, but strewed with briars, she is much better where she is. Alas poor Caroline cut off in the Bloom of life.

She was born on 15th May 1806 so she would have been twenty-one this month. She was such a lively spirit and had always been most affectionate. It would appear that her husband was cruel to her. Why did she marry so young? I remember when my

---

[64] Caroline West was buried at St James, Piccadilly on 31st December 1826.

little brother, George, died in Crouch End. He was fifteen so it hit us hard. My other brothers who died had all been infants. My mother was so very sad to lose George and I doubt my father ever fully recovered from his death. I had moved away by then and was working as an apprentice to George Wellings in Bishopsgate in the trade Citizen Coach and Harness but George's death affected the whole family. And now poor Caroline is no longer with us. When I think of her sister Isabella I would advise her *never to get married, but under very peculiar*[65] *circumstances.*

However, my health has been good this year and I am really very happy here, *planting Indian corn under a burning hot sun, down in a small bottom enclosed on every side with lofty hills whose brush matted tops reach almost to the clouds.* My situation here is *a small farm in a wilderness with smiling peace and plenty all around. Be content and there is nothing to mar your happiness, not even your repose, but some people will not be happy anywhere not even in Paradise… I feel no inclination ever to return to England.*

Life on the farm suits me very well so long as my health holds up *which thank God has been very good for this last twelve months.* There's great satisfaction to be had from growing what you need, and though I often wish for more company we do well

---

[65] Peculiar in the sense of financially secure.

enough here. My companion does her share of work very willingly and our neighbours are keeping an eye out for her with the baby due soon. I am truly amazed by that little miracle, it will be another mouth to feed but then someone to help on the farm, and someone to leave it to. It really encourages me to make a go of it. I realise I must be discreet about the baby to those at home, but I must also make sure we have enough money to make everything secure.

Edward complained in his letter about *my having drawn the interest that was due to me* but I really need a much larger sum. I suppose I will have to send a receipt to George Cowell for some money for the family in England, though they will have to wait until the next interest payment is due.

It would be really helpful if my sons could come out here and help me on the farm. Edward is stuck in an office in smoky London. As I told him *I formed an acquaintance with some of the most respectable people in this place who … informed me that a Clerk's situation is very easily obtained and liberal salaries given, there are several manufactures carried on and some upon a very large scale. I have been solicited to take a berth in one lately erected, but I must confess with all the disagreeable I prefer my little farm.*

I had a great inconvenience last month when I had a first rate horse stolen from my stable. I had three in the stables at the time. A man from Bristol had been staying with me for a short time, who had heard in Bristol that I had drawn all my *children's money and set off to America, beside some other unpleasant anecdotes.* What gossips people can be. *I shall never regret leaving a country where there is no other prospect in old age but a miserable workhouse... I take a weekly paper which gives me a text of all the political occurrences, noble deaths in the old country, and am acquainted with the formation of a new Cabinet under Mr Canning and hope it will be for the better*[66].

Summer 1828: Edward continues to write to me asking for more money and doesn't seem to understand *it is really as much out of my power to send remittances to [his] Mother as it is in her power to send remittances to me….We have victuals and drink but no money, no not a cent at this present time and all I can do is to get sufficient to pay for wearing apparel and other necessities.*

I have some idea of leaving this part of the country if I can sell my farm but unless someone from the old country should be coming this way with a little money, it may be some time. It would be no use my returning to England as I am too old for work, and would only be

---

[66]George Canning was British Prime Minister from 10th April 1827 to 8th August 1827 when he died suddenly from pneumonia.

an encumbrance but my wife *is welcome to enjoy the interest of my Father's legacy as long as I am able to do without it.*

I still wonder what happened to dear Caroline. *Indeed I thought it strange her coming back to that husband after the ill usage she received from him.*

A most melancholy circumstance took place on the river Ohio a few months ago..... .one George Cooper a short time before from London with a wife and an interesting little girl about four years old came to Wheeling. After making a short stay he bought an old skiff and embarked with his wife and child.. to go down the river the Lord knows where. However after being gone about nine days the skiff was picked up without a soul on board.... Sometime after their bodies were found in the river. He was stabbed in three places. There were no marks of violence on his wife and child. It appears he was a freeman from the City of London, a doctor of Physics... How he could be such a fool to wish himself in an open boat on such a dangerous river I cannot conceive, when there are so many commodious steam boats continually going up and down.

England 1827 and 1828

We have all been very affected by Caroline's death. Edward was very unhappy as he felt he should have done more. He had been working very hard for Mr Paget and had found a room of his own in the last few months of her life so she was on her own with her husband. Edward was only two years younger than her. George is also upset and sometimes I wonder if he was the person who had introduced her to that dreadful husband of hers. I will never understand why she agreed to go back to him.

I was worried that Frederick would be in touch with George Cowell again, asking for Caroline's inheritance on her twenty-first birthday, so I persuaded Edward to write to his father about her untimely demise. He took some persuading but Edward finally wrote in the March after she died, so he would have received the letter before her birthday.

I am still finding it very hard to get by in Gloucester. How can Frederick imagine I feed myself and little Percy and Isabella? We have had no new clothes for some time, but Isabella has taken to visiting the draper's in West Street. She sometimes comes back with some little ribbons or fancies for her hat, which the proprietor has given her. It would appear he has taken a fancy to her gentility, but of course we are so shabby! It is most frustrating. In reality the poor girl has few prospects and she is no longer in her bloom.

She has written to her father expressing a strong inclination to go to live with him. I am hoping that he will understand that we are quite desperate for money. As he has a

149

farm he should at least be able to provide some food for her. George is also thinking of going out as soon as circumstances permit. He and Emma had another little girl in July, whom they have called Emma after her mother. These dear babies are the only joy in my life. George wants to go and see exactly what the situation is with his father and why he insists on keeping all the interest from his father's inheritance for himself. It is no good making false promises that he will send a receipt to George Cowell for the interest to come to me, when nothing happens. I am slowly coming to the realisation that I will have to get a situation or else we will simply starve. I hope I can find something suitable for a woman of my years and standing. I will talk to my sister-in-law, Isabella about it. Her husband, George Cowell might know of something or someone who can help. I doubt that Percy will be able to come with me. He is ten now, and I believe he could stay with one of his brothers, so long as he continues with his studies. If Isabella does not join her father, she will have to come with me.

In his letters Frederick is always trying to persuade Edward to come out and help him but I do not think that is very likely now. Although he finds it hard working in an office all day long, Edward is starting to do well and Mr Paget[67] is giving him more responsibility. He has also starting courting a young woman who goes to his church, so his heart will not be turned towards adventure overseas.

Martha in Earls Colne 1829

I have been most fortunate. Through the kind offices of George Cowell, I was invited by Henry Holgate Carwardine to help him in his work at Colne Priory in Earls Colne, Essex. Henry's father Thomas, who was Lord of the Manor before him, was a good friend of George Romney[68], who lent some money to Ince & Mayhew, Frederick's father's firm. George Romney's son, John, was involved with the 1824 financial settlement of the firm's business, and through his kindness I have received this offer. Henry Carwardine is a surgeon and tends the people of Earls Colne. He has allowed me the use of a cottage in the village, so Isabella will be able to be with me while she waits to hear back from her father.

---

[67] John Warren Paget was a Barrister at law and Publisher of The Law Advertiser, later the Law Journal which commenced publication in 1822. It comprised a weekly publication of Reports in all the Courts, together with a Digest of all the Cases, a supplement to Burn's Justice and an abridgment of every Act of Parliament.
[68] Henry Holgate Carwardine 1779-1867) was a FRCS and worked as a surgeon in Earls Colne. George Romney painted a portait of Henry's mother Anne and his brother Thomas as a baby. George Romney and Thomas Carwardine are mentioned as friends in the Humphrys papers.

Edward was not very happy in his work, but now he has married his dear Annie Finnie, on 24th January 1829 at All Souls Marylebone, and Mr Paget has recognized his talents and is involving him more in the publication of the Law Journal[69]. His firm publishes all the decisions at the Inns of Court so it is very important work as the law is based on those decisions. He has been given a rise which makes life a little easier for him, and he was twenty-one in May and able to inherit his share of his grandfather's money as soon as Frederick signs it over to him.

Fred has gone to Dudley where he is working hard to make a success as a coach-maker. He has the backing of Ely Ellis but I am not certain he has provided all the contacts he promised. They need more capital to keep up with the latest designs, but no-one in this family is able to help.

George will soon be leaving for America. He is determined to find his father and find out whether any of the rumours are true about the way he is living. He has promised to let me know whatever he discovers. I hope he will be able to make a living out there. He seems to think life will provide him with whatever is needed. He is going to take Emma and little George and the two girls. I shall miss all my grandchildren, with Fred in Dudley and now George going away. It was lovely to learn that Edward and Annie are in the family way[70], but Edward had to write to his father in November, sending him a form to sign so that Edward can receive the money he is entitled to.

Turkey Run 1829

I should very much like Edward to come out and start helping me on the farm. Isabella has written to say she would like to come here. *She can draw poor Caroline's share coming to her to help to defray her expenses.* Edward could travel with her. He would be a better companion than George, who *may not perhaps be able to come as soon.* I wrote to Edward to tell him *I will do the best in my power to make everything comfortable. If you like farming you may find plenty to do besides good health and a keen appetite, if not the town will find you employment; by no means think of getting a wife till you have seen America.*

The dear boy seems to be very confused about the money. He has written to me expecting me to release my life's interest, wholly in his favour. *I must confess I never expected such a request neither will I agree to any such thing most probably I am as much in want of money as [he] is, and until [he] is willing to give up the half it will remain as it is, as long as I live. I am sorry to be so very laconic on the subject, but so it must be.* Perhaps

---

[69] In 1829 Law Journal Reports Printed for J. W. Paget 5 Quality Court Chancery Lane.
[70] Henry Bret Ince born 7th December 1829.

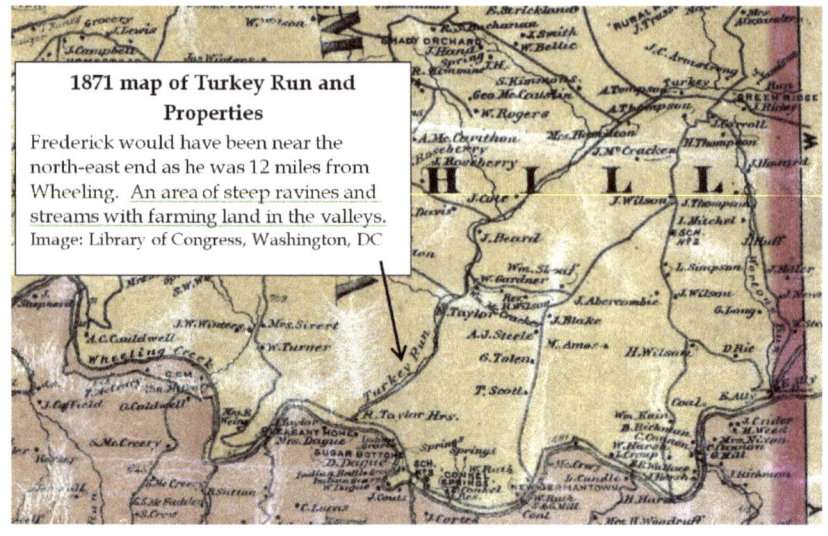

1871 map of Turkey Run and Properties
Frederick would have been near the north-east end as he was 12 miles from Wheeling. An area of steep ravines and streams with farming land in the valleys.
Image: Library of Congress, Washington, DC

when he comes out here we could set up in business together *in any other way of business than farming, that might be thought more agreeable and more productive.*

If any of the family come over here they should bring *a reasonable stock of wearing apparel, a good fowling piece and accoutrements, a thermometer for me as I have had the misfortune to break mine, a barometer would also be a useful article if [they] can meet with one reasonable.*

The winters here can be extremely cold. However *I was never as well in my life as I have been for a considerable time past a*nd I would be glad to live here until I reach seventy or eighty. *If there be a paradise on earth it is a Farmer's Cot, a Farmer's home.*

I do hope Fred manages to make a success of his business in Dudley but *from the knowledge I have of coachmaking the chances are twenty to one against him unless he has a capital to begin with or has got into business with a person who has made his fortune and wishes to retire… however he has my good wishes and may God bless and prosper him...* Martha's brother, John de Bar, made a poor do of his mastership and now works for Makepeace in Bristol. *It will al*ways *be a great difficulty to succeed… in that overtaxed country, it is only for Gentlemen and beggars.*

My son George arrived unexpectedly in December. He had come over on the Ship Brighton from London to New York. He stayed for *five days when he departed for New York where he had left his wife and family and his friend Mr Carlisle his wife and Tom* [his son]. *I lent him my Mare Dolly and accompanied him on my young Mare Nelly as far as Claysoille where we slept, and breakfasted early on a Saturday morning he on Dolly for N.Y. about 450 miles and I to my home about 12 miles – I fully expected him back with his friends, but from some occurrences that took place during his absence he was induced to stay at N.Y. Of course I anxiously expected to hear how he got thro his journey, but week after week passed away and month after month. I at length wrote him two letters and concluded he must be dead.*

However at last I received a letter saying he had taken a grog shop[71] and had paid out all his money. ...He said he would send me the price of the Mare, but has not yet done it which has put me to great inconvenience, wanting another in her place.

George informed me in December last that Isabella shortly expected to be led to the altar. If so I hope they may live long and happily together.

Turkey Run February 1830

I have received Edward's letter with the deed for his inheritance all drawn up and ready to sign. I have to find a witness so it will have to wait until I next go to town. It is a good opportunity for me to claim the money I need to pay my debt on the farm. We have lived here for nearly five years now and if I am unable to pay the final amount we shall be obliged to leave.

I have persuaded my friend Thomas Jones to witness my signature and have sent off the deed to Edward for him to send to George Cowell.

This is what the deed said:

In consideration of the sum of fifty pounds .. paid by Mr George Cowell the surviving Executor under the will of ..Wm Ince.. I do release ..the said George Cowell his heirs [etc]and the Estate and effects of the said Wm. Ince and every of them for ever. .. On account of my right to claim or interest in or to a sum of one hundred and forty three pounds ten shillings and sixpence Bank that share of my son Edward Brett Ince in the sum of £430.11.8. The annuities invested by the said George Cowell in the British funds to answer the share of the said Edward Brett Ince, and my children Caroline Ince and Percy Ince in a bequest made by the Will of the said Wm. Ince, the interest whereof was bequeathed to me for life.

At first I thought Edward might like ten pounds *on account of his not being able to receive his share of his deceased sister*, but I have changed my mind and want Martha to have ten pounds instead. I will receive the remaining £40. I want George Cowell to send it to Messrs Coutts Bank *to be remitted to me through the medium of their agent at Philadelphia Mr Willing, as soon as may be convenient.*

The share of £143 is a third of the total, the other two-thirds being due to Caroline and Percy. Fred, George and Isabella have already had their shares. There does not seem

---

[71] According to Longworth's American almanack, New York register for 1830 George Ince had a porterhouse at 266 William Street.

to be much left from the total I inherited[72]. I regret having broken into the principle, which I had to do to buy my passage to New York. It means there is less interest each quarter.

Martha in Earls Colne April 1830

George has sent me the lovely news of their new baby girl. She was born in New York and they have called her Caroline after George's dear sister. I shed many a tear on hearing that.

It was much harder though to learn the truth about Frederick and the way he is living with that young woman as though they are man and wife. They even have a little boy in the house. George was not sure it was their child, but thought it very likely because he had the look of an Ince.

We also had the difficult news that Fred and his partner went bankrupt in Dudley[73]. All that money he invested gone to waste. Now he has gone back to Bristol to work for Henry Makepeace. Isabella is still being courted by the draper from Gloucester, George Morse. She was hoping for an offer of marriage last year, but apparently he had cold feet. Thankfully he is still in touch and she remains optimistic.

Edward finally heard back from Frederick on 5th April this year with the Deed all signed and ready to be sent to George Cowell so Edward can receive his share at last. I was surprised to hear that Frederick has agreed to give me ten pounds. It was very helpful of George to visit him and remind him of his family obligations.

Turkey Run July 1830

I am so disappointed that I have not yet received the £40 that was agreed with the family in England. They do not seem to understand that I have great need of this money, and if it does not arrive soon, I shall lose my farm, which will be most upsetting as I have been so happy here. I will write to Edward again and explain how *It is now a considerable time since I addressed [him] with the deed enclosed and expected long ago to have heard from [him] whether [he] was satisfied at my filling them up or not.*

Even though now married, he might still be considering coming out here and I must advise him to come via Baltimore as it is *the best and cheapest place to land at to come to*

---

[72] Six lots of £143 11s 8d equals £861 10s, plus the £50 and the money Frederick took to pay his passage.
[73] Frederick Ince and his partner Ely Ellis were declared bankrupt on 14th December 1829 (Birmingham Gazette).

this part of the country...the Mail leaves Baltimore daily for Wheeling which is 12 miles from where I reside at Turkey Run.

I have not heard from Isabella since her letter last July which I duly answered. *On receipt of this letter I must request [Edward] will write her a few lines, telling her I shall be happy to see them in America, should the fates so decree,…. It would be a happy time to see my only daughter again. I have been much disappointed in not having the society of my son George and family but alas how fleeting are all our joys and expectations.*

I am obliged to sell my farm in consequence of the disappointment in not receiving the £40 as agreed to upon the signature of the deed of release. I had devoted it for the purpose of paying certain debts which cannot any longer be protracted, I could wish it had been otherwise and [Edward's] wants had been less, which might have been had [he] sailed four or five years before entering into the Nuptial state. However [they] have my blessing good wishes for both [their] welfares and happiness.[74]

Wheeling December 1830

I received a letter from Edward in August and have finally had a correspondence with the Coutts Bank agent in Philadelphia. I now expect to receive my money in the course of this week. The agent received a letter from the Bank at the end of July, and I expect there was a letter for me at the same time, but it appears that one of my neighbours may have intercepted it. I called at the Post Office every week, when *the Post Master to my surprise told me I have received two letters last week but he could not recollect who he gave the lettters to. I have told him to give no letters directed in the name of Ince to any body but myself.*

I have only had one letter from my son George since I saw him last December. He wrote in March telling me about the opening of *a house, sign, the Ship Brighton, kept by one Alexander, Steward of the Packet in which he and G came over. G presided and sang the song tune Bob and Joan. The other song is to the tune of Yankee Doodle very long, he also presided here and sang the same at a meeting of the firemen of New York…. It appears he swopped my little Mare Dolly for Barrels of Beer and Ale.* George told me he had *purchased a wig for me, and had some other things to send me.. but have never heard anything from them.*

With respect to myself I am quite unsettled at present, having sold my farm, not very advantageously, as I have to wait some time before I get the whole of the money. I am presently living in Wheeling, where I have a number of acquaintances. My plan is to go to Pittsburgh in March and probably then go on to Buffalo on the river Niagara not far from the Falls. *I don't think I shall farm, the labour being too much for my declining*

---

[74]Edward Bret Ince married Ann Finnie on 24th January 1829 at All Souls Marylebone.

years, otherwise I am very partial to a farmer's life. … I have some idea I shall keep school for a time. I continue to enjoy a good state of health but am not as lusty as when I left England.

I will reply to Edward and ask him to remember me to his mother and to Percy and hope they are doing better than myself.

Frederick in Captina Creek 1831

I have been travelling in a small covered waggon and two horses near five hundred miles, together with our furniture thinking to settle somewhere near Lake Erie but the high price of land and the necessaries of life prevented me from doing so.

We set out on the Virginia side of the Ohio, going through Pittsburgh, Marces, Meadville, Waterford, etc, and on our return came through the State of Ohio on the western side of the river, until crossing at Stubenville and returning to Wheeling. *Erie is a pretty place eligibly situated on the lake. You would not know the lake from the sea only from the water being fresh.*

I sold my farm at Turkey Run… for something more than I gave for it, and with a little waggon and two good horses and furniture commenced my travels to Erie on the lake about the middle of April about 200 miles from our residence. It is a pretty place and a fine country, but land and every other necessary of life by far too dear to suit my pocket. I therefore returned a different road back through the State of Ohio to Wheeling which I reached in June 1831 without any accident although we had some hair breadth escapes.

Now we have settled in Captina *a small place situated on the river about 20 miles below Wheeling. I have been induced to come here by a Mr Woods the owner of the place, but I cannot say that I am anyways partial to the place at present. However, I expect to stop here till the first of April next.*

This is a much smaller plot than the Turkey Run farm, 10 acres rent free with five years to come. It will be less hard work and we should be able to afford to stay here.

I was pleased to hear from Edward's letter that Fred is going on again and *hope he will succeed in his undertaking, though I must confess I am not very sanguine owing to the difficulties that a man has to contend with that has no capital. I wrote to George from Erie in May but cannot get a line from him. I shall therefore give it up hoping he is doing well. The old Mare I bought to replace the one I sent him, died a short time after I had her which was 30 dollars lost. [I was sorry to] hear of Uncle Ben's failing, but I believe it is a vice he had been long addicted to. ..I suppose poor unfortunate man he has had his share of trouble in the world, and endeavours to relieve it by the intoxicating draught but I am afraid it is but a poor remedy.*

I often think of the family back in England and *wonder how all branches of the family get on and may God prosper them in their undertakings.*

I have no idea of returning to England, especially as I am getting old *and an old man in England is always in the way, and is at last driven into that wretched asylum the Workhouse, to end his days in service. I have some idea of going down the river to New Orleans by steam the latter end of October next where I intend stopping til May or June next, it is twelve hundred miles by land and I believe 2,000 by the river.* I hope to hear back from Edward before I go.

Martha 1831-1833

My brother Ben has been having problems in Ireland. Sadly he is trying to drink them away and I am not sure he will last much longer. His life was blighted by the stay in prison when he was in London, and our father died before he was released.

A great joy in our lives though occurred when Isabella finally married George Morse in Earls Colne church on 16th January 1833. I was one of the witnesses and Edward came down from London to be the other one. George Morse came over from Gloucester, and had to get a licence as he was not resident in the parish long enough. It was a lovely occasion and I was very touched that George invited me to go and live with them in Gloucester at my convenience. He owns the draper's shop in Westgate Street, so we will finally be comfortable and will no longer have to worry about money.

St. Andrew's church, Earls Colne
cc-by-sa/2.0 - © Robert Edwards

Captina Creek 7th April 1833

It is very disappointing not to have heard from any members of the family. Edward hasn't written since January 1831 and I have heard nothing from dear Isabella since her letter of July 1829, though I have written to her three times. Perhaps she is no longer at her old address, but I will send her another letter as to receive one from her *hand always gives me infinite pleasure and satisfaction.* Hopefully someone in Gloucester will know her whereabouts and be able to send it on to her. I hope *Edward is doing well and may God prosper his undertakings. ... As far as George, I know not whether he is in America or not as I never heard from him although I have written to him several times. I shall not trouble to write to him again unless I hear from him.*

1832 was a very difficult year for me, with a terrible flood in Captina early in the year, after which I was *very unwell the greater part of [the] summer, but thank God am now as well as ever I was in my life. ... I tried a year at the mouth of the creek and was driven out in the month of Feb 1832 by the great flood, was taken out in a boat to a neighbours about a mile off. It made dreadful havoc sweeping away houses, barns, warehouses with every description of property. The steam boats took out several human beings from the floating houses, however the house I lived in remained with the furniture in the upper storey.*

I am at present living on Captina Creek about a mile or so from the mouth which falls into the Ohio river about 20 miles below Wheeling. ... I am at present ploughing and getting in my seeds and dressing the garden. I shall continue here till April next [when] I hope to get something to suit me better. .. I have some idea of keeping school in this neighbourhood, as the school house is now wanting a Master. It will be an easier living than toiling in the field.

I wish I had the means to enable Isabella to come out here; if I could *I would gladly pay her expenses here and back.* Her presence here would *make me completely happy.* I think about my brothers and sisters and wonder *how they all are whither dead or alive, particularly Charles and Henry. I expect Mrs Henry must be dead long before this as she seemed to be in the dropsy when I saw her last*[75].

I took a ride on my grey mare to my old neighbourhood [Turkey Run] this day week about 27 miles, slept there, next morning went to Wheeling 12 miles and from Wheeling to Elizabeth Town on the flats 12 miles, slept there and returned home next morning Tuesday 10 miles. I have to cross the Ohio going and coming in a ferry boat. It was good to have time with my acquaintances in those places, something which is *a comfort and joy* to me. When in Wheeling I saw *a signboard near the Market Place painted in large characters: John Mayhews Eating House: He has lately moved opposite the Market Place. John Mayhew. I have not seen any of them.*

It occurs to me that Caroline's portion of the inheritance is still available. Perhaps it could go to the children's Mother *in the event of my demise, with the consent of parties interested… That is should it come back to the family, she is welcome to enjoy the interest as long as I live.*

Any letters addressed to me *care of J. Smith, Captina Creek near Wheeling* will find me, though officially the name is now Powhatan Point. *We have not had any symptoms of the cholera here, but has been very severe at many places on the river. I believe we have had only one resident of this place that died of it.*

England 1833-1834

Edward has been taking some advice from his legal friends and it seems that we can come to some arrangement about the inheritance money from William Ince, Frederick's father. Frederick left us in September 1824 and George has seen how he is living. He shows no sign of returning to England. Apparently we can look at a legal separation on the grounds of desertion and the children can claim the remainder of their grandfather's inheritance.

According to William's will the money was left to Frederick *to lay out in the Stocks the interest of which to be apportioned for his use and the benefit of his children after him.* The

---

[75]Henry's wife, Ann Elizabeth Saunders died on 14th August 1830 in Presteigne, Radnorshire.

money was finally released in 1824 after the long law case against John Mayhew's family, and as each of Frederick's children reached twenty-one they have received their portion of the inheritance. Frederick, George and Isabella received theirs immediately. Poor Caroline died too early, then Edward received his after chasing up his father in 1830. Percy will be twenty-one in 1837 so his share has to be kept separate.

It certainly does not seem right that Frederick should continue to receive interest to spend in America, when he still has family who are in need here.

Edward has written to George to ask him to give him Power of Attorney so Edward can act on his behalf. I am sure George will agree as he has had to give up the porterhouse, and is now working for a printer as a stereotype founder in New York, making up plates that can be used again.

George signed the Power of Attorney on 19th August 1833. It said he did *make constitute and appoint Edward Ince … my true and lawful attorney for me and in my name place and stead to receive a certain legacy to which I am entitled under the Will of William Ince late of the City of London Upholsterer,* so Edward had full permission to act on his behalf. George's signature on the deed was witnessed by Alexander Aitken, who encouraged George to open the grog shop in New York. George said he was a steward on the Ship Brighton, in which they travelled over in 1829. He set up a company in New York called Aitken & Co. which ran a porterhouse in Fulton. He appears to have made a steadier income than George ever could.

George came over to England to collect the remainder of the money due to him. It was such a joy to see him again after his years in America, but I was sorry not to see the rest of the family. I realised he could not stay long, but I so enjoyed talking with him and hearing about them all. They have grown up so quickly. George Horace is nearly ten, Fanny is eight and Emma is already six, though she was still a baby when they left. Little Caroline I have never seen, and there is also a new baby, Annette, who was born on 14th July 1834. I feel quite sad when I think I shall probably never get to meet them. George travelled back to New York in September 1834, returning on the ship Samson[76].

I do hope the extra money does not cause George to think he will have an easy life now. He seems very reluctant to do any hard work, wherever he lives.

---

[76] As shown on his naturalization papers dated 1854.

Edward has now taken over the publication of the Law Journal as Mr J. W. Paget sadly died in July. His daughters now own the journal and have agreed to its publication for the next fourteen years.

Captina 1835

We have continued well enough in Captina. I have ten acres here and it is rent free for the next five years. Now I am nearly 65 years old it is hard work to keep the farm going and provide enough food, but we manage. Our boy is very willing to do what he can and is very affectionate.

In June 1835 my son George arrived at Captina having walked from New York. I had heard nothing from him since his last letter five years ago. *He was quite broke down. He conceived the idea of taking the adjoining farm and sent for his family for that purpose, and I having the necessary implements for farming everything might have gone on tolerable well if industrious, but however this did not suit his idea. He conceived an idea that my property was not safe, and that I had better give him a bill of sale to secure them.* Sadly this I very foolishly complied with, not suspecting him to be such a villain as he turned out.

He then picked a quarrel with my *housekeeper* gave *her a share of my property and turned her out of doors. She took the little bond boy along with her, so he caught the scarlet fever and died.* This was a very serious loss to me, for he was very affectionate, always ready and willing to do everything that lay in his power to help me.

Alas what was to be done, and after exposing all my affairs we could no longer stay in that neighbourhood[77].

George then took a place near my previous farm on Turkey Run, taking all my property *together with his family who had just arrived.* I was to live with them. However George then started selling off my property *first the cow and calf and everything else in succession although I told them not.* I was very badly off for clothing and necessaries and George *never gave me a cent after thus robbing me.*

I then overheard George's wife, Emma, saying *that the old fellow was come there to eat up the bread from her children.* I was very *nettled* by this and in *the morning I expostulated with George about their conduct. He replied that I was likely to live a series of years and that they wanted the money.*

---

[77]It seems very likely that the housekeeper was the Mrs Smith who had accompanied him from Bristol, and that the bond boy was their son. Why otherwise would she have taken him with her? Presumably she later let Frederick know that the poor child had died. It also explains why Frederick had to leave the neighbourhood.

I replied that I would not live with them a series of hours, but to saddle my mare and I would be off, which was done, and was the only thing I saved out of all my effects.

I tried to get my bed and bedding back, but they had run away to Philadelphia. *Besides what he had now taken from me, there is my mare, that I lent him when he came to see me several years ago and for which I never got a farthing. To put a gloss upon their vile conduct they have told the people about here, that I had a considerable sum of money from him in England, in fact they have done me all the mischief that lay in their power, I most heartily wish I had never seen them here.*

Fork Ridge[78] 1836

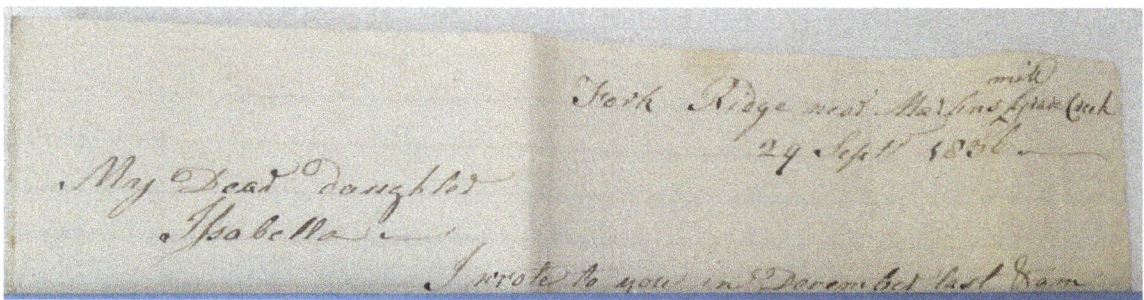

My son George, and his wife, Emma, have, between them, completely ruined me. I wrote to Isabella last December telling her about my situation and ill health, but have heard nothing back from any of them. Now I have decided to write to Isabella again, as to receive a letter from her *is the only solace left me in this world.* I would like to have news of the rest of the family: to know how Isabella is going on *whether happy and prosperous in business*; what Percy's intentions are and what Frederick is doing, *whether with his family; whether Mr G. Cowell is alive and also Mrs G. C.* and news of *Brother Henry and family, Betsy, Brett, etc.*

My health is very poor. *My affliction of the paralysis stroke is much the same as it was a year ago*[79], *my left arm still continues entirely useless, but I make shift to hobble about with a stick but cannot go any distance, otherwise I am tolerably well in health.*

I am *much in need* of money, *I am miserably off for want of clothing, not being able to show myself at public worship for want of it.* If there is any interest due for me I would wish to

---

[78] An 1871 map shows J. B. Martin owned Fork Ridge Farm, and S. Martin owned land to the east. It is possible Frederick was living with either Martin family in 1836. The letter is written in a firm hand with interest expressed in others. He may have died there from another stroke.
[79] The stroke may well have been the result of the emotional upset of George's visit.

have it, and *as for George's share of poor Caroline's money I shall certainly endeavour to obtain it, it will only be a small trifle of what I am entitled to by his unnatural behaviour.*

I was obliged to sell my mare last Winter for necessaries. This was a grievous loss to me as it was the only comfort and joy I had for I could take a ride … and spend a few days with some old acquaintances. .. I am at present residing with people, farmers, where I expect to remain for the Winter... Much of my time I am obliged to spend in the dark.

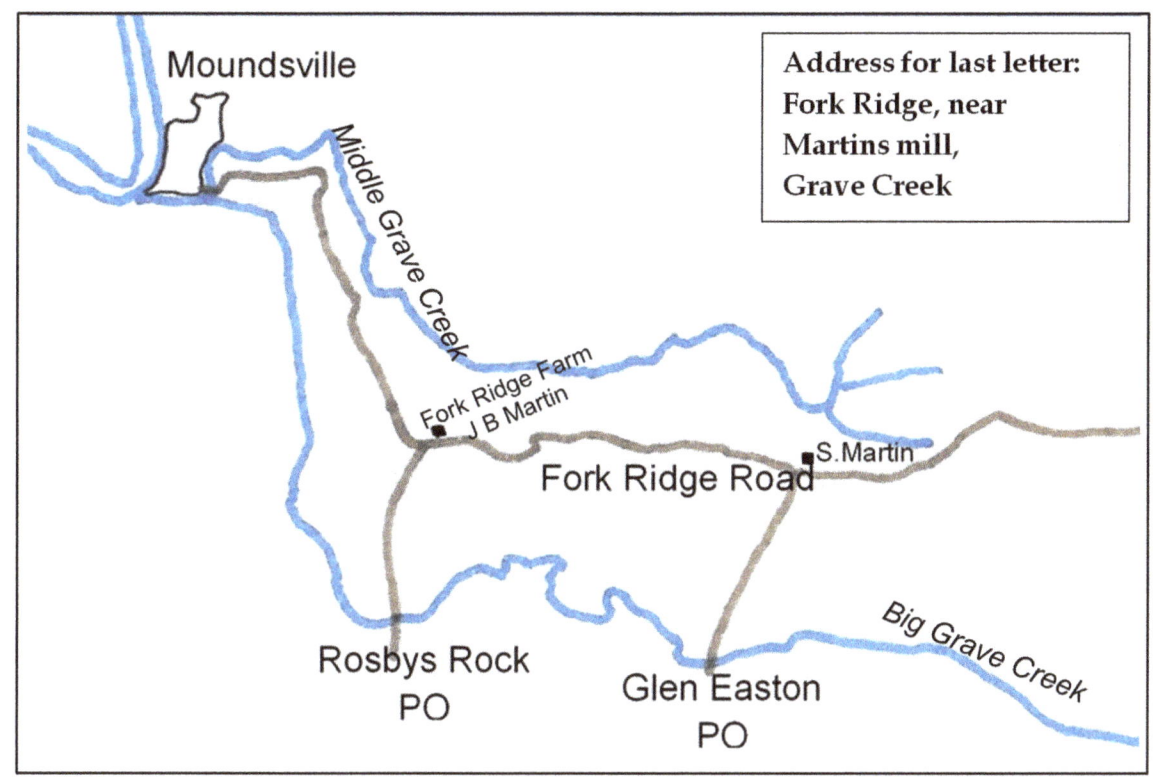

Gloucester, England 1836

Isabella received a letter from her father today. She was very upset as he is in a bad way. He sent a letter last year which we destroyed. He does not seem to realise that just as he abandoned us, so we have had to abandon him.

I am very content living here in Gloucester with George and Isabella. They have a dear little girl who they have called Martha Caroline, and I am probably the happiest I have ever been in my life. I understand Frederick has had another stroke and has been made destitute. I know George was very angry with him, but I am really not sure that taking everything from his father was the correct way to proceed. George told us that the old man took himself off, and that he and Emma were perfectly willing to have him live with them. From Frederick's letter to Isabella, it does sound as though he has brought his downfall upon himself. And typical Frederick to the last, he seems to think he is still entitled to some money, and wants George's share of Caroline's money. I am so glad Edward was able to sort that out a few years ago. The official story from George is that Frederick shot himself, but he may simply have had another stroke and died, or perhaps he is still alive. We do not need to know.

Letters and Documents in the possession of Nigel Ince

	Date	Address given	Postmark	Post Office	To
	28 Feb 1826	Wheeling	1 Mar 1826	Wheeling	Mr Edward Ince, at Mr B Wests 81 Great Portland St Regents Park, London
	16 Jul 1826	Turkey Run	18 Jul 1826	Wheeling	Mr E. Ince c/o J W Pagets Esq 5 Quality Court Chancery Lane
	27 May 1827	Wheeling	28 Jun 1827	Wheeling	Mr E Ince Mr J W Pagets Esq 5 Quality Court Chancery Lane, London
	20 Jul/ 20 Aug 1828		6 Oct 1828		Mr E Ince Mr Pigots Esq 5 Quality Court London England
	17 May 1829	Turkey Run	20 May 1829	Wheeling	Mr Edward Ince at J W Pagets Esq
Release of money to Edward	21 Feb 1830	Turkey Run, Ohio County			Mr G. Cowell North Baker St
Copy of letter by Edward Brett Ince	21 Feb 1830	Turkey Run	rec'd 5 Apr 1830		Mr Edward Ince c/o Mr Pagets Esq 5 Quality Ct
	11 Jul 1830	Turkey Run	14 Jul 1830	Wheeling	Mr E Ince J W Pagets Esq
	12 Dec 1830	Wheeling	16 Dec 1830	Wheeling	Mr E B Ince J W Pagets Esq
	24 Jul 1831	Captina	21 Aug 1831	Wheeling	Mr Edward Ince 5 Quality Court
	7 Apr 1833	Captina Creek	10 Apr 1833	Powhaton Point	Miss I Ince, Mr Hutchinsons West Gate St Glocester
Power of Attorney	19 Aug 1833	New York		from George	
	29 Sep 1836	Fork Ridge	1 Oct 1836	Wheeling	Mrs G Morse, York House Westgate St Glocester

Sources & Picture Credits

Chapter 1

i Houses of Benedictine monks: Abbey of Evesham, in A History of the County of Worcester: Volume 2, ed. J. W. Willis-Bund and William Page (London, 1971), pp. 112-127 http://www.british-history.ac.uk/vch/worcs/vol2/pp112-127 [accessed 10 September 2015]

ii Dyer, Alan D, The City of Worcester in the Sixteenth Century, Leicester University Press, 1973

iii http://list.historicengland.org.uk/resultsingle.aspx?uid=1017254 [Accessed 8 Aug 2015]

iv Dyer, Alan D., op.cit.

v Deeds: A.12401 - A.12500, in A Descriptive Catalogue of Ancient Deeds: Volume 5, ed. H C Maxwell Lyte (London, 1906), pp. 306-325 http://www.british-history.ac.uk/ancient-deeds/vol5/pp306-325 [Accessed 19 August 2015]

vi Carole Shammas, The Domestic Environment in Early Modern England and America, Journal of Social History Vol. 14, No. 1 (Autumn, 1980), pp. 3-24

vii http://www.bbc.co.uk/history/british/tudors/human_reformation_01.shtml [Accessed 24 Aug 2015]

viii Average Annual Nominal Earnings: from Measuring Worth Index http://www.measuringworth.com [Accessed 18 Apr 2015]

Chapter 2

ix http://www.historyofparliamentonline.org/volume/1558-1603/parliament/1597 [Accessed 23 Aug 2015]

x The History of Parliament: the House of Commons 1558-1603, ed. P. W. Hasler, 1981

xi The National Archives (TNA) Public Record Office (PRO) :STAC 8/63/2 STAC 8/35/5

xii TNA:STAC 8/43/19

Chapter 3

xiii TNA: 1/1/34/86

xiv TNA: 1/1/70/25

xv http://www.worcesterpeopleandplaces.org.uk

xvi Diary of Henry Townshend of Elmley Lovett, 1640-1663. Edited for The Worcestershire Historical Society by J. W. Willis Bund by Townshend, Henry; Worcestershire Historical Society; Willis Bund, J. W. (John William), 1843-1928

xvii TNA:E 179/201/312 m.13 v

Chapter 4

xviii 850ELMLEYLOVETT/9845/2/v Indexed transcript of Christenings, Marriages & Burials 1539-1643, 1660-1730/31, by J H L Booker 1898

xix Worcester CRO: 705:95/3964/12/I c.15 deeds and other papers relating to land and property in Inkberrow, Feckenham, Chaddesley Corbett and Shell [in Himbleton]. Bearcroft, Fyncher, Mowle, Ince, Barnet, Jowe, Holden, Walls, Chandler, Roberts, Smith and Carpenter families.

xx Bishop's Transcript for Himbleton

xxi Parish Register for St Mary the Virgin Stone

xxii http://www.british-history.ac.uk/vch/worcs/vol3/pp391-398 [Accessed 2 Aug 2015]

Chapter 5

xxiii Magnae Britaniae Notitia Or the Present State of Great Britain ..., Volume 2 By John Chamberlayne 1725

xxiv White, Jerry *London in the 18th Century* 2012 Great Britain

xxv Espey, Nigel T. *Covent Garden: A short history* http://www.coventgardenmemories.org.uk Accessed 22 Jul 2015 xxvi John Strype, *A Survey of the Cities of London and Westminster*, 1720, vol II, bk. VI, p 93 from britishhistoryonline.ac.uk accessed 22 Jul 2015

xxvii G.L.R.O.(M), LV(W), 1743 britishhistoryonline.ac.uk accessed 22 Jul 2015

xxviii Collyer, J *The parent's and guardian's directory, and the youth's guide, in the choice of a profession or trade* London 1761

xxix TNA: PROB 11/742/310

Chapter 6

xxx Parish Record, Westminster City Archives

xxxi TNA: PROB 11/742/310

xxxii TNA:PRO C 12/711/30 Court of Chancery: Six Clerks Office: Pleadings 1758 to 1800. Purcas and Winter Division   Ince v Bladwell b.r.r.r.

xxxiii TNA:PRO C 12/711/30 Ince v Bladwell

xxxiv TNA:IR 1/19 Register of Duties paid for Apprentices Indentures 1752

xxxv TNA:PRO C 12/711/30 Ince v Bladwell

xxxvi Parish record for 20 Feb 1762 – Westminster City archives: The London Chronicle Vol II William Fuller Maitland

xxxvii City of Westminster Archives Rates for Brook Ward, St George Hanover Square

xxxviii Parish Records St Mary The Virgin, Monken Hadley and St James Piccadilly

xxxix Roberts, H. 1993. Mayhew and Ince And The Westminster Fire Office. Furniture History, 29, pp. 134–139. Retrieved from http://www.jstor.org/stable/23407791

xl London Metropolitan Archives: DRO/020/H/073

xli TNA:PRO PROB 11/1403/207

xlii Dictionary of English furniture makers, 1660-1840 / edited by Geoffrey Beard and Christopher Gilbert: Mayhew, John and Ince, William, Roberts, H and Cator, C. 1986 pp. 589-598

xliii *The Morning Post* (London, England), Saturday, January 07, 1804; Issue 11001. 19th Century British Library Newspapers: Part II.

xliv *The Morning Post* (London, England), Tuesday, November 25, 1806; Issue 11161. 19th Century British Library Newspapers: Part II

xlv TNA:PRO PROB 11/1453/97

xlvi Percy, Reuben and Timbs, John. 1835. *The Mirror of Literature Amusement and Instruction* Vol 25 Image from print 1764 http://books.google.co.uk/ [Accessed 28 Feb 2012]

xlvii Wendeborn, Gebhard Friedrich August. 1791. *A View of England Towards the Close of the Eighteenth Century* Volume 2 G. G. J. and J. Robinson, Pater-noster-Row

xlviii LMA/4472 Whitefield Memorial Church: Burial Registers

xlix Meller, Hugh and Parsons, Brian. 2011. *London Cemeteries: An Illustrated Guide & Gazetteer*

l The Getty Provenance Index Database

li National Archives Currency Converter

Chapter 7

lii TNA:PRO C 109/204 Cowell v Mayham: Articles of partnership and inventories: London

liii Roberts, H and Cator, C. 1986 Mayhew, John and Ince, William.   In Beard, G and Gilbert, C eds. *Dictionary of English Furniture Makers 1660-1840* Leeds,London : Furniture History Society: W.S. Maney & Son Ltd, pp. 589-598.

liv https://www.british-history.ac.uk/no-series/dict-english-furniture-makers

lv Boynton, Lindsay, 1966. *Furniture History* Vol 11 p. 25

lvi Ince, W and Mayhew, J. 1998. *Authentic Georgian Furniture Designs: Universal System of Household Furniture 1762* Mineola, New York: Dover Publications Inc.

lvii Morrison H. Heckscher, English Furniture Pattern Books in Eighteenth-Century America http://www.chipstone.org/article.php/48/American-Furniture-1994/English-Furniture-Pattern-Books-in-Eighteenth-Century-America (Dixon, p.68, no.19)
lviii Davis, Frank, The World of Art in Wartime, Furniture "Convenient to the Nobility and Gentry The Illustrated London News on 25th May 1940
lix https://www.1stdibs.com/furniture/more-furniture-collectibles/collectibles-curiosities/books/ince-mayhew-original-1st-edition-18th-century-furniture-pattern-book/id-f_1124272/
lx Hecksher, M. H. 1974. *Furniture History* Vol X p. 61
lxi Ward-Jackson, P.W. 1984. *English Furniture Designs of the Eighteenth Century* Victoria and Albert Museum
lxii Roberts, H. 1985. The Derby House Commode. *The Burlington Magazine, 127*(986), p. 275-283 Retrieved December 7, 2011, from www.jstor.org/stable/882065
lxiii Roberts, H and Cator, C. 1986 op. cit.
lxiv Streeter, C. June 1971 *Marquetry Furniture by a Brilliant London Master* Metropolitan Museum Bulletin, Part 1, pp. 418-29
lxv Wills, Geoffrey English looking-glasses: a study of the glass, frames and makers (1670-1820) 1965 Country Life
lxvi Kay, Sarah Croome Redefined June 2012 National Trust http://www.933.me.uk/croome/Croome%20Conservation%20Management%20and%20Maintenance%20Plan.pdf [Accessed 2/10/2018]
lxvii Kay, Sarah Croome Redefined ibid
lxviii Wood, Lucy ibid p. 210
lxix Wood, Lucy Catalogue of Commodes p202
lxx Roberts, H. and Cator, C. 1986. Mayhew, John and Ince, William. In Beard, G and Gilbert, C eds. Dictionary of English Furniture Makers 1660-1840 Leeds, London : Furniture History Society: W. S. Maney & Son Ltd, pp. 589-598.
lxxi http://www.goodnestoneparkgardens.co.uk/history-of-goodnestone.php
lxxii BBC At Home with the Georgians: A Woman's Touch Broadcast 10 Nov 2015; also Vickery, A. *Behind Closed Doors* Yale University Press, New Haven & London 2009 p.169 Citation: Bowood Archives, Lady Shelburne's diaries, vol 3 (1766), f.1, vol 1 ff.10,13,15,16
lxxiii Vickery, A. 2009. *Behind Closed Doors* Yale University Press, New Haven & London p. 141
lxxiv Roberts, Hugh 1981. The Ince and Mayhew connection: furniture at Broadlands, Hampshire; *Country Life, 169*(4354), 29 January, pp. 288-90
lxxv Medway Archives: U0565_F002; U0565_F075-U0565_F076 and U0565_F099-U0565_F101 and Roberts, Hugh 2015. 'No Grandeur Was Wanting': The Funeral Of The 3rd Earl Of Darnley *Furniture History 51*: pp. 151-63. www.jstor.org/stable/43946339.
lxxvi Bristol, K. 2001. 22 Portman Square: Mrs Montagu and her 'Palais de la vieillesse'. *The British Art Journal, 2*(3), 72-85. Retrieved February 5, 2020, from www.jstor.org/stable/41615077
lxxvii Exeter MSS.90/51 Messrs Mayhew & Ince, cabinet makers, in full to midsummer 1768
lxxviii Llyfrgell Genedlaethol Cymru = The National Library of Wales E5126-E5128
lxxix Wood, Lucy 1994. *Catalogue of Commodes* London: HMSO
lxxx lxxx Roberts, H. 1993. Mayhew and Ince and The Westminster Fire Office. Furniture History, 29, pp. 134–139. Retrieved from http://www.jstor.org/stable/23407791
lxxxi Etching. Credit: Wellcome Collection. Attribution 4.0 International (CC BY 4.0) https://wellcomecollection.org/works/yd6mxh5z
lxxxii Roberts, H. and Cator, C. 1986. op. cit.
lxxxiii Worcester Historical Society Miscellany 1 1960

[lxxxiv] http://www.british-history.ac.uk/survey-london/vols31-2/pt2/pp196-208
[lxxxv] https://en.wikisource.org/wiki/A_Dictionary_of_Music_and_Musicians/Kirkman
[lxxxvi] http://earlypiano.co.uk/2013/arnold-frederick-beck/
[lxxxvii] http://earlypiano.co.uk/2013/ganer-christopher/
[lxxxviii] http://www.british-history.ac.uk/survey-london/vols31-2/pt2/pp196-208
[lxxxix] TNA: PROB 11/941/191
[xc] TNA:PRO C 109/204 and LMA MDR/1825/4/638
[xci] Boynton, Lindsay, 1966. *Furniture History* Vol 11 p. 25
[xcii] TNA:PRO C 109/204
[xciii] TNA:PRO C13/623/44 Ince v Mayhew. Two bills and two answers
[xciv] TNA:PRO C 13/2770/38 18th June 1811 Cowell v Tennant Bill only
[xcv] TNA:PRO C 13/2795/34 Mayhew v Tennant
[xcvi] TNA:PRO C 38/1292 Chancery: Reports and Certificates. M. Index in IND 1/14942.
[xcvii] TNA Masters Accounts Books C 101/6156 and C 101/5924
[xcviii] LMA MDR/1825/4/638
[xcix] TNA:PRO IR26/83/121 and IR26/118/171
[c] LMA MDR/1825/4/638
[ci] Marcham, W. McB. 1933. *The Village of Crouch End, Hornsey* Transactions of the London & Middlesex Archaeological Society Vol VII
http://lamas.org.uk/archives/transactions/volume07.html [Accessed 28 Aug 2012]
[cii] Clouston, R S The Burlington Magazine for Connoisseurs, 6(19), pp. 47–52
[ciii] Boynton, L. 1966. An Ince and Mayhew Correspondence Furniture History, 2, pp. 23–36
[civ] Streeter, Colin June 1971. Marquetry Furniture by a Brilliant London Master *The Metropolitan Museum of Art Bulletin,* 29(10), pp. 418–429
[cv] Heckscher, M. (1974). Ince and Mayhew: Bibliographical Notes from New York Furniture History, 10, pp. 61–67
[cvi] Roberts, Hugh 1981. The Ince and Mayhew Connection, Furniture at Broadlands, Hampshire, Country Life, 29 January pp. 288-90
[cvii] Roberts, Hugh 2013. 'Precise and Exact in the Minutest Things of Taste and Decoration': The Earl of Kerry's Patronage of Ince & Mayhew Furniture History
[cviii] Fox, Celina 2001. Design in McCalman I. ed *An Oxford Companion to the Romantic Age – British Culture 1776-1832* Oxford: OUP

Chapter 8

[cix] Image of Coach-Maker from 1800 Woodcuts by Thomas Bewick and his School, Edited by Blanche Cirker, 1962 Dover Publications Inc.
[cx] Kent's Directory for the Year 1794
[cxi] Phyllis Hartnoll and Peter Found. "De Bar, Benedict" The Concise Oxford Companion to the Theatre 1996. Retrieved March 30, 2012 from Encyclopedia.com: www.encyclopedia.com/doc/1079-DeBarBenedict.html
[cxii] Fairclough, Oliver. "'In the richest and most elegant manner': a suite of furniture for Clive of India" Furniture History, vol. 36, 2000, pp. 102–114. JSTOR, www.jstor.org/stable/23409994. Ince & Mayhew worked for Robert Clive, probably mostly at Claremont. The firm was owed £459 10s 10 ½d in December 1774. Also £130 0s 4 ½d to 24th May 1776. Ref: Shropshire Record and Research Centre: Powis 552/7/53
[cxiii] The Bombay Artillery List of Officers, Spring, F W M, London: William Clowes & Sons, 1902
[cxiv] The Centre for the Study of the Legacies of British Slave-ownership
https://www.ucl.ac.uk/lbs/

cxv BBC News Magazine: The landmark buildings that never were Jul 2012
cxvi TNA: WWM/F/66/65
cxvii Ziani de Ferranti, Gertrude and Ince, Richard 1934. *The Life and Letters of Sebastian Ziani de Ferranti*, London
cxviii http://www.sebastiandeferranti.co.uk and http://www.ferranti.me/sebastian-1864.html
cxix The Times. 9 May 1889. p. 11. Boase, Frederic (1897). Modern English Biography v. 2. Netherton & Worth. p. 8. Proceedings of the Statistical Society. (1866). *Journal of the Statistical Society of London,* 29(4), pp. 612-613 Report of the Evening Meetings, Session 1881-2 *Proceedings of the Royal Geographical Society and Monthly Record of Geography,* 4(6), pp. 382-383
cxx Gray, Sara, 2009. *The Dictionary of British Women Artists* Lutterworth Press, 2009

Chapter 9

cxxi City of Westminster Archives, Parish Records for St George Hanover Square on microfilm
cxxii Kirkham, Pat. 1974. The Partnership of William Ince and John Mayhew 1759—1804." *Furniture History* vol. 10 pp 56–60 JSTOR, www.jstor.org/stable/23403407 Accessed 10 Jan 2020
cxxiii The Getty Provenance Index Database http://piprod.getty.edu/starweb/pi/servlet.starweb#
cxxiv The Public Advertiser, Saturday 9 Sept 1786, p. 4
cxxv Roberts, H. 1993. Mayhew and Ince And The Westminster Fire Office. Furniture History, 29, pp. 134–139. Retrieved from http://www.jstor.org/stable/23407791
cxxvi *State Trials for High Treason: Embellished with Portraits reported by a student in the Temple* accessed via googlebooks
cxxvii https://monthlyreview.org/2019/11/01/the-trial-of-thomas-hardy/
cxxviii List of members, [Society of Arts, 1791] Transactions of the Society instituted at London for the encouragement of Arts, Manufactures, and Commerce; with the Premiums offered in the year 1791 Vol. IX pp. 329-372   Applies to 1791-1800
cxxix Library and Museum of Freemasonry; London, England; Freemasonry Membership Registers; Description: Register of Members, London, vol I, Fols 1-597
cxxx IR26/171/292
cxxxi http://emuseum.huntington.org/objects/2386/isabella-mayhew?ctx=a0c4be5e-74b1-4091-8a7c-f9cc8f810f47&idx=1
cxxxii TNA Land Tax Redemption Office: Quotas and Assessments, IR23; Piece: 55
cxxxiii Letter from J. Prince, Magdalen Hospital for the reformation and relief of penitent prostitutes, St. George's Fields, Southwark, to the Rev. Dr. Clarke, Great Quebec Street, St Marylebone, about the measures taken to help Elizabeth Greville, notably getting her a position as a nursery maid with Mrs Mayhew, Broad Street, St. James, Piccadilly. Date: 9 July 1798 City of Westminster Archives D.Misc/187
cxxxiv The London Gazette January 1805 and November 1806
cxxxv Accounts and Papers of the House of Commons, Volume 44
cxxxvi https://surveyoflondon.org/map/feature/1270/detail/ accessed 7/1/2020
cxxxvii http://emuseum.huntington.org/objects/2479/james-gray-mayhew?ctx=12bea0e3-5bdf-44ab-905c-651da94bcb35&idx=1
cxxxviii http://www.histparl.ac.uk/volume/1820-1832/member/tennant-charles-1796-1873
cxxxix Thompson E P and Yeo Eileen 1984. *The Unknown Mayhew* Penguin English Library p. 11
cxl Pierce Egan's Account of the Trial of Mr. Fauntleroy: For Forgery at the Session's House, in the Old Bailey, on Saturday, the 30th of October 1824

https://books.google.co.uk/books?id=hhllyhCT9bcC&dq=Trial+of+Henry+Fauntleroy+Mayhew&source=gbs_navlinks_s (accessed 7/1/2020)
[cxli] https://www.oldbaileyonline.org/browse.jsp?div=t18461123-31 and https://www.oldbaileyonline.org/browse.jsp?div=t18461123-32
[cxlii] Burke, Edmund (editor) 1835. *The Annual Register of World Events: A Review of the Year*, Volume 76 Longmans, Green
[cxliii] https://books.google.co.uk/books?id=SscRAAAAYAAJ&source=gbs_navlinks_s
[cxliv] Mayhew, Henry 2008 *London Labour & the London Poor* Wordsworth Edition, Introduction by Rosemary O'Day.
[cxlv] Thompson, E. P. and Yeo Eileen, ibid
[cxlvi] Dictionary of National Biography, Volumes 1-22
[cxlvii] Dental Practice in Europe at the End of the 18th Century edited by Christine Hillam
[cxlviii] Wheatley, B., auctioneer [Sale catalogue. 1835:12:17--19] A catalogue of the valuable library of Irenæus Mayhew, Esq. …Which will be sold by auction by Mr. Wheatley, at his Great Room, 191, Piccadilly, on Thursday, December 17, 1835 [London]:, G. Norman, printer, [1835].

Postscript
[cxlix] Kent's Directory for the Year 1794
[cl] History of the Northern West Virginia Panhandle embracing Ohio, Marshall, Brooke and Hancock counties by Peter Boyd vol one Carnegie Library Steuberville and Jefferson Counties Historical Publishing Company Topeka-Indianapolis 1927
http://www.digitalshoebox.org/cdm/ref/collection/p17043coll1/id/61649

Picture Credits

This book has been a family affair and it has been fun to work with my cousins Derry Mountford and Jennifer Evans on the artwork - I am most grateful to them. Derry drew the wonderful pencil sketches, including the front cover. These are artistic impressions of the scenes based on contemporary sources. Jennifer produced the lovely water-colours of the spaniel and of Elmley church. Thanks also to Patrick Evans for his advice on the Marathon. I would also like to thank my more distant cousin Frances Ross and her husband John for their furniture photos and Chris Ingle for the timeline.

Photographs and graphics are credited in the text or below. Any uncredited are by the author or illustrators. PD means the image is in the Public Domain and has been identified as being free of known restrictions under copyright law, including all related and neighbouring rights. Thanks to the American Museums who have opened up their collections in this way.

Chapter 1
Tudor Weaver Jost Amman Book of Trades 1568 PD
Chapter 3
Elmley Lodge Source: The Moules of Sneads Green, Horace Granville Monroe PD
Church Bell Kindly provided by Richard Cartwright of Elmley Lovett Bellringers
Chapter 6
Font at St Paul's Covent Garden Photo by John Salmon PD
Interior St George Hanover Square photo by John Salmon PD

Old Crouch Hall Photograph by E Scammell 1885 Source: Marcham, W.McB. 1933. *The Village of Crouch End, Hornsey* Transactions of the London & Middlesex Archaeological Society Vol VII PD

Whitefield Tabernacle From a print dated 1764 Source: Percy, Reuben and Timbs, John. 1835. *The Mirror of Literature Amusement and Instruction* Vol 25 PD

Map Screen British Library Thomas Jefferys, Four-fold map screen, with 21 engraved maps attached to canvas and then to a pine frame c.1750 PD

https://www.bl.uk/collection-items/screen-with-engraved-maps-c-1750

Chapter 7

Drawing of Seal on letter to Richard Myddleton from Llyfrgell Genedlaethol Cymru = The National Library of Wales E5126-E5128

Ram's Head by Boulton & Fothergill on I&M commode: The Metropolitan Museum of Art, New York, Gift of Irwin Untermyer, 1964 No. 64.101.1145

Early Issue of Universal System of Household Furniture: The Metropolitan Museum of Art, New York, Harris Brisbane Dick Fund, 1934 Accession No. 34.100

Mirror from Shillinglee Park, Sussex: The Metropolitan Museum of Art, New York, Purchase, Morris Loeb Bequest,1955 Accession No: 55.43.1

Furniture from Croome Court Tapestry Room: The Metropolitan Museum of Art, New York, Gift of Samuel H. Kress Foundation, 1958 Accession Nos: 58.75.131, 58.75.16

Bull Cabinet LL4246 Lady Lever Art Gallery Courtesy National Museums Liverpool

Serpentine Commode: The Metropolitan Museum of Art, New York, Fletcher Fund, 1959 Accession No. 59.8

Serpentine Commode: By kind permission of Lennox Cato Antiques

Two Corner Cupboards: The Museum of Fine Arts, Houston, part of the Rienzi Collection, the gift of Mr. and Mrs. Harris Masterson III

Cobham Hall furniture by kind permission of English Heritage with the assistance of Cobham Hall Heritage Trust

Burghley House furniture by kind permission of Jon Culverhouse, Curator

Lion and Tassel bedpost photo by kind permission of @fringefrogandtassel and Jon Culverhouse

Commode with Siena marble slab top: The Metropolitan Museum of Art, New York, Gift of Irwin Untermyer, 1964 Accession No: 64.101.1145

Corner washbasin stand: by kind permission of Lennox Cato Antiques

Fire Engine: Photo used by kind permission of Sussex Archaeological Society, Anne of Cleves House Museum

A Representation of Mr Joachim Smith's New Invented Machine for escaping from Fire Etching. Wellcome Collection. Attribution 4.0 International (CC BY 4.0)

Serpentine Commode from Reindeer Antiques – thanks to Peter Alexander

https://www.reindeerantiques.co.uk/Item/1121

Chapter 8

Font at St James Piccadilly Photo by John Salmon PD

Coachmaker from 1800 Woodcuts by Thomas Bewick and his School, Edited by Blanche Cirker, 1962 Dover Publications Inc.

Sir John Fallstaff, characterized by Mr. Ben De Bar: Welcker, F., fl. 1858-1871, artist; Hall, George R, b. 1818, printmaker; Virtue & Yorston, publisher Source: Cornell University Library PD

The Residence of Mrs Ince: kind permission of Daphne Ince Photo by Karen Hitchlock

Bombay: c.1731 by George Lambert (1710-1765), and Samuel Scott (1701-1772) PD

Annette Ince: Photo: Billy Rose Theatre Division, The New York Public Library, retrieved from http://digitalcollections.nypl.org/items/510d47de-fb20-a3d9-e040-e00a18064a99 PD

1000 Light Dynamo from Life and Letters of Sebastian Ziani de Ferranti 1956

London Electric Supply Corporations Works at Deptford 1889 Illustrated London News

Joseph Murray Ince: King's College Chapel, Cambridge, 1843 - in the Fitzwilliam PD

Chapter 9

Canal Token Photo by kind permission of The Basingstoke Canal Society

James Gray Mayhew: https://collections.britishart.yale.edu/vufind/Record/3650138

James Gray Mayhew, 1771–1845, A Project for a Triumphal Archway with Classical Figures in Foreground undated, Pen and black ink, watercolor on slightly textured, thick, beige wove paper, Yale Center for British Art, Paul Mellon Collection. PD

Henry Mayhew: from London Labour and the London Poor (1861)

Postscript

Ship Charles W. Morgan Photo: Mystic Seaport, The Museum of America and the Sea Source: commons.wikimedia.org PD

The National Road at Willis Creek, just west of Cumberland by Carl Rakeman, an artist with the U.S. Bureau of Public Roads. It shows a stagecoach and two Conestoga wagons. Picture courtesy of Federal Highway Administration, United States Department of Transportation

Rates of Travel 1932 Atlas of the Historical Geography of the United States https://www.mnn.com/green-tech/transportation/stories/how-fast-could-you-travel-across-the-us-in-the-1800s

St Pancras New Church 1820 PD

The south and east front of St James's Church, Piccadilly in London. Published 1814. Engraved by Joseph Skelton. Plate 55 in *Architectura Ecclesiastica Londini*.PD

F.W. Beers & Co & Lathrop, J. M. (1871) *Map of the "Panhandle" embracing counties of Hancock, Brooke, Ohio and Marshall, West Virginia*. [S.l.: Geo. Nichols, I. D. Hall, D. L. Miller, W. R. Dumond, I. F. Manchester and C. J. Corbin] [Map] Retrieved from the Library of Congress, https://www.loc.gov/item/2007633928/.

St. Andrew's church, Earls Colne, Essex cc-by-sa/2.0 - © Robert Edwards

Law Journal Report 1838

https://books.google.co.uk/books/about/The_Law_Journal_Reports.htm

Efforts have been made to acknowledge correctly and contact the owner and/or copyright holder of each picture.

Index

Acton, Sir John 14, 16, 17, 20
Acton, Sir Robert 3, 8, 16
Adam, Robert 45, 64, 67, 75, 100
Adderbury House 84
Alscot Park 48, 84
America 3, 1, 55, 58, 78, 104, 105, 106, 109, 110, 111, 132, 136, 140, 141, 146, 148, 151, 155, 166, 173
    Captina Creek 156, 158, 159, 161
    Fork Ridge 162
    New York 138
    Ohio river 140, 149, 156, 158, 159, 171
    Turkey Run 142, 146, 153, 154, 161
    Wheeling 104, 110, 134, 138, 140, 143, 144, 145, 149, 155, 156, 158, 159
Ansell, Charles 124, 125
Austen, Jane 71

Birmingham .. 1, 37, 38, 47, 61, 67, 84, 85, 154
Blake, William 86, 102
Boulton, Matthew 61, 67, 84, 91
Bow Street, London 41, 42, 44
Bristol ... 41, 103, 104, 134, 135, 136, 138, 140, 141, 148, 152, 154
Broad Street 48, 57, 65, 86, 103
Buckingham Palace 70
Burghley 75, 76

Cape of Good Hope, the ... 103, 110, 134, 141
Chancery Court 46, 50, 91
Charles I 19, 22, 29
Charles II 23, 24
Chingford Mount Cemetery 56
Chippendale 48, 62, 63, 87, 131
Chirk Castle 78
Church Bell 25
Church Warden 1, 6, 20, 23, 25, 51, 56, 115
Civil War 1, 13, 18, 19, 21, 22, 23, 25, 29, 103, 111

Clandon Park, ... 45
Cobham Hall 72, 73, 99
Commonwealth Gap (1640 to 1662) 31
Compton Verney 84
Covent Garden 1, 32, 33, 38, 41, 44, 46, 47, 48, 130, 131, 166, 171
Cowell, Charlotte Grace 115
Cowell, George 51, 52, 53, 59, 92, 108, 109, 110, 115, 136, 148, 149, 150, 153, 154
Cromwell, Oliver 24
Croome Court 65, 84
Crouch End .. 45, 51, 53, 56, 85, 88, 89, 93, 94, 95, 134, 169, 172

Daylesford House 84
de Bar, Ben (1813-1877) 105
de Bar, Martha 102, 104, 134, 150
de Ferranti, Sebastian 112
Death Duty Register 94, 123
Dentist Extraordinary 128
deserted village 4, 19, 20

Earls Colne, Essex 106, 150, 154, 158
East India Company 107
Eaton, Elianor 27, 28, 31, 32, 35, 130
Eaton, Humphrey (d.1687) 32, 33, 35
Eaton, John 29, 30, 31, 32, 33, 35, 130
Elmley Lodge 5, 21, 171
Elmley Lovett 1, 3, 4, 5, 6, 8, 13, 14, 15, 16, 17, 18, 19, 20, 21, 22, 24, 25, 27, 32, 33, 37, 47, 166, 171

Feckenham 28, 29, 31, 32, 33, 34, 35, 130, 166
Fire engine 82
Fox, Charles 55
Freemasons 121
Frost Fair 39

George III 45, 99

glass-grinder . 1, 32, 33, 38, 39, 40, 42, 46, 47, 55, 130
Gloucester... 106, 115, 142, 149, 154, 158, 163
Grafton, Duke of 55

Handel, George F 52, 58
Hartlebury Castle 85
Hearth Tax 1, 20, 22, 24, 28, 30, 36
Himbleton 28, 29, 31, 33, 166
House Auction 56
husbandman 14, 34, 39

Ince & Mayhew... 1, 45, 61, 65, 66, 67, 72, 73, 75, 84, 85, 87, 88, 91, 98, 99, 100, 108, 136, 150, 169
Ince Family Grave 45, 55
Ince, Ann .... *See* Stephenson, Ann
Ince, Annette (1834-1892) 111
Ince, Charles (b 1768) 108
Ince, Charles Percy RBA RI 114
Ince, Frederick (1769-1836).. 94, 96, 102, 103, 106, 112, 113, 114, 132, 134
Ince, George 150, 152, 160
Ince, George Horace (1824-1863) 110
Ince, Henry Bret MP 113
Ince, Henry Robert 108
Ince, Isabella (1773-1852) 109
Ince, John (1591-1666) 19, 22, 23, 24, 28
Ince, John (1699-1745) ……..32, 37, 39, 43, 44, 46, 47
Ince, John (brother) 36, 37, 38, 47, 55
Ince, Joseph Murray 114
Ince, Maude1, 3, 5, 8, 9, 10, 11, 12, 13, 14, 15, 19, 25
Ince, Stephen 14, 15, 16, 17, 18
Ince, Thomas 1, 3, 5, 6, 8, 14, 34
Ince, William (1633-1715) 23, 24, 25
Ince, William (1667-1728) 25
Ince, William (1737-1804) 1, 45, 46, 48, 51, 61, 89, 91, 130
    will of 52
Ince, William (1765-1808) 107

India 3, 1, 58, 78, 94, 107, 169
Kidderminster. 1, 5, 16, 17, 23, 33, 35, 37, 39, 46, 47, 84
Kimbolton Cabinet 67

Lady Lever Art Gallery 100
Lady Shelburne 72
Land Registry Document 1825 .... 51, 94
Law Journal, The 112
Lincoln, Abraham 105
London Labour and the London Poor 127
Longmore, Elizabeth 14, 18
Lord Palmerston 72

marriage bond 5, 8, 14, 50
Marshall Street .. 50, 53, 55, 56, 61, 85, 86, 88, 93, 95, 102, 134, 136
Marshalsea Prison 47
Mayhew, Charles 125
Mayhew, George 125
Mayhew, Henry 127
Mayhew, Irenaeus 128
Mayhew, Isabella 123
Mayhew, James Gray 92, 93, 124
Mayhew, Jane Margery 127
Mayhew, John ... 45, 48, 50, 51, 56, 61, 88, 89, 92, 118
Mayhew, John George Winsley 124
Mayhew, Joshua Dorset Joseph 125
Metropolitan Museum of Art 63, 66, 68, 100
Mowle, William 29, 35, 36
Museum of Fine Arts, Houston 71

National Trust 45, 100

Osterley Park 65

Paget, J W 112, 149, 150, 151, 160
Pitt, William 45, 55
plague 20, 21, 23, 25
Poor Man's Guardian, The 126

Prince of Wales, The 71
Punch Magazine 127
Pyramid Cemetery....................................110

Restoration, The 27
Romney, George 88, 95, 150

Sandwell Park 84
Severn river 5, 14
Shell .. 27, 28, 29, 30, 31, 32, 33, 34, 35, 36, 37, 38, 130, 166
Sherborne Castle 72
Ship Marathon..................................136, 138
Slave Trade, The...109
South Africa...3, 1
St Faiths under St Paul's 40
St James Piccadilly .. 50, 51, 56, 102, 124, 146, 167, 172
St Martin in the Fields 40, 50
St Mary the Virgin Monken Hadley,.......118
St Mary's Hornsey 51, 56, 115, 123
St Pancras...141
Star Chamber...............................1, 14, 16, 17
Stephenson, Ann 45, 49, 102
Stephenson, George.....................................49
Stone 16, 28, 34, 35, 37, 38, 39, 43, 47, 166
Sun Fire Insurance 88

Tapestry Room 66
Tennant, George................................123, 125
Townshend, Henry......1, 5, 20, 21, 22, 23, 24, 166

Universal System of Household Furniture
......................................62, 63, 100, 131, 167
Upholder...61

Victoria and Albert Museum 67, 100

Warwick Castle 84
Welch, James 39, 40
Wesley, John 55
West, John 48, 131
Westminster...54
Westminster Fire Office 73, 82
wheelwright............33, 34, 39, 43, 46, 47, 130
Whitefield Chapel...........................45, 49, 55
Willson, Thomas 103, 110, 134
Woods used 81
Worcester ...3, 5, 14, 15, 16, 17, 20, 21, 22, 23, 28, 35, 59, 85, 108, 166, 168

yeoman 16, 20, 29, 39

www.ingramcontent.com/pod-product-compliance
Lightning Source LLC
Chambersburg PA
CBHW042035100526
44587CB00030B/4428